The Origin and Development of Jazz

Third Edition

Otto Werner

Colorado State University

KENDALL/HUNT PUBLISHING COMPANY
4050 Westmark Drive Dubuque, Iowa 52002

To my lovely wife, Jeanette, in thanks for her encouragement and support over four decades of hearing all that jazz!

Cover: Miles Davis Bronze by Ed Dwight, Sculptor.

Copyright © 1984, 1989, 1994 by Kendall/Hunt Publishing Company

Library of Congress Catalog Card Number: 94-76902

ISBN 0-8403-9567-1

Printed in the United States of America

10 9 8 7 6 5 4 3 2 1

Contents

Preface

With this book, Otto Werner has performed a service for jazz which is rare and valuable. Over the past 40 years, I have read most of the literature on jazz and time and again in that reading I have been struck by how arcane the writing must be to the jazz beginner, the person whose ear has just become excited by its first sounds of jazz. It is almost inevitable that such a person will turn to a book to learn more about his new found musical passion, and it is odds on that the first book he chances upon will prove to be a confusing disappointment. The neophyte, seeking help with the arithmetic of jazz, has found a book dealing with its algebra.

Most of jazz literature is written by experts writing for their peers, or semi-experts. And much of the writing is too narrowly focused, it deals in-depth with only one or two facets of jazz, often failing to implant those facets in a perspective of jazz in the round. This paucity of material, which could inform and enchant a newcomer to jazz so that he becomes `hooked' and does not drift away after a brief, puzzled exposure to the music, is one of the many reasons jazz in the United States, its homeland, is an art form with a much smaller audience than it deserves.

Of course, writing about jazz is difficult. Take these facts for starters: No one really knows where jazz began, who began it, when it began or what the roots are of the word jazz or 'jass'. And if one refers to definitions of jazz in leading dictionaries, one finds widely differing, even contradictory, statements. So, jazz is, inescapably, an elusive, murky subject which strongly resists literary efforts to over-intellectualize it.

The central brilliant concept in forming this book was Otto Werner's original perception that a book on jazz *exactly* like this one was badly needed coupled with his unswerving determination in writing the book to stick to his original perception.

I know Otto Werner well. He knows a lot more about jazz than he puts in this book. Can you imagine how seldom a writer on a subject (and make no mistake, Otto is an expert on jazz) leaves out much of his knowledge on the subject? There is an almost overpowering compulsion when writing a book to include not only every little thing you know about the subject but to throw in a lot of extraneous conjecture to boot.

With rare self discipline, Otto keeps it simple. He admits right off that jazz is, finally, special sounds in sequence and time. There can be no substitute for 'active' listening to the music itself. But, in addition, he points out that there is a mind that wants to know something more about those sounds it likes than just the sounds themselves. It may be almost enough to experience the sad and beautiful and joyful and exciting sounds of jazz alone, but the human mind is inquisitive. What are those sounds? Who is playing them? What is jazz all about? And when the jazz beginner asks those questions, he is also implicitly couching them within an appeal: "If you can answer my questions please answer them in a way I can understand. I'm new to jazz. Give it to me simple."

Well, in THE ORIGIN AND DEVELOPMENT OF JAZZ, Otto Werner has pulled off a remarkable achievement. He has made jazz and those who play it best, understandable and human, and fascinating to those who know little or nothing about jazz.

Jazz needs this book and I take enormous pleasure in recommending it to you.

Dick Gibson

Foreword

The Origin and Development of Jazz has enjoyed enormous success since its release in 1984. Students of jazz have profited by the insights, experiences, and interpretations of Otto Werner, Professor of Music at Colorado State University. What I admire about Otto is the fact that he remains very active as a performer, scholar, and writer in the field of bands—concert, marching, and jazz. To perform, study and write in an area of musical expression help to integrate the diverse and complex phenomena comprising the many different musical forms, but in particular, this thing we have all come to know as jazz. He surely has done this with great distinction over the past thirty-three years.

Through personal interviews with Dave Grusin and myself, the book comes alive with stories and personal anecdotes. The reader is able to more fully integrate the significance of each of the developmental movements through the personal reflections of those who "were there" and were a part of the scene when it was happening.

The lists of suggested recordings are a rare composite of important works representing each of the historical periods. Many of these recordings are being re-released by the major recording companies and in some instances are even "up-graded" in tone quality due to new innovations in the technology of recording (compact disc).

Of particular significance is the section on "Women in Jazz." Werner has presented some exciting developments in terms of very important contributions of women, both vocalists and instrumentalists. This section contains a valuable composite of some of these often neglected historical elements of jazz. Given the more enlightened environment in which to work in recent years, we will continue to see more prominent women performers.

I am particularly delighted to be a part of this effort. In talking with Otto during my interview, much of the nostalgia associated with the big band era took on a new dimension for me, as I contemplated what a book of this nature means for the student seeking an understanding and insight into the field of jazz.

We in the United States have much to be proud of, especially in cultural and scientific fields. Surely, one of the truly significant "American" contributions to the world of music is the development of jazz as both a formal and informal area. We may be importing some raw materials and products from other countries around the world, but one of the prime exports from this great country of ours has to be jazz. Its message has reached around the globe and touched the human spirit of people of every type of cultural heritage. Jazz is an undeniable link to others and something that represents the American energy that has been the driving force of our heritage.

I feel pleased to have been a part of this great development. As I reflect back upon the development of jazz from its beginning through what I feel were its greatest moments during the peak of the big band era, I have an inner sense of personal pride that my fellow bandleaders and I helped mold the style and direction of our art form. We played for large audiences in theaters, nightclubs, and ballrooms throughout the country. They always enjoyed our music and felt they were a part of it. They supported our efforts and showed their appreciation by coming and listening and dancing. After all, in the beginning this music called jazz was born for dancing, regardless of the time and place. During the big band era, more professional musicians were employed in the hundreds of dance bands than at any other time in the history of jazz. The tragedy is that it came to such an abrupt end at the close of World War II, leaving many fine performers unable to pursue their vocation.

People, places, and events helped develop jazz as we know it today. It has taken many forms and many styles. From the area of Storeyville in New Orleans to the concert stage of Carnegie Hall, jazz and its people have continued to develop new sounds and combinations of sounds for the listener. Who can tell what form jazz will take in the years to come? This book should enhance the reader's curiosity in what might lie ahead. It tells us what has happened and leaves us with a feeling of curiosity about the future.

When, in the twenty-first century, historians chronicle significant trends of our century, jazz is certain to hold a prominent place as a vital communicative direction. It is wonderful that colleges and universities recognize this importance by adding courses about jazz history to their curricula. This new edition by Otto Werner is a valuable contribution to the study of jazz history, and it blends current directions with past achievements. This is the type of book that people can read and enjoy or use as the basis for a detailed study of American's music, jazz. I recommend it to you and know that it will provide interesting and valuable insights into where we have been, where we are now, and where we are going in the field of jazz.

Les Brown, Leader

"The Band of Renown"

Introduction

This book is designed as an overview of the origin and development of jazz. It is written for the non-musician—the individual who has an appreciation for jazz in one form or another but has had little or no formal musical background. The book does not delve into the complex theories of the music but rather encompasses the people, places, and events that contributed to the development of the art. Those who made worthwhile contributions and are regarded by jazz historians as the leaders in their specific eras are briefly characterized. It is impossible to list every individual and event which is significant to the history of jazz. Suffice it to say that this book merely projects the 'tip of the iceberg'.

Compared to classical music, jazz is in its infancy. In little more than 100 years, it has undergone extreme changes in style and format. From its establishment as an art form in the days of the work songs through the performances of contemporary jazz rock groups such as the "Electric Thunderpigs", society has been given a variety of musical offerings. Because an era ends does not mean that the particular style of music is no longer played. It continues on while making way and evolving into something new. This is the fascination of jazz. Today we have a wide variety of musical styles from which to choose. These styles will continue to undergo changes over relatively short periods of time. Even at this writing, somewhere, someone is creating something new for our listening pleasure.

As with many endeavors, what one hears or sees is only a small part of the total. Jazz is more than music, whether that is listening to a compact disc or a live group. As with a painting, a book, a well-tuned car, or a prized box of chocolates, it is of interest to ask "What went into this music?" "What are they thinking?" It often has been said that understanding or at least knowing enhances appreciation. Jazz is no different. In this book jazz is explained and explored for the reader. It is an American music form important culturally and socially in the international scene as well.

From early funeral bands where the music paid homage to a deceased person and reached those in or witnessing the procession to the electronic technologies of television and sophisticated recording techniques, jazz now reaches many more people on a daily basis. Air travel allows musicians to put far more miles than hours between performances. Music, technology, and business have come together so that some people term today's jazz more an entertainment business than a musical performance. Thus, jazz is a complex and dynamic part of our culture. Studying the music without understanding the broader contexts overlooks the people and their impact on America's development.

In a list in *Fortune magazine* entitled "100 Products that Make America Best" jazz took a place with 99 other consumer and industrial products (from all-electric plastic injection-molding machines to washing machines and pianos to jet engines). Jazz is unique on the list. It is the only 'product' that was not identified with a manufacturer or brand name (i.e., Levi Strauss, Steinway, 3M). Likewise its quality is not as dependent on the platitudes of "managing the technology, the labor force, the managers themselves" to the extent of the other products. Jazz is on the list as it similarly relates to the "sales-force bromide: know your customer." There is a better educated, more cynical buyer out there with little patience for poor quality. This buyer wants products that work the first time and is willing to pay for them. Substitute the "jazz consumer or listener" for the customer and the message is clear. Jazz has had to change in form and presentation. The big bands have adapted to the "customers" changing demands and lifestyles as well as to the competition of television, movies, and recordings which bring music to the listener, though most often not in person.

As American as apple pie and baseball, neither were on the "best" list. This sets jazz apart. Jazz is recognized. It often has its own column in major newspapers, information telephone lines in large cities, and a section in the "what is going on where." The pictures and commentary in this book provide perspectives into the personalities of jazz, its performers and entrepreneurs. The pictures and thoughts compiled here provide a very vivid illustration of how jazz has evolved. Granted some changes were and still may be seen as negative while others are termed the best thing that has come along. We also may say the same about some of the personalities. This is not negative. We only need to remember that similar doubts as well as praise were expressed about early automobiles and every U.S. president. If jazz had remained as it was in the early 1930s, who would be performing today? Where would they be performing and for whom? Would you be reading this book?

Marilyn Marchall's article in *Ebony,* "Are Blacks Giving Jazz Away?" asked some serious questions. Basically, her view is that jazz is a very important part of African-American culture that could be lost. If jazz becomes part of white American culture, it may lose its identity with the black community. She challenged the black community to strengthen their appreciation of jazz. Besides the serious questions that she poses for maintaining jazz as black culture, she encourages the inclusion of jazz in the interest of blacks. The reader should relate similarly questioning jazz and other aspects of our heritage and interests.

Jazz does reflect on the heritage of another group. Providing means of identity for women in a field that was not readily made for them. Jazz did not open the door and roll out the red carpet, at least not as nursing or elementary teaching. It took hard work and risks, yet, jazz can be a model for other fields where women still have the door nearly shut to them—major league sports and officiating, the highest offices of this country, and administrative positions in many companies and organizations.

Jazz, as other music and art forms, is affected by social, political, and economic forces in society. Some jazz artists have found greater opportunities and acceptance in other countries due to the political and social messages of their songs; messages deemed unpopular in the United States. Theolonious Monk had to overcome not only limited acceptance of his style of music by musicians, but also the consequence of being in the wrong place at the wrong time.

Ask yourselves these questions. How much better do I understand an era of jazz, such as minstrelsy or the big bands, by knowing more about the people and reflections on their careers in jazz during the height of the era? Isn't it exciting to know what they are doing today and what they project for the future? Often we separate the music from the personalities, forgetting the people. Their daily trials and tribulations have made success a very big challenge. Most pictures in this book express the positive side of jazz. The hours of travel, rehearsals, pleading for jobs, trying compositions again and again, overcoming the physical and mental anguish of drugs, alcohol, or chronic health conditions often do not show either in the pictures or the music. Yet, it was a very real part of their lives. Many have overcome much to bring us jazz. How has jazz evolved since your birth? Who was in the spotlight then? Who will you be listening to 25 years from now?

As students reading about jazz and/or in a course on jazz, your understanding of jazz is greater than that of most people. Share that knowledge with others to increase their appreciation of jazz as both a music form and an important part of black heritage and American culture. Don't be satisfied with what you read here. Be sure you go to performances of college jazz groups, those of area high schools, and don't miss the bands of Les Brown, Maynard Ferguson, and/or Count Basie when they come to your campus or city. Be there! If well known performers do not come to you, look at the entertainment calendar of the nearest large city. Watch for the listing of festivals, campus jazz competitions, and television programs featuring the personalities and their music.

What is important is the overall effect jazz has had on society—its origins, developmental stages, and the purposes of the music. It is an art form conceived in the United States for the populace. For students wishing to enhance their knowledge of the subject, a bibliography offers sources for further study and a discography provides reference to the aural facets of jazz. A glossary of terms is included at the end of the book which gives the reader insight into the language used by jazz musicians and provides general musical definitions.

Remember jazz is music, people, and heritage,

References

Knowlton, Christopher. "What Makes America Best?" *Fortune,* March 28, 1988, 40–45.
Marchall, Marilyn. "Are Blacks Giving Jazz Away?" *Ebony,* 43 (February 1988), 90–98.

Otto Werner
Carole J. Makela

Acknowledgments

As people made jazz, people and their efforts made this book a reality. The book provides background for the jazz listener and the youthful performer to understand the origins and development of the music. While it is not a history separate from the daily lives of people, places and events of the times, it cannot go on endlessly with anecdotes and stories losing the music to the interesting bits.

Often when writing a book one finds that people make the difference in shaping it and in putting it all together. When I reflect back in time, I realize that the opportunities to listen to, to play gigs with, or to merely talk with many of the great jazz personalities provided me with materials and memories helpful in my teaching and in writing this book. It is with sincere appreciation that I recall the many occasions when the people named herein as well as many others, shared their time, music, skills and thoughts with me. These performers were jazz to me. At the other end of the spectrum were the students throughout the years wanting more than just hearing jazz. For some, understanding its history and desiring to perform it brought them into my classes and ensembles. Their interest, enthusiasm, questions and desire to learn about jazz has been my reward.

The cooperation of academic and music colleagues made this book a project of people, not that I, alone, conceived, created and completed. Not unlike the musician who needs the composer, lyricist, vocal and instrumental accompaniment, and/or the many people in recording, broadcasting, or production to complete the song, this book is the product of cumulative efforts.

To keep the reader from seeing only words, illustrations and photographs show the people, instruments, music, and places of jazz. I recognize the assistance of Pat Dietemann and Amy Helm for their sketches of African and American instruments and of composers; Dr. Peter Jacobs for consultation of the art work; Ed Dwight, sculptor from Denver, Colorado, for allowing me to photograph his bronzes of jazz people; and the following for making photographs available to me—Sammy Nestico, arranger/composer, Paul Jennings, Jensen Music, Inc., Nadine Gardner of Kendor Music, Inc., Jack Maher of DOWNBEAT MAGAZINE, Carl Schunk of the Willard Alexander Agency, Jim Steinblatt of ASCAP, Dan Morgenstern of the Institute of Jazz Studies, Rutgers University, Armand and Rab Zildjian of the Avedis Zildjian Cymbal Company and Robert Dunham.

The discography was developed with the able assistance of Joe Speace, Radio Station KCSU (Colorado State University) and Wil Huett, Radio Station KCOL (Fort Collins, Colorado), and Dr. John Powers, saxophonist. Dick Gibson shared ideas, historical perspectives, allowed me to photograph jazz artists during his jazz party, and also wrote the preface.

It is impossible for an individual alone to write a book of this type. With this thought in mind and with the guidance of my editor and many colleagues, I enlisted the advice and help of people considered tops in their fields. I thank the individuals who gave of their valuable time to grant me interviews relative to their careers and jazz in general. Les Brown, bandleader; Davi Grusin, composer; Dick Gibson, jazz producer. These men are very active in the music business and are influential in the direction jazz is taking.

Special thanks to the National Association of Jazz Educators executive director Bill McFarlin for permission to reprint Herb Wong's article on Woody Herman. Also thanks to Jim Steinblatt of ASCAP for use of photos and the article on the Gershwin Brothers.

Also appreciation to Dan Morgenstern of the Institute of Jazz Studies at Rutgers University for again letting me use their priceless photographs. Thanks to each of the following for allowing me to use photographs from their private collections: Ingrid Herman Reese; Tom Cassidy, Artist Management; Dr. Herb Wong; David Shaner; Les and Stumpy Brown.

For the technical details of writing and organizing as well as continued support to make the book a reality, I credit Dr. Carole Makela, consumer scientist and jazz fan, Colorado State University. Also gratitude for their efforts in typing, editing and computer expertise go to Nancy Branlund, Sharon Sparks and daughter Pamela Blue. Without their diligent screening of my typing, this would never have been completed.

To all the individuals named above, and the unnamed others who in their unique ways made a contribution to my work, my sincere appreciation. I could not have led this ensemble if you had not played your part.

Thank you!

CHAPTER 1

Listening to Music

A number of years ago, I attended a Ramsey Lewis Trio performance at the London House in Chicago with a group of musician friends. As jazz enthusiasts, we were anxious to hear the trio and anticipated the sounds to come.

When the performance began I was quickly swept up in the musical exchange. Halfway through the first set, however, several persons at the table next to us became restless and started talking and soon their conversation became loud enough to distract our attention from the music. We asked them to hold the conversation down, but were quickly told they were entitled to their conversation and would certainly continue as they pleased.

So, along with the fine music of Ramsey Lewis, we were treated to a discourse on the purchase of the best radial tires. This incident stuck in my mind not only because it was annoying, but because it served as a perfect example of the three methods of listening to music: active, passive, and a combination of the two.

The performance began with active listeners concentrating on the music and its various aspects. Those at the next table became passive listeners, pushing the music into the background. The distractions provided by their conversations kept other listeners from devoting their entire attention to the performance forcing us to combine both active and passive listening.

Methods of Listening

The best way to study music is to listen to and analyze it. Verbal discussion of music is no substitute for the aural experience. It should or rather must be heard a number of times in order to get the complete scope. Some forms of music are accompanied by a written score. When this is possible, it enhances the listeners perception of the music as both the visual and the aural senses are stimulated. The listener can see the score, follow it as the performance goes on, and thereby get an overview of the total composition. If improvised music is being performed there is no score for in-depth study. The music is immediate and when the sound is gone, there exists only a memory of it. Recognizing the need to use the senses, three methods of listening are used.

1. The *active* listener concentrates on all facets of the music without outside interference. He/she notes the basic musical components as well as the orchestration or arrangement. Active concentration allows the listener not only to enjoy music, but to appreciate the creativity and interpretive talents of the performers.

2. The *passive* listener hears the music and may have a basic appreciation and understanding but concentrates on other activities at hand. At home or in the office, people may have the radio on all day long while doing their work. Although aware of the music, the center of each person's concentration is on the tasks at hand and the music is secondary.

3. Most listeners use a *combination* of active and passive methods, sometimes concentrating and then, at different points, allowing their attention to be drawn to other activities.

Of the three the active listener is the most sought after by the performer. In becoming a more active listener, we take control of the kinds of music which we allow into our lives and begin to understand our needs in relationship to music. In becoming more aware, the listener needs to dissect the music, understand the various facets involved, and appreciate the relationship of each facet to the others.

Scales

Music is sound and sound is based on seven notes, which performed sequentially, constitute a scale. By altering the basic seven notes, through raising or lowering these notes, chromatics or half-tones are added, giving a total of 12 notes. This total is all the composer has to work with to develop music. Even though the piano has 88 keys, the sound is only a repetition of the notes in various octaves: there are only 12 notes including the chromatics. The *diatonic* scale is comprised of the basic seven notes with the first note of the scale being repeated at the end to create the octave such as the "DO" (diatonic) scale itself; DO RE MI FA SOL LA TI DO. Numerically, they are 1, 2, 3, 4, 5, 6, 7, 8, with eight being a repeat of one, one octave higher. Letter names follow the first seven letters of the alphabet: A, B, C, D, E, F, G, and A. A, placed at the end, is a repeat of the prime (1 or DO).

The Keyboard:
Notes in bracket constitute the C Major Scale

F G A B C D E F G A B C D E

| 1 | 2 | 3 | 4 | 5 | 6 | 7 | 8-1 |
| do | re | mi | fa | sol | la | ti | do |

C D E F G A B C

Utilizing these notes with the possibility of raising or lowering any of them, the composer constructs melodies. The notes will vary in duration depending upon the melody. They will vary in range, some being higher or lower than others.

Techniques

Composers and performers also enhance music with techniques that alter the sound quality of notes. Included here are eight techniques.

1. **Vibrato.** The wavering of a note after the initial sound/tone has been established. Warmth and color are provided, whereas a pure sound without any embellishment can sound cold. The tones of an acoustic piano or any instrument which relies on tactile sound production cannot be altered once it has been struck. The electric piano and the vibraphone, however, have a resonator which can produce a vibrato electronically.

2. **Bend.** The bending of a note in either direction from its initial sound.

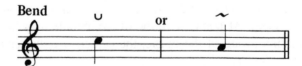

3. **Fall.** The dropping of a note after it is sounded on its original pitch. The note can be given either a long or short fall. The note's ending is indefinite.

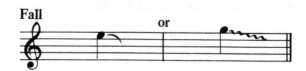

4. **Doit.** The raising of a note from its original pitch after the note has been sounded. It will not culminate on a definite pitch.

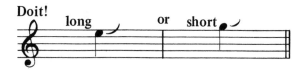

5. **Dynamics.** The loudness or softness of a tone or succession of notes altering the intensity of a passage/phrase.

6. **Accents.** The specific punctuation of a note or notes to indicate emphasis.

7. **Glissando.** Moving from one note to another without stopping the sound. A number of notes can be spanned with this technique.

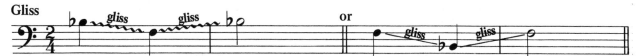

8. **Scoop.** Coming from below the desired note and sliding into pitch. This was used a great deal by blues singers, particularly on blue notes.

Considering the possibilities listed above, it is easy to see that musical sound is best studied through listening and analyzing. Reading and/or discussion does not substitute for the aural experience.

Parts of a Composition

The components of all music are *melody, harmony* and *rhythm.* The listener must be able to hear all the components at the same time because they are related. Classical music and jazz have their own priority order in relation to the components. Classical music uses melody as the prime component, leaving rhythm as last, while jazz places rhythm as the most important. Early classical composers centered their concentration on the melodic line and its harmonization. This accomplished, composers would then fill in a percussive part. Listen to a Mozart Symphony, the percussion instruments play a very diminutive role. Contemporary classical composers have realized the potential and have included the percussive elements as integral parts of their compositions.

The *melody,* a line of successive notes, carries the theme (melodic line) of the composition and provides the continuous thread that holds a piece together. The melody may, at times, take a back seat to other facets, but it is woven in and out of the entire piece giving a feeling of continuity. The melody creates the basic idea or mood for a composition.

3

Melody – "Hymn to Joy"   *Beethoven*

A chord, which is a combination of three or more notes, can be built on each note of the scale. This provides the *harmony*. To harmonize a melody, the composer or arranger adds notes to be played with the melody, and chords are created. The chords of a particular melody, known as progressions, may vary depending upon the melodic line. A composer/arranger may use the same chord for several notes in a melody or may change the chord with each note.

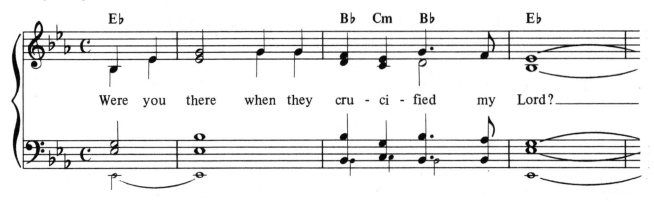

A basic chord consists of three notes built upon a root. These are placed in thirds (every third note in the scale). Beginning with DO (1) using a "C" chord built upon the "C" scale, for example, the notes would be a C (1), E (3), and G (5).

Basic Chord – C Major

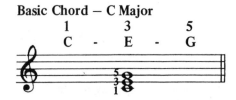

The note placement of a chord, often called voicing, is determined by the composer/arranger. The chords may be held in a 'closed' or 'open' position. If closed, the notes are placed as close as possible to each other. Barbershop quartets are characteristically known for their closed harmony. When the distance between notes is wide, the chords are termed open. For example, the timbre or sound of various members of a saxophone section (alto, tenor, baritone) may be voiced in an arrangement from high to low tones, giving the listener the rich, full sound of open harmony.

Voicing – C Major Chord

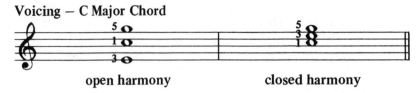

open harmony   closed harmony

Other changes than can occur are those using chromatic alterations. Sharping or flatting a note in the chord can change the chord from *major* to *minor* to *diminished* to *augmented,* depending on the desires of the composer/performer.

4

Chromatic Alterations

The combination of notes for harmony can be described as two-part harmony when it consists of a melody note and one harmony note. Three-part harmony consists of one melody note and two harmonic notes and so on. Standard church hymns are usually harmonized in four-parts. Soprano has the melody throughout, while also is given the notes immediately below the soprano. Tenor is assigned the notes immediately below the alto and the bottom notes just below the tenor are the bass. A five piece trumpet section can consist of one melody note (the lead part) and four harmony parts making up a five note chord.

Harmony

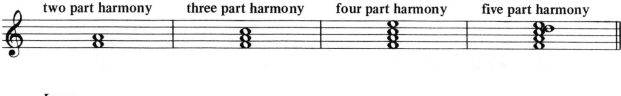

The third musical component, *rhythm,* is often misconstrued as the 'beat' of the music. This is a common error made by the lay listener and has become accepted as a substitute term. But the main idea is that the rhythmic structure of a composition gives it flow. Compositions can be performed with a variety of rhythmic styles. Regardless of Gershwin's original concepts, "Summertime" could be played as a swing tune, a rock tune or as a Latin tune according to the performer's choice and taste.

There are three basic forms of rhythm. Swing is the uneven pulsation with an even primary beat, consisting of a long followed by a short beat. On the other hand, rock is an even pulsation or succession of beats while Latin is a series of patterns made of groupings of long and short notes with accents on the first, third, and fourth beats of each measure.

Determining Rhythmic Patterns

In determining rhythmic patterns, the composer also uses meter, tempo, and form.

Meter. is the time in which a composition is structured. Innumerable meters are available. Musical format is based on the quarter note—one note gets one beat. So, if a composition is written in 2/4 time, there will be two quarter notes as the basic meter in each measure of the music. (Most marches are written in 2/4 time and much of early Dixieland was written in this meter). 4/4 time uses four quarter notes (beats) in a measure. 3/4 time has three quarter notes/beats per measure. (Waltzes are composed in 3/4 time). 6/8 time indicates there are six eighth notes in each measure and so on.

Meters

The speed of the music is *tempo*. Classical composers used Italian terms for the tempo of their music with *largo* being very slow, *allegro* moderately fast, and *vivace* as quite fast. Metronome markings are often placed at the beginning of each selection/movement. Metronomic markings indicate the number of notes/beats per minute as M.M. ♩= 120 (120 quarter notes or beats occur per minute), and M.M. ♩= 78 (78 quarter notes per minute). Therefore the larger the number the faster the tempo.

Jazz composers use English terms (slow, moderately slow, moderately fast, and fast) and often give a tempo suggestion with a specific metronomic marking, M.M. ♩= 90 or a range by writing M.M. ♩= 120 to 140. This range gives the performer choices of tempo.

Form is also determined by the composer. A symphony's form is different than that of a concerto, and a concerto differs in form from an overture. In jazz, forms differ according to when it was written and the style. In classical and popular music, themes of various measures in duration are used. A total composition may have as few as one basic theme or be comprised of as many as four or five separate-though-related themes. The forms of music found in jazz will be discussed later.

Once the composer/arranger has decided the meter (2/4, 3/4, 4/4, etc.), the tempo and the form, the rhythmic pattern that will best accommodate the music to give it flow is chosen. The choice of the rhythmic pattern determines the 'flavor' of the piece. Church hymns are usually written in a simple rhythm—either 3/4 or 4/4 time—and designed for congregational singing. Jazz and classical rhythms can become quite complicated, both for the performer and for the listener. The same melody can be varied in style by substituting a Latin rhythm in place of a rock rhythm.

A performer's playing style will often determine a rhythm or rhythmic combinations. The performer may elect to play a complete chorus in a swing style and then follow with a chorus in a Latin rhythm. A common practice among contemporary composers is to begin a piece with a 'free time' introduction, work into a definite time/tempo at the beginning of the first chorus, move into Latin or rock with the second chorus and then use swing for the closing.

Most listeners are conditioned to a straight 3/4 or 4/4 meter to which they can keep time by walking or dancing. Odd meters and rhythms, such as 5/4 or 7/4, seem to create tension for listeners who are trained to feel the even pulsation of downbeat and upbeat in a double or triple meter. Dave Brubeck's "Take Five" composition is an excellent example of the odd meter, with five beats in each measure played in a 5/4 meter. Brubeck's "Blue Rondo ala Turk" also demonstrates the odd meter. He begins with 9/8 time, combining nine notes of two plus two plus three. The selection then changes to a three plus three plus three. A brief interlude in 4/4 follows and then the theme returns to the original 9/8 meter. This music is impossible to dance or march to but can be very exciting for the active listener. The 9/8 section creates the tension; movement to 4/4 relieves the tension.

Rhythmic Pattern — "Blue Rondo ala Turk"

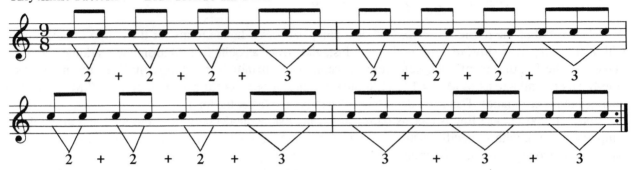

Variations. Two other methods of varying a melodic theme include countermelody and improvisation. The countermelody is a secondary melodic line used to enhance the main theme. This is sometimes used in the manner of 'call and response' where one instrument or voice calls and another responds accordingly. When musicians improvise, they play or sing extemporaneously, that is, without prior preparation. Using improvisational techniques, the melodic lines are varied and colored.

Neither melody, harmony nor rhythm can be considered more important than any of the others. Different music forms establish different priorities for components. Jazz composers use percussion and rhythm as equal elements. In fact, the basic instrument in jazz is the drum. Even though crudely constructed, the drum played a dominant role in African music. African drummers, the musical ancestors of jazz drummers, were revered as descendants from the gods and treated accordingly. This influence and image of the instrument carried to the New World where drums became the foundation and basis of jazz.

The Musical Groups

This history of jazz has given many names to the groups that performed the music. Instrumentally speaking, they come under the basic heading of bands and orchestras. Using the word orchestra in the title (The Glenn Miller Orchestra) is a misnomer. Musicians and listeners alike seem to make a generalization of the term. By definition, a band is a group of instruments utilizing wind blown and percussion instruments as the prime source of sound. An orchestra utilizes these same instruments as part of the total ensemble, but adds the stringed instruments (violin, viola, cello, and double-bass or string bass) as a major section of the group along with brass, woodwind, and percussion. It is true in some cases that strings were added to the jazz band. Paul Whiteman utilized strings a good portion of the time, he himself was a violinist. Often, for specific functions (movies) a bandleader would augment his band with a string section, then it could rightly be called an orchestra. Jazz bands were named bands or orchestras at the discretion of the leaders, the journalists, or the listening public, without concern for the actual instrumental composition. Today we have several names given to the concert band, including, wind ensemble, wind symphony, neither of which include the word 'band' but in reality are just that.

Historically, each era had its own identification for the groups prevalent within it. In Dixieland, a band had a specific name (Red Hot Petters, Creole Jazz Band, Original Dixieland Jazz Band, etc.) with a specific leader (Jelly Roll Morton's Red Hot Peppers). Similar names were used during the big band era (Harry James and his Music Makers or Les Brown and his Band of Renown) although not all leaders used names for the bands they led (Count Basie, Benny Goodman, Duke Ellington).

THE STARS AND STRIPES FOREVER. MARCH.

By John Philip Sousa.

PIANO 2 HANDS 50.
PIANO 4 HANDS 1.00
PIANO 6 HANDS 1.50
ORCHESTRA 1.00
MILITARY BAND 50.
ZITHER SOLO 50.

ZITHER DUET 90.
MANDOLIN SOLO 40.
MANDOLIN & PIANO 60.
MANDOLIN & GUITAR 50.
MANDOLIN-PIANO & GUITAR 80.
2 MANDOLINS & PIANO 80.

2 MANDOLINS & GUITAR, 70.
GUITAR SOLO 40.
GUITAR DUET 50.
BANJO SOLO 40.
BANJO DUET 50.
BANJO & PIANO 60.

PUBLISHED BY

THE JOHN CHURCH COMPANY.

CINCINNATI. NEW YORK. CHICAGO. LEIPSIC.

9

The Stars and Stripes Forever.
March.

JOHN PHILIP SOUSA.

12

Summary

You do not have to be a music student or a musician to understand and appreciate music. The ear can be trained to listen and discriminate between the musical components of a composition. As the listener hears and begins to understand the role that each facet of music plays, he/she will begin to develop not only a stronger appreciation, but a more selective process for choosing the kinds of music suited to his or her needs and personal tastes. A more intelligent and perceptive audience will place more of a demand on the performer. As performers strive to meet an audience's demands, the state of the art of music is expanded and upgraded.

That is how music is nurtured and how it grows—through the musician's experimentation and expansion and through the audience's reaction. The following chapters will show the birth, the nurturing and the growth of jazz, from its roots in Africa to the beginning of the rock era. The reader will explore song forms and each era's music as we follow the development of jazz chronologically.

Discussion Topics

1. What should a person listen for when hearing new music for the very first time?
2. What is meant by the statement, "We tend to enjoy and identify with the music heard during our formative years"?
3. How can you detect the type of listener a person has become?

CHAPTER 2

Song Forms

Within each segment of music (classical, jazz, etc.) exists a variety of musical forms. This variety occurs because music is based upon themes or statements. A number of separate themes may occur within a composition, related either by words or music. These themes may vary in length depending upon the composer's concept of the total composition. In exploring the different forms of jazz, a comparison will be made with classical music to help the reader understand the relationship of the two.

Regardless of whether the music is classical or jazz in origin, the themes are the makeup of the total composition.

Song Form — "Deck the Halls"

Classical music is characterized by the symphony, suites and marches. Symphonies usually have four movements with or without related themes. Each movement has a different tempo and a different tonal center (key). Suites have three to four movements. The separate themes may be related or unrelated. The different (contrasting) tempos are used for each movement, usually in different keys. In marches there are three or four themes with one or more key changes. The themes are 16 measures in length (some have eight measure themes repeated to make a 16 bar theme). The march style was copied both by ragtime and Dixieland composers.

Major Song Forms

The major song forms most used in jazz are the work song, spiritual, gospel, blues, ragtime, Dixieland, and popular songs. The first song form in jazz history was the *Work Song,* which as the name implies, was sung by the slaves as they worked in the fields. The lyrics of the work songs related to human rituals: work, birth, death, marriage, and to other events in the slaves' lives in the New World.

The form was quite free, using repetitive short phrases with no definite number of measures. Even though the lyrics have been preserved there is little record of the melodic lines of the work songs. The melodies underwent numerous changes as this period progressed. The music was not written, but rather passed on from group to group and generation to generation, allowing many melodic changes.

The work song lowered notes in the diatonic scale (3rd, 5th, and 7th notes of the scale). This along with the bending, sliding, scooping of notes that originated in the work song, helped form the beginning of the blues. These songs were based on the convenient ranges of the singers, rather than a specific key.

Lyrics were descriptive of the days' events, the labors at hand, and, often, involved the 'double entendre'—the double meaning of a word or phrase. A classic example of the double entendre is "Follow the Drinkin' Gourd" which gave directions for escaping to the North by following the North Star off the end of the Big Dipper.

Lyrics: *"Follow the Drinkin' Gourd"*   traditional

Follow the Drinkin' Gourd
Follow the Drinkin' Gourd
For the Old Man is Awaitin'
For to Carry You to Freedom
If You Follow the Drinkin' Gourd

When the sun comes back and the first quail calls
Follow the Drinkin' Gourd
For the Old Man is Awaitin'
For to Carry You to Freedom
If You Follow the Drinkin' Gourd

Other lyrics of work songs included description of plantation life and anticipation of the hereafter. Work songs often involved a method of 'call and response' where the call was sung by the leader and the remainder of the group answered with the response.

From the work songs, spirituals and gospel music evolved. *Spirituals* were a contribution to religious music, reflecting the emotional and social viewpoints of the blacks. From a technical standpoint the slaves' music was illiterate. They sang as they felt, pouring out their religious feelings in a descriptive fashion rather than fitting their music into an existing musical pattern. Minor keys were used (the influence of the blues tonality). Repetition was also predominant. Some lyrical examples include "Do Lord", and "Were You There When They Crucified My Lord".

Gospel evolved from early European church music. Men like Bach who served as Kappelmeisters (church musicians/choirmasters) spent a great amount of their time writing original hymns for their church. The music was basically gloomy and serious, preaching about salvation/damnation. By the 19th century, the traveling evangelists were active on the religious scene in the U.S. Their music brightened the church setting as cheery and emotional. The 'hellfire and damnation' message was eliminated. In the late 1800's, evangelist Dwight L. Moody and composer Ira D. Sanky joined forces as traveling revivalists. Before Moody's sermons, the congregations were 'warmed up' with Sanky's music. The music was written in major keys with predominantly eight measure phrases utilizing a two theme format (theme A and B). The lyrics often spoke of the wonderment of heaven.

The *blues* were not a specific era in jazz, but rather an evolution of music. While there were individuals who made major contributions by either singing or composing the blues as a style of music, the blues were really an outgrowth from African roots and the developments which occurred during slavery via work songs.

The blues, as we know them today, are based upon a 12 measure series of chordal progressions. The form has a specific structure much the same as the march, the popular songs of tin pan alley and the rags of Scott Joplin and Jelly Roll Morton.

16

The basic blues chords are the first, fourth, and fifth chords of a scale, which act as a roadmap or guide to the performer indicating position in a chorus, thereby assisting creative improvisation. The chord progressions were played by such instruments as the piano, guitar, banjo—parts of the chord could also be played by the bass one note at a time. In ensembles (big bands), the chord progressions are played by various sections such as saxophones, trumpets, trombones, etc. True blues performers adhere to the *tonality* of the blues scale with its lowered notes (3rd, 5th, and 7th). Not all of today's blues performers, however, adhere to this true tonality, but rather simply follow the chordal structure of the blues. The blues have undergone considerable changes from the early blues choruses of eight measures in length to the later 16 measure choruses.

It is a common practice for a performer to use two 12 measure choruses in succession giving the opportunity to develop a solo over a 24 measure period. Added to the 12 measure format are extensions such as *introductions* and *tag endings* or *interludes*. Today's blues have settled into a 12 measure chorus. The important part of modern blues is the chord progressions used.

Blues Chord Progressions—12 measures long

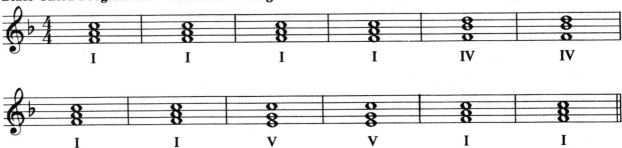

The *lyrics* of blues are divided into those treating either city or rural subjects. City blues deal with the various socio-economic problems of the urban dweller, with sexual innuendo being popular. The problems and activities of rural life—farming, hard work, and religion—are the subject of the rural blues.

Blues Lyrics

I'm goin' down and lay my head on
the railroad track (4 bars)
I'm goin' down and lay my head on
the railroad track (4 bars)
When the train comes along, I'm gonna
snatch it back (4 bars)

or:

I woke up this mornin' with an awful achin' head (4 bars)
I woke up this mornin' with an awful achin' head (4 bars)
My new man had left me just a room and a empty bed (4 bars)

Bought me a coffee grinder, got the best one I could find (4 bars)
Bought me a coffee grinder, got the best one I could find (4 bars)
So he could grind my coffee, cause he had a brand new grind (4 bar)

Ragtime music was primarily written for the piano although bands were quite capable of playing rags. Ragtime's form was based on the march style but incorporated a medium called syncopation. The primary beats of a measure were played by the left hand, while the right hand played melodic lines constructed on the subdivisions of the beat. In simple terms, this amounted to playing off and around the beat, or on the 'upbeat'.

Ragtime was composed like the march with 16 measure themes or phrases. Several themes were often used in one composition, A—B—C—D. There is, however, no specific formula. 'A' theme would reappear

Syncopation

or

in the middle or at the end of a composition as a recapitulation. This compositional device appears in Sousa's "Stars and Stripes Forever" where theme 'C' is again stated at the end giving the selection a structure of A—B—C—D—C. Introductions and endings were used at the discretion of the composer. Ragtime used simple, basic chord structures. As the music was written for the piano, no lyrics were involved.

The **Dixieland** era parallels ragtime chronologically. A Dixieland band would often use themes of a march and 'jazz them up' to the point that the original themes would be difficult to discern. Many of the musical cliches heard in Dixieland are direct 'steals' from the march.

This: — — — —

— — — became this

The interludes separating march themes were also found in Dixieland. In marches everything was written on paper for the performer to follow, while Dixieland was characterized by improvisation.

Dixieland, like ragtime, also used multiple themes, often related musically. Themes were either eight or 16 measures in duration with a portion of the composition left open to accommodate solos by one or more members of the band. Musical gimmicks such as stoptime, breaks, and cadenzas were also used. Another favorite was the call and response, with the 'call' being played by the lead instruments and accompanying instruments 'responding'. As in ragtime, Dixieland was instrumental in nature and, so, lyrics were seldom used.

Popular songs, *'pops',* were an outgrowth of the 'tune factories' of tin pan alley where songwriting teams 'mass' produced music to meet the public demand. Demand was high as the songs of the period were primarily vocal and helped develop the Broadway musicals. At this time, solo singers had begun to make their mark in the musical world and needed new material. Radio needed to fill airtime and music, preferably vocal, seemed the most logical and popular filler. The consumers' needs were most efficiently met by songwriters who adopted a standard formula for songs.

Unlike the art songs of Schuman and Schubert which had one melodic line from beginning to end, tin pan alley songs had a basic 32 measure formula with two themes (A and B). Each theme was eight measures in length with theme A used three times, and then B acting as an interlude (bridge). The basic structure was Theme A (eight measures), Theme A repeated (eight measures), Theme B (eight measures) and Theme A (eight measures), totalling 32 measures. An introduction of four measures and a tag-ending of four measures could be added at the discretion of the performer/arranger. Each eight measure section had different words so while the musical theme repeated itself, the words were a continuation.

During this period, there was a move toward chromatic alterations. Adding 6th, 7th, and 9th notes in a chord and altering chords from major to minor by lowering or raising notes, gave chords 'color', enhancing the melodic line.

"Birth of the Blues"

Theme "A" – 8 measures

Theme "A" – repeated

Theme "B" – 8 measures

Theme "A" – 8 measures

'Pop' lyrics rhymed and verbal themes were often synonymous with social events, romance or fantasy. Songs written for musical shows were related to a central theme or story.

While songs written during the various eras of jazz were composed by songwriters, some of the instrumentalists as well as vocalists delved into the songwriting field, primarily to enhance their repertoire and in so doing become associated with a particular composition. This was not a common practice in that most of the musicians both vocal and instrumental were very busy performing and touring. Some of the artists did make notable contributions to the songs of their era such as Lil Hardin's "Struttin' With Some Barbeque," Mel Torme's "Christmas Song," Duke Ellington's "Sophisticated Lady," "Prelude to a Kiss," and "Black, Brown and Beige," Charles Mingus' "Foggy Day," Jelly Roll Morton's "Milenberg Joys," Charlie Parker's "Relaxin' at Camarillo," and Dizzy Gillespie's "Night in Tunisia."

In today's musical scene, many of the touring bands and their members spend a good bit of time composing songs for their particular group. Entertainer Dolly Parton alludes to the fact that much of the material she used in her shows was written by her. The lyrics of the songs written today are still along the same general themes as those from past eras; social problems, lost loves, economic woes, dissatisfaction with society, moral issues and a young society endeavoring to cope with impending adulthood.

The form of today's music compared with the music of ragtime, Dixieland and Tin Pan Alley is quite different. Whereas ragtime and Dixieland followed a structure of sixteen measure themes (or repeat of eight measure themes), and Tin Pan Alley song writers favored the thirty-two measure formula with two or three principal themes, today's composers actually use a free form where the lyrics seem to dictate the length of phrases and total compositions. The song "Evergreen", composed by Pat Williams and Barbra Streisand, is a classic example of the new style of composing. Where the two themes in the song, "Misty", are only eight measures long and easily remembered, "Evergreen" has several excellent melodies which, however, are extended into a rather long composition. It is a challenge for musician and listener alike to remember the complete work. There are a number of composers/performers who follow the structure of the traditional twelve measure blues and compose songs in that form.

In any event, through the vast history of jazz, we in society have a rather large variety of styles and forms from which to choose for our own personal listening. The changes in song forms will continue to take place as one era gives way to another and one style evolves into another. The harmonic structure seems to remain rather simple, perhaps for the benefit of the listener as well as the performer. Maybe the adage, "less is more," enhances much of the forward flow and drive of the music and lyrics. There are cases where the harmonic structure gets somewhat involved with abrupt key changes which in turn changes the focus of the tonality from one center to another. This is apparent in the standard song, "Body & Soul," in which the composer moves to another key during the bridge (theme B) and then returns to the original key when the song moves back into the last eight measures (theme A). Another example of tonality change is in Whitney Houston's recording of "Didn't We Almost Have It All?", in which the melody changes key at the beginning of each phrase. A unique and enjoyble as well as interesting structure is the result.

Summary

The song forms discussed here were the basis of the development of jazz. Some of these forms are still used today. In terms of form and technique, each era seemed to develop from the last, keeping some basic ideas, adding others, and blending them with the particular tastes of the day. The following chapters will look at each era, so the reader can begin to see how each was influenced by the past, and how each differed with time and the audience's demands.

Discussion Topics

1. Should songs written during a particular era retain their original form, rhythmic accompaniment and harmonic structure when performed/recorded by contemporary artists/groups?
2. Can songwriters who are also performers, perform both functions equally well, or is there a possibility that a flaw could develop in one or the other endeavors? Each involves separate study and skill. Cite examples of people, past and present, that performed both functions equally well.

African Drummers (Ed Dwight, Sculptor).

CHAPTER **3**

From Africa to the New World

The first Africans arrived in the English Colonies in 1619, in Jamestown, Virginia. It marked the beginning of the slave trade in the New World. For the next 200 years they arrived in small groups and large shiploads. They came in bondage to perform laborious tasks to which they were unaccustomed. They were little more than prisoners in unfamiliar surroundings. They were the pawns in a game not of their choosing.

Slavery was not invented by the citizens of the New World. Slavery was practiced in Rome and Greece, centuries before the New World was discovered. Slavery was not relegated to blacks alone. It encompassed all races and religions.

It is perhaps blunt to state that the development of jazz probably would not have occurred had it not been for the African slave trade to the New World. There was the influx of European ethnic and folk music that was brought to America by the many immigrants. While the folk music of Germany and Ireland is far removed from the sounds and styles of today's jazz, there is the relationship that both are music of and for the people.

The Africans that were brought to the New World came from the West Coast of Africa also known as the Gold Coast, the Ivory Coast, and the Slave Coast. It was the area south of the Sahara Desert and included the states/nations/kingdoms/tribes of Dahomey (Benin), Togo, Nigeria, Ghana, Angola, Guinea, Senegal, Camaroon, and the Congo.

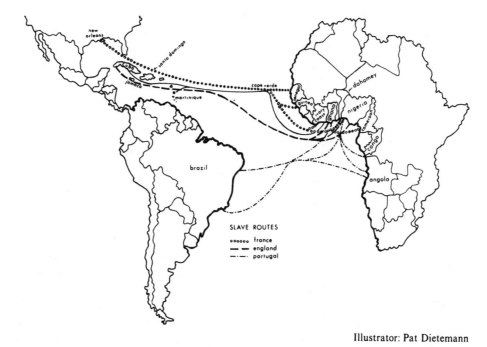

Illustrator: Pat Dietemann

Slave Routes.

In the fifteenth century, the Portuguese were the first to bring slaves from the West Coast of Africa and take them to Europe. They were sold in large numbers to the Spanish who in turn would season and educate them to the ways of Europeans. Many of the slaves that were sent from Spain to the West Indies had been Christianized and spoke Spanish, which helped them adjust to the cultures of Haiti, Cuba and Puerto Rico. The demand for slaves in the New World was continually growing, and Spain did not have an adequate supply to meet this demand. As a result, direct voyages were undertaken by traders from Africa to the New World. Arabs and other Africans became the principal slave traders and kept a warehouse of slaves in fortresses along the West Coast of Africa until they were transferred to slave ships and sent to the West Indies and directly to America.

In the sixteen hundreds, the colonies had little use for slaves, since they had an ample supply of indentured servants to fill their labor needs. However, with the growth of plantations in Virginia and other Southern colonies, the need for unskilled labor grew rapidly. The numbers of slaves brought from Africa increased in the following numbers; by 1750, 300,000 black slaves had been brought to North America, by the end of the century the number had increased to 800,000. By the mid-eighteen hundreds the figure had climbed to nearly 4,500,000. It has been estimated that by the end of the importation of slaves from all sources (Spain, Africa, West Indies) 15,000,000 slaves had been brought to North America.

The Spanish colonization of the West Indies in 1510 created a demand for slaves because of the agrarian development in Hispanola (Dominican Republic) and Haita. The first delivery of African slaves was in 1518. The West Indies later became a marshalling area for the slave trade to both North and South America. Again, agricultural development being labor oriented, created a demand for cheap labor and the African slaves filled that need. America imported 70,000 slaves annually. By 1870 almost 10 million slaves had arrived in the New World either directly from Africa or via the West Indies.

The West Indies became a human warehouse of Africans. It was called the 'middle passage' as it was a stopover between Africa and the final destination of North or South America. The ships stopped at the various islands of the West Indies including, Haiti, Martinique, Jamaica, Hispanola, and Cuba. While in these marshalling areas, the slaves were 'seasoned' to work and obey masters. After this training they were transferred to North or South America when the demand was created by buyers. A slave might be in a marshalling area for a few days, weeks, months, or even a year or more. It was here that a blending of music from the different tribes occurred and intensified.

The music during this period was dominated by the tribes from Dahomey and Nigeria (Arad and Yoruba). It formed a common base of music and the results would become the jazz that developed in New Orleans. The New Orleans slave population included approximately 18 different tribes representing the Agwas; Arados (original voodoo worshippers); Ashantis; Awassas; Cotocolies; Fantis; Fidas; Fonds; Foulahs; Iboes; Mandingos; Mines; Nagoes; Popos; Senegalese; Sosos; and Yorubas. This blending of music from many tribes also resulted in the 'steel bands' in the Carribean, calypso music, and the samba in Brazil, known in America as the 'Spanish tinge' and later called Latin music.

African Music

Music played a very important role in the function of African societies, much like it did in European societies. At the time, African tribes were illiterate. They had no newspapers. There were no schools. The main form of communication was through music and that primarily through the sounds produced and projected by the various drums and horns. The music was attached to various ceremonies which marked important transitions in life or the seasons. Examples of these ceremonies were birth, death, work, marriage, manhood, victory or defeat in war, and the harvest.

African music was quite repetitious rhythmically and melodically—somewhat akin to the traditional American song "Ninety-Nine Bottles of Beer on the Wall". As African tribes used music to tell stories the music could and did get quite long, it lasted until the story was finished.

Even today we can hear this repetition. On a cruise ship in the Caribbean, the author had an opportunity to listen to a steel band playing calypso music. The band played the popular "Yellow Bird" for over 15 minutes, one chorus after another. The lead player noted the fact that the songs have numerous choruses and verses which tell a story and in leaving any segment (verse) out would be like omitting a verse in a poem. The words tell a story, and if it take 50 verses and choruses to tell it, 'so be it'.

There was no notation to African music. It was learned by rote from generation to generation. The music was primarily vocal in nature, utilizing rhythmic accompaniment by various types of percussion instruments. The singing was done either by a solo voice or by a group of singers. It utilized the form of call and response, which became very popular during the work song period and which found its way into all forms and eras of jazz from its beginnings through jazz today. One voice states the call or phrase and is in turn answered by a chorus of voices, either repeating the same phrase or voicing a contrasting phrase.

Drums were the most common of the African instruments. There are included in the instrument family instruments which could carry a melodic line with a percussive sound such as the xylophone. There were also plucked instruments such as harps or the thumb piano, also called the kalimba or sansa. There were reed blown instruments resembling flutes and whistles. Animal horns with their overtone qualities were also in evidence. Stringed instruments resembling violins, guitars and banjos were less common.

The format of the music was simple but effective. The use of an ostinato was very popular. The continuous repetition of a short rhythmic pattern was the basis for much of the music. In later years during the ragtime era, the beginnings of boogie woogie were found, which is based upon the same structure of a short repetitious rhythmic pattern played by the left hand while the right hand plays a melodic line.

The vocal music was usually accompanied by rhythm instruments, however, singers could/would often augment the accompaniment by using the parts of the body as a rhythmic instrument. This was executed by foot stomping, hand clapping, thigh slapping or finger snapping. This, too, was to find its way into the music of the slaves when they were bereft of instruments with which to accompany their dancing and singing on the plantations. At that time it was given the name "patting juba."

Traditionally, African music, whether vocal or instrumental, is based upon repetition of rhythmic and melodic patterns. It has little contrast in melodic lines. Melodies did not go through a developmental process as did European music. Harmonies were very conservative. The African had no written history. His music was his history. Take away his music and you have taken away his past.

To the African, music and life are inseparable. Englishman Richard Jobson wrote "There is without a doubt, no people on earth more naturally affected to the sound of music than these people."

An African writer sums it up characterizing his people as: "A nation of dancers, musicians, and poets. Thus every great event, such as a triumphant return from battle, or other cause of public rejoicing is celebrated in public dances which are accompanied with songs and music suited to the occasion."

Music was so much a part of their native culture that when they were brought to the New World, they continued their musical activities by singing and dancing whenever possible. On board the slave ships they sang songs of sadness lamenting their predicament, including fears of being mistreated and never again returning to their homes. When finally being assigned specific work as slaves, they sang while they toiled and developed their new societies, which produced the foundation of the era known as the work song.

Women in African Music

Unlike the music of Europe, where women played relatively small roles in music, the Africans gave the women in the villages major roles in producing the music for the various tribal functions or rituals. The European women were utilized in the choral area as either vocal soloists in songs, or as members of an opera cast, or as soloists in religious works such as masses and requiems. They were given very little consideration in the field of composition/orchestration or as instrumental specialists either as orchestra members or chamber musicians.

In African music women were employed in virtually all the musical activities. As instrumentalists, they performed on the mallet instruments (xylophone), the thumb piano, the aerophones (windblown instruments such as flutes) and the chordophones which were stringed instruments (fiddle types, harps, zithers and lyres). But perhaps the most important role of women musicians was that of singers. The female voice when performing in a high range has much better projection power than that of men. Without any form of amplification or acoustical treatment, voices should have the capacity to project over distance as well as above any form of accompaniment. While the quality and musical development could not be compared to their European contemporaries, they did perform an important function for the tribe. Their roles in tribal dances were equally important to that of the males. There are instances where tribal women were also members of the drum ensemble, but these occasions were quite rare.

Rhythm

In African music the eighth note is the basic rhythmic unit. Modern rock is based on the repeated eighth note. African music emphasizes the weak beats (2, 4) with hand clapping. This gave American jazz a pulse for the backbeat and a primitive feeling of syncopation. European music uses the quarter note as the basic rhythmic unit and the strong beats (1, 3) are emphasized.

Polyrhythm is the playing of two or more separate rhythms at the same time, such as two beats being played over the same time span as three beats. This is commonly known as two against three. The African drum ensembles would use several different meters simultaneously which might seem quite disjointed, but it always had a focal point at which they all came together.

Melody

The songs of the Africans deal with their social activities as birth, death, marriage, etc. While the African did not use the diatonic scale as we know it today, they sang their melodic line with tonal inflections. Unfortunately the music of the tribes of this period has been lost. Unable to write or record the music, it

was passed down from generation to generation and lost through the development of the nations themselves. In recent years, researchers in ethnomusicology have traveled to Africa with the express intent of recording and preserving what remains of the early tribal music.

The native African would be puzzled on hearing American jazz, as we are when hearing the blending of African music from the various tribes. Compared to the music of ragtime, Dixieland and swing, African music is very complicated rhythmically. Kaufman and Gukin in AFRICAN ROOTS OF JAZZ stated:

> To the African, complex musical rhythms are meaningful and expressive. The cross rhythms of various instruments played against each other develops an intense exuberance which is evident in the mutual excitement generated between the musician and the audience.

26

This total involvement can only be appreciated in light of the knowledge that not only his philosophy of life, but communication itself is influenced by and expressed in terms of the musical elements of tone, pitch and rhythm found in conversational African languages.

There is a general misconception that American jazz was built upon rhythms from Africa and melodies from Europe. Jazz today is a development which may have had its roots in Africa and Europe, but once it arrived at what we today call jazz, it is far removed from its origins. Many of the melodic characteristics of African music became a part of the blues; the field hollers, the cries, scat singing, and the bending and sliding of notes. The shouts and falsetto breaks used in modern jazz trace their roots to the tribes of Africa.

Africans did not use the total diatonic scale used by Europeans. They had no scale but rather sang in terms of notes that were high, medium, or low. The African scale is a five note or pentatonic scale, compared to the European diatonic scale. The five note scale was not a true scale but rather had some of

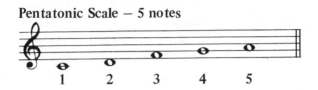

Pentatonic Scale — 5 notes

its notes a bit lower than the comparable note on the diatonic scale. As the blues scale developed in America, the full diatonic scale was used but certain notes were lowered (3rd, 7th, and sometimes the 5th) to create the blues tonality and the blues scale. Intervals used in African music seem to be centered around the five note scale. The melodic line would dictate whether the notes were sung high, medium, or low.

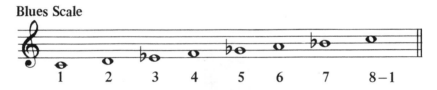

Blues Scale

Harmony

The harmonies used by Africans in their music varies depending on the locale. In general, European harmony was based upon the interval of a third, major or minor. The construction of basic chords in European and American music is based upon the intervals of thirds. Africans used the thirds also but as stated, depending on locations, harmonies also included intervals of fourths, fifths, and sixths as the basic harmony. The interval of a third did not seem to appear in African music until Europeans arrived in Africa.

Harmonic Intervals by Areas

Interval	Area(s)	
Unison	Senegal, Nigeria, Dahomey, Cameroon	
Thirds	Ghana, Nigeria, Liberia	
Fourths	Ghana, Nigeria, Togo	(Example below)
Fifths	Ghana, Nigeria, Togo	

Unison – Sengal etc.   Thirds – Ghana etc.   Fourths – Ghana etc.   Fifths – Ghana etc.

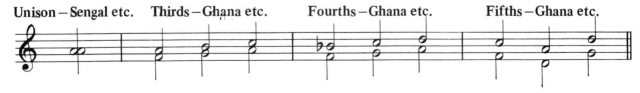

When the slaves came to America, they used the intervals of thirds for their harmonies, thus finding it easy to adapt their songs to the harmonies of Europe.

Form

African music's form was based in part on the call and response which became commonplace in the work song, in Afro-American church music, and in jazz styles where it was used both instrumentally and vocally. Kaufman and Gukin recognized four types of call and response: "1. exact choir repetition of the soloist's verse, 2. choir repetition of the soloist's refrain, 3. soloist sings the first half and the choir sings the refrain, 4. choir vs choir." All of these are found in jazz today.

Instruments

Instrumental ensembles are structured to produce melody, harmony, and rhythm. The string quartet, clarinet quartet, woodwind quintet or similar groups do not use rhythm instruments. The instruments themselves provide the rhythm. Beethoven, while not utilizing percussion instruments as modern composers do, used the wind and string instruments of the orchestra to provide the rhythmic element of his music. The base of African music is the percussion instruments. In searching for sounds, the African developed instruments to fit these particular needs. The basic instrument was the drum. Unlike the modern drum the African drum was made from materials readily available in nature. Though varying in size they were made from a hollow log, with an animal skin stretched over the top fastened to the log with rope or pegs. They were played either with the hand (open or closed) or a striker (beater).

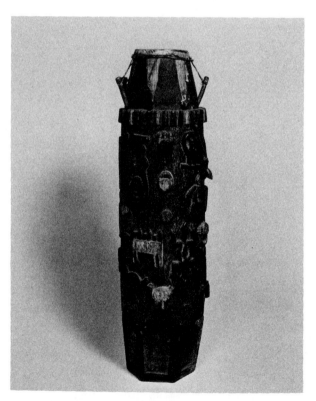

African Senofu Drum from the Ivory Coast (Courtesy: Denver Art Museum).

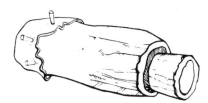

Illustrator: Pat Dietemann

Atumpan—African Drum.

Illustrator: Pat Dietemann

Ababigla—African Drum.

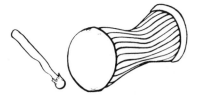

Illustrator: Pat Dietemann

Gan Gan—African Drum.

The xylophone was the most common melody instrument, it was built upon the pentatonic scale.

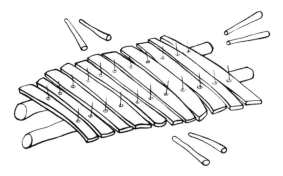

Illustrator: Pat Dietemann

African Xylophone.

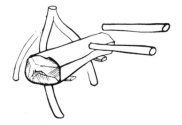

Illustrator: Pat Dietemann

Ekewe—African Instrument.

Horns made from either hollowed animal horn or wood had a limited overtone series similar to the bugle.

The kalimba or thumb piano, a series of flat metal springs stretched over a hollow box (similar to the Spanish guitar), was plucked with the thumb or thumbnail.

Kalimba, African Thumb Piano.

Woodblocks, rattles, gourds filled with pebbles, and clay pots were also used by the African musician. The clay pots were filled with water to various levels to create different pitches and struck across the mouth with the hands or brushes to produce sound.

Illustrator: Pat Dietemann

Udu—African Instrument.

While the village musicians had the responsibility of providing melodic and rhythmic music, it was the task of the tribal "griot" to develop the history of the tribe through song. He, in effect, became a musical historian, and in so doing, would embellish the events of the tribe in such a manner that it would impress visitors to the village. The same activity took place throughout Europe where they were known as the folk singers, and in Ireland where they were named "bards." The Sioux Indians name their crier "Eyabaha." The name "bard" was later given to singers on the street corners of New Orleans, where they would sing of the news events of the city and country, their only reward being monetary handouts of passersby.

The master musicians of the village or tribe had positions of high stature. They were virtuoso performers and were required to present music for the very formal activities of the village. They were assigned to the court of the kings or chiefs, positions that were handed down from father to son. They were categorized as horn blowers, drummers and/or praise singers.

Musical Ensembles

As with all types of musical ensembles, there was one person who assumed the role of director/leader. The leader's responsibility was to select the music to be performed; decide upon the tempo; rehearse the music; teach the music to the other performers (rote learning); and correlate/coordinate the activities of the ensemble. In an African drum ensemble, the task was performed by the 'master drummer'. The members of the ensemble learned their parts from the master drummer. During slavery, if one member was caught the leader had to find and train a replacement. If the 'master drummer' was caught, a major problem existed unless there was an understudy who could remember all the music of the tribe and assume the role of 'master drummer'. In the tribal hierarchy, musicians held almost godlike status. They had an important role in the social functions of the tribe. The loss of the musical ensemble to a tribe would be like a dance without music.

While the master drummer and his ensemble handled the rhythmic responsibilities, the 'bard(s)' handled the lyrics. They sang the folk songs, history of the tribe. Much like the folk singers of Europe and America they extolled the virtues and accomplishments of the tribe to members and visitors. The bard was the musical historian for the tribe. In the New World the 'bard' became the songleader on the plantation during the era of the work song.

Discussion Topics

1. If there had been no slave trade to the new world, how long, if at all, would it have taken for any form of jazz to develop in this country?
2. Besides the rhythmic contributions to jazz of African music, what could be considered equally important factors that made significant influences to the eventual development of jazz?

Banjo Lesson (Ed Dwight, Sculptor).

CHAPTER 4

The Work Song

As the name implies the work song was sung to accompany daily labor and tasks. The lyrics of work songs ranged from those that dealt directly with the specific task ("Michael Row the Boat A Shore") to those that were intended to allow the singers to take their minds completely away from the work at hand. In both melodic structure and lyrical content, the work song as developed in the United States became an important influence on the development of jazz. Europeans did not typically accompany their work with songs. Perhaps this was due to difference in work conditions as compared to the American slaves. The people of Europe usually confined their individual and group singing to religious services. An exception was the 'sea chanties' sung by European sailors.

The time period of the work songs was the 1800s until emancipation. After the 1860s, the work songs that developed were the 'prison songs' and 'chain gang' songs composed by prisoners. Work songs have been called 'Black American Folk Music'.

The adjustments that had to be made by slaves in their new environment were tremendous. Not only did they have to overcome their capture and transport to a location far from their homesites, they also had to cope with the problem of having families divided and sold to separate plantations with no contact with

Boone Hall mansion. The plantation at one time owned 1100 slaves. The plantation encompassed a large number of acres of pecan trees, tobacco fields, a brick factory and pastures for grazing of plantation livestock.

Front entrance to the Boone Hall mansion. The building was constructed of bricks
made in the plantation brick factory.

each other. They also had to begin learning, often with the endurance of physical abuse, the methods of labor required of them with no formal language instruction. The language that they were taught dealt primarily with the functions they were to perform on the plantation. The skills a slave was taught related to the work he/she was assigned and nothing more, unless, he/she showed exceptional talents and potential and was then moved on to new tasks in which he/she could be of greater benefit to the plantation owner or foreman.

Musical talents were utilized during free time and for functions of the slaves, whether religious, ritualistic (many of the slaves still secretly practiced voodoo), ceremonial or recreational. In so doing, slaves with musical talent began to become celebrities both with their fellow slaves and the plantation owners. In both cases, talented slaves were often called upon to perform for their peers or upon orders from the owner. This practice was similar to that of European royalty and people of monetary means who had composers/musicians in residence to perform for social affairs, often premiering new works. It became a status symbol to have men such as Mozart, Haydn and Bach in their employ. And so it was with plantation owners who utilized talented slaves for performances at social functions and plantation events.

The Boone Hall plantation mansion near Charleston, South Carolina had one wing of the building structured for music concerts/recitals which also included performances by slaves.

In her book, *Music of Black Americans,* Eileen Southern describes advertisements for slaves for sale and also advertisements for escaped slaves, describing their musical talents. These advertisements appeared in newspapers such as the *Boston News-Letter* and the *Virginia Gazette:*

TO BE SOLD. A valuable young handsome Negro fellow about 18 or 20 years of age; has every qualification of a genteel and sensible servant and has been in many different parts of the world. . . . He . . . plays on the French horn. . . . He lately came from London, and has with him two suits of new clothes, and his French horn, which the purchaser may have with him.

TO BE SOLD. A Negro Indian Man slave, about forty years of age, well known in town, being a fiddler.

RUN AWAY. A Negro Man about 46 years of age. Plays on the violin and is a Sawyer.

RUN AWAY. A likely Negro Man named Damon . . . was born in the West Indies, beats the drum well, which he is very fond of.

RUN AWAY. Negro man named Zack . . . speaks English, plays on the fife and German flute, had a fife with him.

34

The West wing of the Boone Hall mansion, which housed the music room in which slaves were required to perform for social events of the plantation.

Slave quarters on the Boone Hall plantation near Charleston, South Carolina.

RUN AWAY. Dick, a mulatto fellow . . . a remarkable whistler and plays the violin.

RUN AWAY. A Negro man named Derby, about 25 years of age, a slim black fellow, and plays away on the fiddle with his left hand, which he took away with him.

RUN AWAY. A negro fellow named Peter, about 44 years of age . . . he carried away a fiddle, which he is much delighted in when he gets a strong drink.

RUN AWAY. A Mulatto fellow named John Jones, about 26 years old . . . is a mighty singer.

RUN AWAY. A Negro man named Robert . . . speaks good English. Is a fiddler and took his fiddle with him.

RUN AWAY. A black Virginia born Negro fellow named Sambo, about 6 ft. high, about 32 years old. He makes fiddles, and can play upon the fiddle, and work at the carpenters trade.

Ms. Southern cites one example of a female escaped slave and the description cited in the newspaper advertisement. "She was fond of Liquor and apt to sing indecent and Sailors' songs when intoxicated."

A large number of historical writings about slavery often described the musical talents and activities of the slaves.

In the North, there was little opportunity for people to observe the work songs and little interest in it. In the South, slave owners considered works songs suited to the labors being done and their view was, "if their singing keeps them happy and content, by all means let them sing". The work songs gave the slaves an opportunity to develop their vocal and/or instrumental talents. Slaves were characterized by their musical skills.

Catholic slave owners showed little concern for the slaves' musical activity and let them sing as long as the work was accomplished. In contrast, Protestant slave owners restricted musical activity. They considered work songs 'devil music'. The Protestant owners made an effort to Christianize the slaves and exerted their musical influence through hymn singing. 'Spirituals', which became an integral part of our musical heritage, developed from this blending of the secular and religious.

Unfortunately the early work songs have been lost through time. There were no recording devices, nor were the lyrics or music written down to preserve this musical form for later generations. Song collectors including Colonel Thomas Higginson, Lucy McKim Garrison, and James Hungerford did compile the lyrics of numerous work songs into collections such as The Old Plantation and Slave Songs of the United States. The problem, however, was in writing the exact notation. The songs were not based on the diatonic scale, although, the European influences of tonality, meter, and scalic intervals did have an effect on the melodic structure of the songs. The variances in pitch (bending of notes) and approaches to a note (scoops) did not allow for accurate renditions of the songs for reproduction using the European scalic structure. Song collectors also found that a song was seldom sung the same way twice, and if it became a standard song, a song leader would vary the melodic line a bit each time it was sung. This variance of a traditional melody is found today in the improvisations of musicians, who will seldom play a song the same way twice.

Types of Work Songs

While work songs were usually based on agricultural activities, the social and recreational life of the plantation were also influences. Work songs also depicted; woodcutting, domestic work, shipping, railroading, etc. These were often composed by the laborer performing the task, whether slave or free, black or white.

The themes of the work songs built upon sacred and secular music. A derivative of African music, the songs served a variety of purposes:

Communication
Expression of Feelings
Relief from Loneliness
Ease the Daily Labors
Stimulus
Advertisement

Story Telling
Depression (Prison Songs)
Future Life—Life after Death
Mysticism
Rituals—Marriage, Death, Birth

Work song lyrics:

(Patty-roller, was slang for patrols established by slave owners to guard against escape by the slaves)

The day is done, night comes down,
You are a long ways from home;
Oh, run, nigger, run,
Patty-roller get you.

Yallow gal look and tryin' to keep you overtime;
The bell done rung, oversee hollering loud;
Oh, run, nigger, run,
Patty-roller get you.

Run, nigger, run, the patty-roller catch you,
Run, nigger, run, for it's almost day;
Massa was kind and Missus was true,
But if you don't mind, the patty-roller catch you.

Many of the work songs were characterized by the use of double entendre. This allowed for communication between the slaves, the slaves understood the words one way, the owner or overseer heard something else. As mentioned in Chapter 2 (Song Forms) "Follow the Drinkin' Gourd" is an example of the use of double entendre.

Gospel Music

The clergy, both Catholic and Protestant, were continually invited to the plantations by the owners. It was an effort to establish Christianity among their slaves. This was done in the hope that by Christianizing the slaves, they would then become docile and content in their new environment. It was a continual concern of plantation owners to keep the slaves on their property. The escape of slaves from their environs was an ever present problem for the owners. They felt they had to somehow protect their investment and not have to worry about losing workers. Hiring security personnel was an added expense that owners could well do without.

In the presentation of Christianity, music became an integral part of the program. Group singing about God and His people had a soothing effect on the individual's personality. In time, many of the hymns were taught to the slaves in a form of teaching called "rote" (teacher sings a phrase, student repeats phrase, etc, etc,). The slaves began to improvise around the melodies and rhythms of the hymns, thereby creating the earliest form of gospel music. Some of the music was included in dances developed by the slaves.

Author, Tom Heilbut, in his book "The Gospel Sound", written in 1975, in the preface writes about the effect gospel music had on the development of jazz.

"The assertion that gospel singing supplied the roots for much of contemporary music was not widely accepted; today it seems a received truth. But, paradoxically, though the gospel sound is now universal, the culture that produced it appears increasingly a thing of the past. At its best, the black gospel church provided the richest form of American folklore. Its language combined the stately periods of eighteenth century prose with the richness of southern country talk and ghetto slang. More than this, the gospel culture with its rituals, images and psychological assumptions, allowed generations of untutored artists to express themselves in a manner as free and improvisatory as they cared to make it. Virtually alone among popular forms of folklore, it recognized the importance and creative capacity of women. A cynic may scoff at the gospel church as matriarchal—though some of gospel's greatest exponents are male—but the indisputable fact is that in church singing women could be peerless artists, not by denying their social situation, but by drawing upon all its elements as resources."

Gospel music has given much of today's rock music its very foundations. The elements found in gospel music can be found in all the components of rock, from the basic beat, structured upon the even eighth-note pattern as the pulse, to the shouts and the drama exhibited by performers, including the dance steps which seem to be a derivative of the dances performed to the slaves gospel songs.

True lovers of gospel music are a clan unto themselves. They feel they have their own music. Heilbut theorizes that fans of gospel music have a distinctive language, special rhythms, and complex sense of ritual and decorum. Gospel music has its own very superior aesthetic standards. Their musical sophistication is remarkable. Universal approval comes from honesty and emotion. Church people understand spirit and soul better than anyone. They feel that all the music calling itself soul is really nothing but warmed-over gospel. Church people invented it. The lyrics of gospel music center around the plight of the poor man. This can easily be traced to its origin in slavery. Many of the lyrics decry the hope and desire to simply stay alive. There are, of course, songs which touch upon warmth, humor, play, love and sex. Gospel singers can be the most physical performers, on a par with and even surpassing some of the most physical rock entertainers.

Some of gospel music's better known singers include; Mahalia Jackson, Marion Williams, Sallie Martin, Willie Mae Ford Smith, Bessie Griffin, Sister Rosetta Tharpe, Clara Ward, Ruth David, Dorothy Love Coates, Shirley Ceaser, Thomas A. Dorsey, Sam Cooke, James Cleveland and Jess Dixon.

Call and Response: Singing utilizing the solo singer and the chorus. It was used in field work songs and in religious services (called 'lining out') in which the soloist sang the theme (text) and the chorus would respond with an answer.

These inflections have been refined and used by jazz singers throughout the development of jazz, 'Scat singing', which became popular in the 'bop' era had its origin in the 'field hollers'.

Lyrics

The words to the songs of this era were primarily related to the events at hand, either sociological or ritualistic. The lyrics were meant to tell a story. The majority gave an insight into the life of a people brought to this country in bondage and their attempts to be assimiliated into society. The lyrics of work songs were sometimes unprintable. Almost a century later in the blues, certain lyrics could not be broadcast.

Unprintable lyrics:

On to Glory

There's Chloe Williams, she makes me mad,
For you see, I know she's going on bad;
She told me a lie this afternoon,
And the devil will get her very soon.

or:

Hyprocrite and the concubine,
Living among the swine;
They run to God with the lips and tongue,
And leave all the heart behind.

The lyrics contained intense messages of individual and group personal experiences. While we think of the work song as being sung in the fields while picking cotton or shucking corn, it was also found in the cities. These were the songs and cries of the handicapped and the poor, sometimes accompanying themselves on guitar or banjo, standing on the street corners of New Orleans or other Southern cities, hoping to receive money for their musical talent and effort. The unemployed used their singing to advertise for a job, others sang to announce a local or national event much like the wandering minstrels of Europe. The 'balladeers', and 'story tellers' used their improvisational ability to sing about common problems facing society. They were often called 'spirit lifters' as they made light of problems facing mankind.

Instruments

The instruments used to provide accompaniment for the vocalists were homemade, purchased, or provided by the plantation owner. When instruments were not available the body was used as a percussion instrument. A carryover from Africa, 'patting juba', a form of hand clapping, thigh slapping, and foot stomping created the simulation of a drum to provide an aural stimulus for singers and dancers.

Primitive though they were, a number of the homemade instruments were adequate enough to provide the rhythmic accompaniment for singing and dancing. Most were designed after their African counterparts, a shell covered with hide and struck with either the hand or a wooden beater. They were made in a variety of sizes to give the players a selection of pitches. In addition to drums, modified household items were used as rhythmic instruments.

Whenever available, possibly the most popular instruments on the plantations were the banjo and the fiddle. In some instances, slaves purchased these instruments themselves with money earned. In other cases, plantation owners, realizing the benefits to slave morale, purchased the instruments for the slaves, and in other cases, craftsmen emerged who had the talent to manufacture these instruments from the very basic materials; pine board, animal intestines, gourds, animal hides, animal horns, horse-hair, canes, jawbones of horses/cows, pieces of metal and hollowed out lengths of logs. From all of this, although quite primitive, wind, string, and percussion instruments could be and were fashioned to provide the tools for making music.

Guitar, left, Banjo right (Sketches courtesy Amy Helm, Illustrator)

Washboards: Scraped and struck with a hard stick or metal rod.

Tub Bass: An inverted washtub with a string attached to it, the other end attached to a broom handle. The string was plucked much like a string bass.

Jugs: Narrow necked jug played by blowing across the open mouth, producing a bass-like tone.

Fiddles: Wooden boxes, similar in size to a violin, with a fingerboard attached and wires streched over a bridge, played with a horsehair bow.

Some instruments had been given to the slaves as rewards or incentives to contribute to their musical activity and their contentment, necessary to ensure continual productivity. There are instances where owners would purchase instruments for their slaves and in some cases pay for musical training. Purchased instruments used as accompaniment to the work songs included:

Harmonica: 'Blues harp' was capable of producing the pitch varients used in their singing.

Guitar: Limited in the 'projection' of sound it provided a subtle background accompaniment. Sometimes used with 'bottle necks'—necks of bottles broken off with sharp edges filed smooth—put on a finger and slid across the strings to give the effect of sliding and bending notes and producing a sound much like the steel guitar.

Banjo: With its greater projection capabilities, was used as chordal as well as rhythmic accompaniment.

Wind instruments: Clarinets, French horns, trombones, and cornets were sometimes found as accompaniment to the work songs.

Dancing

The Africans regarded themselves as dancing people. For the major part of their musical activity, dancing was integrated into the performance. So, also, dancing was a large part of the slaves' musical activity. Europeans likewise utilized dancing with much of the musical activity, whether as part of the social affairs of nobility, or the folk dances of the commoners. It has been stated by some historians that folk music, both African and European, was composed/designed for dancing. That was the case in the slaves social/religious activities on the plantation. Such was also the case of the music composed and performed during the eras of ragtime, Dixieland, minstrelsy and swing.

Writer Lewis Paine relates a moment in Georgia history when, after a logrolling contest, masters and slaves began dancing at the same time. As the slave musicians became more intoxicated with the spirit of dancing, they played faster and wilder until finally the whites could keep up no longer and withdrew from the dancing. This was exactly what the slave dancers desired! They sang out, "Now we show de white man what we can do!" and threw themselves with wild abandon into their frolic.

Where often there were no rhythm instruments to aid the slaves in their dancing, using parts of the body as instruments became popular. It was called patting juba (juber) and was performed by; foot tapping, foot stomping, hand clapping, finger snapping, thigh or stomach slapping, or knee slapping. It was most important to keep steady time for the dancers. One of the songs during this patting was recorded by a former slave named Solomon Northrup:

"Harper's creek and roarin' ribber,
Thar, my dear, we'll live forebber;
Den we'll go to the Ingin Nation,
ALL I want in dis creation,
Is pretty little wife and big plantation."

Dances during holidays were literally all night affairs. When the musicians got tired, the slaves resorted to patting juba and continued until such time as the fiddlers, banjoists, guitarists, and drummers could again provide necessary accompaniments. Many of the dances were copies of the African tribal dances. Others showed the influences of the white society. The most common dances were:

Ring Shout: A dance in which the women would form a circle, surrounded by a circle of men, seated, providing instrumental and vocal accompaniment. The dancers would work themselves into a frenzy until they would collapse from exhaustion. (Similar to a dance marathon.)

Cakewalk: A form of dance contest, in which the winner(s) were awarded a cake as the prize, also seen in later jazz eras.

Calinda: Two lines of dancers facing each other, moving forward and back in time with the music, similar to some square dances.

Bamboula: Couples danced together in a spirited fashion, similar to western dances.

Juba: A form of 'jig' in a duplet meter similar to the quadrille. A very lively dance.

Form

The general structure of a work song was musically simple. The musical pitches used can be characterized as; high on notes that began the song, medium for the main thrust of the lyrics (blue note area), and low to give finality to a phrase verse, or the entire song.

The melodic line and the notes were of short duration, notes were often repeated in a phrase, and a great deal of pitch variation (bending, scooping, and shouts) was used. There were no specific number of measures, the length of a phrase or verse was dictated by the length of the lyrical line. The performance of these songs on an instrument of fixed pitch, capable of producing only whole or half tones gives an inaccurate impression of the songs.

The rhythms of the work songs showed the influence of the polyrhythmic music of Africa. However, much of the music took on the duplet and triplet meter of European music. This is perhaps due to the influence of hymn singing.

The work song era was primarily vocal in nature. Instruments, when used, served as accompaniment. The voice was used to create inflections not found in European music but found in later jazz eras. The inflections found in the work songs included:

Falsetto Break: Somewhere similar to the 'yodel' of European music. The use of the voice in the extreme upper range where the singers original tone quality is changed to sound like another voice.

Shout: The accenting of words of a song with non-tonal sounds. It provided impact by the singer. It was used in religious music to provide 'impact' to the service.

After the Civil War and emancipation, the prison songs developed. The blues singer Huddie "Leadbelly" Leadbetter composed a number of songs while incarcerated. There is a tale that while in prison he composed a song pleading for his release and sung it to the state's governor, who was visiting the prison. Supposedly, his efforts earned his release.

Historians feel the end of the work song era came with the mechanization of agriculture, the end of slavery, and the decline in the need of field workers. Seasonal demand and migrant workers, living elsewhere, did not have the same bonds as did the plantation slaves, the bonds that led to the work song form.

One of the most important musical developments stemming from the work songs was the blues as we use them today. The work song provided the foundation for the blues scale, the lowering of notes in the diatonic scale brought from Europe. Both the use of the drum as an important rhythm instrument and the banjo as an accompaniment instrument resulted from the work song era.

In their musical activities, the slaves engaged in a great deal of singing about fictional characters such as Brer Rabbit and all his animal friends. They sang of slaves called Jack, John, Zack or Sambo. They also sang about Biblical heros. But, they did not sing about themselves very often. They felt they had no heros or heroines. They were not in control of their own bodies.

He knew of his future and what was in store for him during the remainder of his lifetime. As a result, what folk songs he sang about himself were about the sadness in his life, the toil of his existance and occasionally a little bit of mirth and satire of the Master and Mistress. Songs about fictitious animals that were half spoken and half sung became the foundation for their repertoire of narrative and song. Their songs were a delight for the young and old alike. Their musical activities and at times their performances for the "Massa" during his social functions also gave the slave the foundation of one of the mainstays of jazz, improvisation! Slaves possessed of that ability were of great value to their own society as well as that of the Masters. One account is as follows; Charlie could make up songs about de funniest things. Marsa say, "Come here, Charlie, and sing some rhymes for Mr. H." "Don't know no new ones, Marsa," Charlie answered, "Come on, you black rascal, give me a rhyme for my company, one he ain't heard."

Summary

To the slave, music was important. When he sang, when he danced, whites were under the impression he was happy. Too often that was not the case but rather just the opposite. When asked about what appeared to be good humor, the slave answered, "We endeavor to keep ourselves up as well as we can. What can we do unless we keep a good heart? If we let it weaken, we should die."

Discussion Topics

1. By what means and through whose efforts, did the Northern states become aware of the roots of jazz that were developing throughout the South?
2. Why is the drum considered the basic instrument of jazz when in effect it cannot produce a melodic line?
3. The popular melodic-type instruments associated with early jazz were the string instruments; fiddles, banjos and guitars. Why, with the exception of the guitar, are they seldom heard in jazz today?

Minstrel Man (Ed Dwight, Sculptor).

CHAPTER 5

Minstrelsy

James L. Collier, in his book THE MAKING OF JAZZ best describes an introduction to Minstrelsy. He states:

> White Americans have, for most of the country's history, been curious about, and at times fascinated by, the black subculture in their midst. This fascination with the black subculture has manifested itself, almost continuously since about 1840 and perhaps before, in an interest in black music.

Prior to the advent of the minstrel shows and their eventual transformation into vaudeville, the black slaves entertained themselves and their white owners through music either in the form of songs or dances, or instrumental performances on instruments of far lesser quality than those used by musicians today. In addition, whether by accident or design, they engaged in mimicry and joviality, making light of an impossible situation regarding their personal and social lives. This was the basic format of the minstrel shows. The original plot of a minstrel show was to entertain the white audience with a generalized picture of 'plantation life' encompassing both its sadness and hilarity.

Prior to and during the Civil War, minstrel shows served as a propaganda vehicle for the Northern cause by vocally and visually illustrating the trials and tribulations encountered by slaves (breakup of the family, loss of loved ones, cruelty of masters, death of slaves from inhumane treatment). Minstrelsy started in a theater in New York. The originators had heard about slaves' life on the plantations and decided that it would make popular entertainment for white audiences. New York had its stage programs of sacred and secular music. It had its ballad operas which were English in origin. And John Gay's "Beggars Opera" had been quite popular.

The first minstrel troupes were comprised of white men in black face (using anything from burnt cork to forms of shoe polish to darken both face and hands). The first black minstrel troupe was not formed until 1855. The positive aspect of minstrelsy as it relates to jazz history is in the opportunity it gave the blacks to become entertainers in their own right. It gave the exposure necessary to the public to establish the blacks in the entertainment industry with black and white audiences alike.

The time frame for minstrelsy was from 1840 to the end of the century. While there were still minstrel shows in existence after 1900, vaudeville was to replace it as a major form of entertainment.

Form

The musical form of the songs used in minstrelsy was diatonic. However, the blues tonality was utilized by those singers who become characterized as specifically 'blues singers'. The harmonies utilized simple chords, possibly again an offshoot of early hymn singing and spirituals. For a major part of the era, the lyrics utilized the 'black dialect' and composers (for the most part white—Stephen Foster) wrote the words in dialect.

Lyrics in Black Dialect.

Lyrics fit "Turkey In The Straw"

O its old Suky blue skin, she in lub wid me,
I went the arder noon to take a dish ob tea,
What do you tink now, Suky hab for supper,
Why chicken foot an possum heel, widout any butter.

I tell you what will happin den, Now berry soon,
De Nited States Bank will be blone to de moon,
Dare General Jackson, will him lampoon,
An de bery nex President, will be Zip Coon

In later compositions written for minstrel shows, the dialect was dropped for commercial reasons, so white audiences, purchasing the sheet music of minstrel show songs, could sing the songs without the dialects.

The theme of some of the songs included spirituals. The call and response patterns used in the work songs were used between soloists and chorus. A song written by composer Will S. Hays titled "Early in de Morning" is an example of the call-response pattern:

I hear dem angels a callin' loud,
Keep in de middle ob de road.
Dey's a waitin' in a great big crowd,
Keep in de middle of de road.

Many sentimental ballads were written for minstrel shows. Some were designed purposefully to elicit tears from the audience. An example was "Miss Lucy Neal" by James Sanford. It contained nine stanzas, the first and last of which were:

I was born in Alabama,
    My Master's name was Meal
He used to own a yellow gal,
    Her name was Lucy Neal.

One day I got a letter,
    And jet black was the seal
It was de announcement ob de death
    Of my poor Lucy Neal.

Many of the plantation songs were lyrical portraits of slave women as: "Darling Nelly Gray" (B. R. Handy); "Dearest Mae" (L. V. H. Crosby); and "Melinda May" (Stephen Foster). Not all the satirical songs used in minstrelsy were directed at blacks. Numerous songs aimed their lyrics at other ethnic groups including the Irish, German, Chinese, and American Indians.

Show Format

Themes of minstrel shows were to portray the blacks as illiterate, shuffling individuals who were the objects of ridicule and jokes. They presented stereotypes in several manners: a ragged, uncouth but joyous individual who appeared on the stage as 'Jim Crow'; a man of elegance and manners called 'Zip Coon'. From the latter, a song by that title was written for minstrel shows which following the Civil War was changed in title to become "Turkey in the Straw".

Northern audiences had little concept of plantation life. To them it was distantly removed from their everyday activities of work and play. Minstrel shows provided them with a form of light entertainment available to the whole family, quite diverse from opera, concerts, and the theater. There was little music or stage performances available for passive home entertainment. Neither the phonograph nor the movie camera and projector had been perfected and not everyone was into classical music. The minstrel show filled a gap.

Sheet Music Cover: "Turkey in the Straw." Copyright 1920.

Sheet Music: "Turkey in the Straw." Copyright 1920.

While minstrelsy was an undeniable form of racial bigotry, it did give rise to a form of popular music and became the predecessor of vaudeville. Composers, like Stephen Foster, were given the opportunity to write much of the country's folk music. The traveling minstrel shows proved very entertaining to audiences and gave individuals prominence in the performing arts.

Minstrel shows involved numerous facets of performance; vocal, instrumental, dance, and theater. The performances included individuals, small ensembles, and whole casts. This is the basic form of Broadway musicals and can be compared to both opera comique and grand opera. Since minstrel shows per se began in the New York area, it is conceivable that the format for the shows was based upon European theater and musical drama.

The first minstrel troupes contained a cast of four performers. Each member of the cast had specific charges in relation to the total performance. They were multi-talented and could either perform solo or as part of a combination of instruments or voices. The program, which had to encompass a whole evenings entertainment, included the following:

Songs: Solo, duets or full chorus
Dances: Tap dancing to instrumental accompaniment
Jokes: Between members of the cast, or solo
Satirical Sketches: All members of the cast
Skits: All members of the cast
Instrumental: Solos by banjo and fiddle, sometimes accompanied by tambourine and bones.

From this small beginning, the minstrel shows grew to massive stage productions including large choruses, featured soloists, both vocal and instrumental, and a large pit orchestra of up to 60 members.

In both the vocal and instrumental portions of the show, the songs exemplified by the works of Stephen Foster and described in the next section were used. 'Flag wavers' were played by the pit orchestra

47

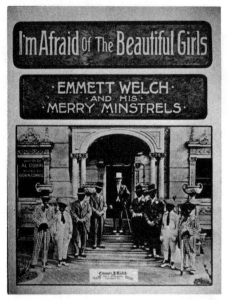

Sheet Music Cover: "I'm Afraid of the Beautiful Girls."

at the beginning of a show or between acts. 'Walkarounds' were used to close the show, during which the entire cast 'walked' among the audience singing.

The Cast

Minstrel shows, when they were at their most popular point, were quite elaborate productions with large casts. It was the forerunner of the variety show and included the same aspects with the exception of acrobats and trained animals. Music was the primary component which necessitated singers and instrumentalists as both soloists and ensembles. The typical cast included:

The Interlocutor: A master of ceremonies, usually dressed in white and sitting in a thronelike chair at center stage.

The End Men: Two men located at either side of the stage who engaged in repartee with the Interlocutor and other cast members. One was called Mr. Bones, and depicted the black man as a poor recipient of jokes. He had a set of animal bones in his possession and would rattle them during the 'punch line'. The other was Mr. Tambo, a well dressed cast member who portrayed the role of the 'city slicker' often called 'Jim Dandy' who played the tambourine in the same manner as Mr. Bones.

The Chorus: Men in blackface (it should be noted that when all black troupes were formed, the chorus still put on blackface) serving as accompaniment to the soloists. Members of the chorus were at times given vocal or instrumental solos or other featured parts of the show.

The Soloists: Singers, dancers, and comics who were the featured soloists of a show.

Pit Orchestra/Band: Instrumentalists who provided the 'warm up music' prior to the opening curtain, played all accompaniments for soloists (singers and dancers) and acted as an advertising group playing programs in the community including a minstrel show parade just prior to show time.

Stephen Collins Foster (Sketch courtesy Amy Helm, Illustrator.)

Olio

Olio was the part of the minstrel show which kept the audiences entertained between acts. While the main curtain was drawn during costume and scenery changes, members of the cast were given the opportunity to display their talents as soloists or in small ensembles. A member or members of the chorus were allowed to perform as 'olio' stars during these intermissions. They were accompanied by the orchestra or a piano during their performance. The important contribution of olio in the total picture of minstrelsy was that while it entertained the audience during intermission, it also gave individuals an opportunity to get solo exposure and perhaps find future employment as a feature attraction.

W. C. Handy who started as a six dollar per week cornet player with Maharas' Minstrels relates in his book FATHER OF THE BLUES the racial discrimination that faced the black minstrel troupes. The minstrel band was often attacked by 'white gangs of toughs' during the parade prior to the show. Handy also tells of the problems faced by blacks on tour in finding traveling, eating, and sleeping accommodations.

The Pioneers

One of the first minstrel troupes was a group called the Virginia Minstrels which included in its cast a **Daniel Decatur Emmett** (1815–1904). Emmett, born in Mt. Vernon, Ohio, helped form the Virginia troupe in 1843. He had played fife and drums in the army. He was a composer for the show and today is known best for his composition, "Dixie". He originally titled it "Dixies Land", and it was a favorite with audiences in the South. An interesting sidelight to this particular composition was the fact that besides making Emmett a well known composer, the song was adopted by the Confederacy as a 'rally' song. While Emmett resented this use, it became one of the better known compositions of the time and remains popular today. The Virginia Minstrels popularity in this country gave them an opportunity to tour England where they achieved enormous success.

In 1844, **E. P. Christy** formed a troupe called Christy's Minstrels. This group was quite small at the outset but as popularity of the minstrel show grew, he expanded the group and it became one of the more prestigious minstrel groups. He hired a young man named Stephen Collins Foster as his composer/arranger, to write 'Ethiopian Songs' for the show. Foster wrote for a number of minstrel shows including the Sable Harmonists. In so doing, he gained the necessary popularity to establish himself as one of the leading if not the leading composer of music for minstrel shows. His works were classified in three categories: Sentimental songs with slow tempos—"Beautiful Dreamer", "Massa's in de Cold Ground", "My Old Kentucky Home", "Old Black Joe", and "Old Folks at Home"; comic songs—"Camptown Races", and "Oh! Susanna"; and war songs—"Willie Has Gone to War". Many of the songs of Foster, as well as other composers, were 'tear jerkers' used to create emotional responses from the audience.

Following **Stephen Foster,** a young black songwriter came into the minstrel show spotlight. **James Bland** (1854–1911) became known as the 'world's greatest minstrel man' and the 'idol of the music halls'. His songs were a favorite of the minstrel audiences and the general public. He was a victim of plagiarism. Many of the white performers for whom he wrote songs published them under their names, without giving Bland credit for the compositions. Stephen Foster was also a victim of this plagiaristic exercise. Some of Bland's memorable songs include: "In the Evening by the Moonlight"; "Carry Me Back to Old Virginny", and "Oh, Dem Golden Slippers". He gained much of his fame when his music was performed during European tours of the minstrel shows. The Germans considered him one of the top three Americans who impressed them most with their music. The others were John Philip Sousa and Foster. When minstrelsy faded in the early 1900s, so did the music of Bland. He continued to compose but never again reached the level of popularity he had during minstrelsy.

Charles Callander, an organizer and promoter, formed Callander's Consolidated Colored Minstrels in 1882. He split the original group into three shows and toured America and England. Charles Hicks, a minstrel performer, organized his own show and following tours of America, his troupe toured Australia, China, Japan, Java, England, and Wales.

Thomas D. Rice, a white entertainer, made up in blackface, did a song and dance routine in which he portrayed the real or imagined facets of black life. His dance was quite rhythmic and included leaps and jumps as well as shuffles. He named the song and dance "Jump Jim Crow" which was very popular and in a sense set the pattern for solo acts in minstrelsy.

Other early minstrel troupes which performed in this country were: The Congo Minstrels; Ethiopian Melodists; Ethiopian Mountain Singers; Kentucky Minstrels; Metropolitan Minstrels; and the Billy Rice Minstrels.

While the general scope of the minstrel show was centered around the male performer, women blues singers were employed by various shows as an important feature. Renowned blues singers such as Bessie Smith and "Ma" Rainey were members of minstrel shows.

In addition to these female 'blues singers', several instrumentalists began their careers as minstrel performers and went on to become giants in jazz. W. C. Handy became one of the nations leading composers/arrangers and conductors. Lester Young, tenor saxophonist, performed in all jazz eras including the big bands and be-bop. Bunk Johnson a noted Dixieland trumpeter and bandleader and Jelly Rolly Morton a leading ragtime/jazz pianist and composer/bandleader had their musical roots in minstrelsy.

Minstrelsy hit its peak prior to the Civil War. The show casts became much larger and included bigger bands/orchestras. All black troupes were formed by 1855 and these became the training grounds for black musicians. The black entertainer became a true 'professional' during this period and the music began showing the pre-jazz traits of ragtime and blues. One of these traits was the banjo players utilization of syncopations in their playing which ultimately reached its major popularity in ragtime.

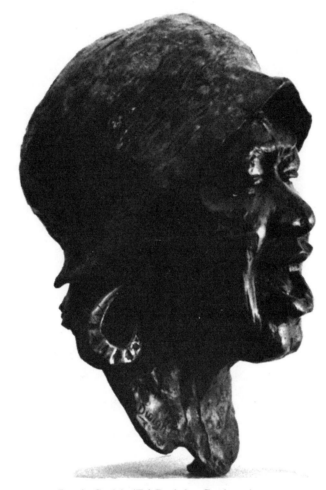

Bessie Smith (Ed Dwight, Sculptor).

CHAPTER 6

The Blues

To best describe the blues, the following excerpt from Paul Oliver's THE STORY OF THE BLUES should be noted.

> The blues are a state of mind. Furthermore, they are music which expresses this condition. The blues reflect the cry of the forgotten man and woman, the shout for freedom, the boast of the virile man, the wrath of the frustrated, and the ironic chuckle of the fatalist; but this is not all: they also reflect the agony of insecurity, the poverty and the hunger of the workless, the despair of the bereaved and the cryptic humor of the cynic.

> But let there be no mistake, the blues are a social music. Today, they are of paramount importance as an entertainment. They are the ideal music for the enjoyment of dining and dancing, and, at the other extreme, they are the songs of a certain segregated class—the American Negro—for in them he can find an outlet for his problems. Thus, the blues can be a music of creative artists within the folk community. It makes little difference whether it be in the deep rural South, or in the teeming ghettos of Chicago and Detroit, Blues are all things to all men of the race; they are the songs of the primitive guitarist sitting beside the railroad track; they are, too, the sound of some barrel-house pianist pounding away far into the Mississippi night; they are commercial Rock of the blues bands; they are the ribald 'dozens' of the medicine show, or the cabaret blues of the edge-of-town club; they are certainly contained in the show-biz routines of the traveling troupes, and in the latest hit of the recording star, or an unknown field worker singing his toils.

The blues had their origin in the days of slavery. At the turn of the century composers were putting the music on paper and onto recordings. Each era of jazz has utilized the blues as an integral part of its music.

True blues when properly performed adhere to the tonality of the blues scale with its lowered notes (3rd, 5th, 7th). However, not all of today's blues performers follow the true blues tonality, but rather simply follow the chordal structure of the blues.

The blues have undergone considerable changes over time. Early blues choruses were eight measures in length, then they developed into 16 measure choruses, and have today settled into a 12 measure chorus. The important part of blues are the chord progressions which are used in many of today's musical styles.

Added to the 12 measure format are extensions such as introductions and tag endings or interludes. Commonly, a performer plays two 12 measure choruses in succession to 'develop' a solo over a 24 measure period.

Blues Types

There are essentially two types of blues—city and rural. Both are based upon the format of lowered notes in the scale. The lyrics distinguish each: city blues, often called classic blues, deal with the socioeconomic problems of the urban dweller. Rural blues with the problems and/or activities of rural life; agriculture, slavery, work, and religion. See Chapter 2 (Song Forms) for details on blues lyrics.

The following is a comparison of the two types of blues as outlined in the *Introduction to Jazz History* by Donald Megill and Richard Demory:

Country vs City Blues

	Country Blues	City Blues
Accompaniment	Sparse, usually a single guitar	Several instruments or piano
Rhythm	Quite Free	Rigidly controlled, 12 bar structure
Lyrics	Earthy, dwelling on hardships	Sophisticated mature observations on love; verses carefully constructed to fit meter & rhythm
Vocalism	Underdeveloped, but highly expressive	Refined, carefully considered.

Performers

A number of individuals popularized the blues in both performances and recordings. Instrumentally, pianist Jelly Roll Morton, trumpeter "Satchmo" Armstrong, clarinetist Sidney Bechet played and recorded the blues. The blues main thrust was through the vocalist. The blues singer gave the blues the popularity needed to make it a true art form, and the basis of jazz as we know it today.

While the blues were sung by both men and women, it seems the women dominated the style and period. Most performed during the era of vaudeville and were part of the many traveling shows that appeared throughout the country. While vaudeville encompassed the entire country, the blues singer favored and was more popular in the South. A number of them were unknown to northern audiences. The **T. O. B. A.** was the primary booking agent for their public appearances. The race recording companies, Black-Swan and Paramount were their major outlets although other companies such as Columbia utilized the blues vocalists. Supposedly, Bessie Smith helped keep Columbia Records in business with her popularity and high record sales.

The "moaners", as they were called, were forerunners of the "torch singers" of later eras. It was a style in which the singers performed with great feeling in the vocalizing. The singing was designed to involve the listener in the emotion of the song, much as Stephen Foster utilized melody and lyrics in the songs described as "tearjerkers." The blues singers employed verbal and physical emotion in the melody and lyrics of a song. Each singer had her particular songs for which she was popular with audiences, both in live performances and on recordings. As is the case today, many of the blues singers were also adept at writing their own songs for their particular performances (shows). Many of the blues singers were involved in vaudeville. In this setting, they were not just singers of the blues. Their repertoire had to have variety and as such had to include songs other than blues. It was the female blues singers that were the first to record, albeit race recordings for labels such as Black Swan, Bluebird, Paramount and Pace.

As new eras of jazz appeared and developed, the traditional blues singers faded into oblivion. While they did not disappear altogether, their popularity diminished. Women blues singers made the style of the blues a notable fixture in jazz history.

There were a number of male blues singers, among them; Charlie Patton, Bukka White, Mississippi John Hurt, Skip James, and Blind Lemon Jefferson who, historians feel, was an influence on Huddie "Leadbelly" Leadbetter.

Many composed the blues, quite often extemporaneously. But one man stands above the rest as perhaps the most prominent composer—**William Christopher Handy.** He was a musician with quite a diversified background; instrumentalist (trumpet), college bandleader (Huntsville A. & M., Alabama), minstrel

W.C. Handy (Courtesy: Downbeat).

show musician, arranger (spirituals, folk songs), author (NEGRO AUTHORS AND COMPOSERS OF THE UNITED STATES, FATHER OF THE BLUES), and music publisher (Handy Bros. Music Co., Pace and Handy Music Publishers).

Born November 16, 1873, Huntsville, Alabama, Handy's music helped glorify the blues, and leaders such as Paul Whiteman gave it meaning to white audiences. A partial listing of his blues compositions include:

Beale Street Blues
Memphis Blues
Jogo Blues
Hesitating Blues
Yellow Dog Blues
St. Louis Blues

Handy's autobiography, FATHER OF THE BLUES, is a very informative history of the development of the blues.

Vocalist **Mamie Smith,** 'The Blues Queen,' was born in Cincinnati, Ohio, in 1883. She made the first recording by a black blues singer in February 1920, "That Thing Called Love," by P. Bradford. Her other recordings included "You Can't Keep a Good Man Down," and "Crazy Blues," both written by Bradford and recorded on Okeh records.

Bessie Smith (Courtesy: Institute of Jazz Studies, Rutgers University).

Lucille Nelson Hegamin was born in the early 1900s in Macon, Georgia. 'The Georgia Peach' recorded with Cameo Records. Some of her recordings are:

Rampart Street Blues
Land of Cotton Blues
Down Hearted Blues
Bleeding Heart Blues
St. Louis Gal

Ma Rainey was born **Gertrude Pridgett,** April 26, 1886 in Columbus, Georgia. Known as 'Mother of the Blues', she performed with the "Rabbit Foot Minstrels" and "Tolliver's Circus". After marrying William "Pa" Rainey, they performed in minstrel shows as "Ma and Pa Rainey". She became the first female band leader, as vocalist with the "Georgia Jazz Band". A partial list of her recordings follows:

Ma & Pa Poorhouse Blues (Paramount Records)
Counting the Blues (with Louis Armstrong)
Jelly Bean Blues (with Armstrong)
See See Rider (with Armstrong)
Cell Bound Blues

Historians of jazz regard **Bessie Smith** as the greatest of all the blues singers. Born in Chattanooga, Tennessee on April 15, 1898, she spent the early part of her career singing in minstrel shows on the T. O. B. A. circuit. She recorded for a label which produced the race recordings sold in the black communities. The record company was a subsidiary of Columbia Records. It has been theorized that her recordings alone kept the parent company, Columbia, in business until more of the white citizenry patronized the recording industry. Her original recordings have been rereleased as L.P.'s under the Columbia label. They contain a large amount of her original repertoire. She was a great inspiration to singer Billie Holiday. Given the honorary title, "Empress of the Blues," Bessie Smith was regarded the leader of the style. An automobile accident while on tour caused her untimely death in 1937. It is rumored that she was not allowed into an all-white hospital for emergency treatment. By the time she was taken to a hospital that accepted blacks, it was too late.

Some of her recordings include:

Empty Bed Blues
Send Me to the 'Lectric Chair
Gimmie a Pigfoot
Downhearted Blues
St. Louis Blues
Back Water Blues

Lizzie Miles, was born in New Orleans in 1895 and performed as a Creole (French) singer. Her most memorable recording is "Bill Bailey".

"The World's Champion Moaner", **Clara Smith,** was reportedly born in Spartanberg, South Carolina, in 1895. A top headliner for the T. O. B. A., she recorded several duets with Bessie Smith. Her recording on the Columbia Records label is best remembered for these blues songs:

Jelly, Look What You Done Done
Shipwrecked Blues (with Armstrong)
Salty Dog
My Brand New Papa

Victoria Spivey, birthdate and place unknown, became known as 'Queen Victoria'. She was a blues composer as well as singer. Her compositions dealt with sad, morose subjects; death (suicide), drugs, alcohol, sadism, illness, and sex. Spivey had her own record company, Spivey Records, and at one time or another recorded the songs of Alberta Hunter, Lucille Hegamin, Memphis Slim, Roosevelt Sykes, Big Joe Williams, and the "Muddy Waters Blues Band". Her recordings on the Okeh label include:

Black Snake Blues
Let Me Roam
Black Belt
Brooklyn Bridge
T. B. Blues

One of Paramount Recording Co,'s first vocalists, **Ida Cox** was born in Knoxville, Tennessee, around 1900. The 'Uncrowned Queen of the Blues', she spent several years performing in vaudeville. Cox, who became very successful financially, formed her own road company, "Raisin' Cain". For her recordings she used the very best of the instrumentalists; trumpeter "Hot Lips" Page, J. C. Higgenbotham on the trombone, pianist James P. Johnson, King Oliver on the trumpet, and Coleman Hawkins playing tenor sax. Her best known blues recordings are:

Last Mile Blues
I Can't Quit that Man
Cherry Pickin' Blues
Moanin' the Blues

Alberta Hunter recorded for both Paramount and Black Swan. In addition to her recordings, she was one of the best known travelers among the singers of her day. She found success in the stage play, *How Come*. Her songs were full of sentimental yearning. One of her favorite accompanists was ragtime pianist and composer Eubie Blake. Born in Memphis, Tennessee, she traveled worldwide. She looked upon herself as not just a blues singer, but a singer of broad musical/vocal capabilities. Sometimes recording under an alias named Josephine Beatty, she avoided contractual problems. She starred with Ethel Waters in the broadway musical *Mamba's Daughter*. During World War II she traveled about the country and the world, entertaining troops. Her efforts brought her a well-deserved decoration. She retired and began working as a nurse in the Goldwater Memorial Hospital on Welfare Island and gave up singing and acting. Following a period of retirement, she did a recording for Prestige during which she recorded "I Got Myself a Working Man," and "Got A Mind To Ramble."

In the 1980s, Ms. Hunter attempted a brief comeback. Having appeared on television, she won the heart of Americans. She passed away several years ago and was named the "last of the Great Blues Singers."

A brief list of some of her recordings include:

Don't Pan Me
Daddy Blues
Down Hearted Blues
I' Going Away Just To Wear You Off My Mind
Jazzin' Baby Blues
Crazy Blues

Lonesome Monday Morning Blues
You Can't Have it All

Many of the blues singers were accompanied by some of the top jazz instrumentalists. Artists who had made a name for themselves in Dixieland and/or in the big band era accompanied the blues vocalists in recording sessions and live performances. Following is a list of some of these instrumentalists:

Pianists: Willie "The Lion" Smith
Fletcher Henderson
Jelly Roll Morton

Clarinetists: Buster Bailey (also played the sax)
Benny Goodman
Don Redman (also sax)
Sidney Bechet (also sax)

Trumpeters (Cornetists): King Oliver
"Hot Lips" Page
Roy Eldridge
Charlie Shavers

Saxophonists: Coleman Hawkins (tenor)

Drummers: "Baby" Dodds
Cozy Cole
Sonny Greer

Blues vocalists were in their heyday during the 20s, 30s, and early 40s. Their recordings are a lasting momento to the period.

The period of the traditional blues as a primary force in popular music drew to a close about 1935. But, similar to other eras, it never died out completely. There have been several resurgences in recent decades. The advent of rhythm and blues with such stars as B. B. King and Muddy Waters has kept it alive. The music of rock and roll is based in some large part upon the blues. Other forms of the blues can be found in country music and modern versions of Gospel. The themes of the lyrics no longer concern themselves with slavery but rather with the social concerns of the time. Popular subjects of blues lyrics are poverty, social and moral issues, political issues (The Vietnam Conflict), racism and love.

The late Muddy Waters (real name, McKinley Morganfield, 1915–1983) performed in the style of rural blues. A worker in cotton fields in the south, he was discovered by folklorist Alan Lomax. Coming to and performing in Chicago in 1943, he recorded on the Aristocrat label. In the late 1950s he recorded a selection titled "Rollin' Stone," which in turn inspired Bob Dylan's "Like a Rolling Stone," which in turn became the name of a British rock group and finally gave the name to a periodical. In the 1960s personalities such as Ray Charles, B. B. King, James Brown and Aretha Franklin turned this music into a style called, jazz-blues-rock!

During the fifties and sixties, many of the rock stars utilized the blues in their styles and fashions. Fats Domino, Chuck Berry, Bill Haley and the Comets and Elvis Presley relied heavily on the format of the blues in many of their selections.

Discussion Topics

1. The blues as a form of music have undergone changes since their inception during the work song era. What are the specific changes that have taken place since that time to make them a style in today's music?
2. The original blues singers utilized numerous vocal gymnastics in their performances. What was done different vocally in singing the blues in their traditional manner, and singing popular ballads created in Tin Pan Alley?

Scott Joplin (Ed Dwight, Sculptor).

CHAPTER 7

Ragtime

The ragtime era began toward the end of the 19th century. It was a 'happy' style of music. Rhythmically it was quite complex compared to the redundancy of blues songs, work songs, and hymns. While it was primarily composed for the piano, banjo, and guitar, Dixieland bands played ragtime and the professional concert bands of Sousa, Pryor, and Gilmore featured 'ragged tunes' in many of their concerts. Ragtime was the new jazz that swept the country. It not only became popular in America but spread to Europe and became the popular music form. It even influenced some classical composers to try their hand at this new music form. Aided by published music, its popularity was greatly enhanced both in this country and Europe. Ragtime pianists were in demand throughout the country and music publishers had a heyday! A new form of piano playing developed with spinoffs such as 'boogie woogie' and 'stride'. The term syncopation became a household word in relation to the music which had a rhythmic flow seldom heard in classical piano compositions. The player piano became the 'essential' part of household furniture and ragtime pianists were kept busy performing live and recording piano rolls. Ragtime pianists became composers as well. The musical 'stars' were born.

The period of ragtime paralleled Dixieland, but, ragtime seemed to come to a rather abrupt halt with the end of World War I, while Dixieland survived until the swing bands took the spotlight.

The origin of the name of the era is questionable. Historians will never totally agree upon the real meaning of the term. One theory is that it is named after the piano dance music that was popular in the Northeastern states in the early 1800s inappropriately called "jigtime." Another theory is that it developed from the custom of flying a white flag, or "rag" at houses where there was dancing and music. "Ragged time" is another name given to the style. To "rag" a tune simply meant to "jazz it up." "Ragging" is associated with black clog dancing, also associated with "patting juba", using the hands and feet for slapping and stomping to produce syncopated rhythms. In "ragged time", the rhythmic style is loose and ragged, compared to the strict structure of the rhythm of marches and hymns as well as European piano compositions. Whatever the historic origin of the term, it became a style of jazz in which the solo pianist, banjoist and guitarist had to assume the role of the complete ensemble, providing all the musical components; melody, harmony and rhythm.

The timing was right for the style of music. It was lively and spirited, although in its truest form it was a somewhat subtle and relaxed style, with a happy flavor. It followed the depression of 1890, a time when the country needed and wanted a mental 'uplift'.

Historians place its geographical origin in Sedalia, Missouri. Nearby St. Louis can also be noted as being the home and nurturing place of ragtime. Sedalia was at the time a railroad hub between the East and the West. It contained a large population, all of which were in some manner associated with the railroad. As a result, the various forms of vices found their way into and around the city. Saloons and bawdy houses were everywhere. The effect on the development of ragtime was a natural. Most saloons and sportin' houses hired piano players (professors) to entertain the customers. The popularity of the music soon spread to other cities including St. Louis, Chicago and New Orleans.

An interesting aspect in the development of ragtime was its concentration upon the piano. During slavery, blacks had virtually no contact with keyboard instruments. When once freed, and developing a society of their own, they exhibited a tremendous interest in the development of their music. That whites could hardly understand the music was of no concern to them. Families purchased pianos and organs so their children could learn to play and develop musically. These purchases often were at the sacrifice of some of the basic household necessities. W. C. Handy and Eubie Blake began their musical training in just this manner. The irony of the development of the style of the music and the fact that a pianist could entertain as a soloist had an adverse effect on the development of jazz bands. Saloon owners soon found that their customers were just as satisfied in hearing and dancing to a solo piano playing this new type of popular music, and that hiring additional musicians playing wind and rhythm instruments was not necessary and much more costly.

Syncopation

This is characteristic of ragtime. In very simple terms it is the playing of a melodic line on the 'upbeat'. It is also described as putting the emphasis in the melody (the notes of longer duration) on the upbeat. Alternatively it is described as playing parts of the melodic line just before and just after the beat. A form of short-long-short melodic structure, while the bass line (played by the left hand) emphasizes the beats in the measure, either in a stride (walking) fashion, or a boogie-woogie (repetition of patterns) fashion.

Syncopation can be traced back to the African 'cross rhythms' with their complicated rhythmic structures of a three note figure played over two beats.

Syncopation as such was a device used by European composers for centuries prior to the development of jazz in this country. In reality, ragtime, rhythmically and harmonically was a fusion of African and European musical styles. It must be remembered that ragtime was pianistic in nature and the piano and piano compositions were a European export.

Form

The form of ragtime compositions are similar to the march. Why this is the case is unclear, unless it was through the development of Dixieland and the popularity it achieved. Ragtime pianists in their effort to simulate the music of a complete ensemble, copied the musical structure of Dixieland music, which in itself was patterned after the marching bands and their music.

Unlike the work songs and the blues with one central theme, ragtime composers utilized multiple themes similar to marches, even to the point of the duration of the phrases (themes). Most of the themes were 16 measures in duration, often repeated. The trio of which, like the march, modulated into another key. At times the melodies of the themes were related, but this was not a compositional rule. Introductions were optional and used at the discretion of the composer, along with 'tag' endings.

The harmonies were European in nature, utilizing chromaticism, and a number of the 'rags' were labeled 'marches' by their composers.

The 'blue notes' were discarded in favor of the European harmonies and melodic structure. The piano did not have the ability to 'bend' a note once the note was struck, nor could it perform with vibrato. The banjo and guitar had these capabilities, however, the piano was the more popular of the instruments even with its shortcomings.

Sheet Music Cover: "Great Crush Collision March."

Location

While Sedalia, Missouri is considered by some to be the home of ragtime, St. Louis had a greater effect on its development and popularity due to its location on the Mississippi River. St. Louis was a popular docking point for the riverboats on their way north from New Orleans. The riverboats carried two items—passengers and cargo. It was for the entertainment of the passengers that the riverboat owners employed musicians. Ragtime pianists found ample opportunity for employment on the riverboats, as well as in the towns and cities between New Orleans and St. Louis and overland to Chicago. Ragtime pianists were hired in places that could not afford a complete band for dancing and entertainment. The brothels, honky tonks, cabarets, speakeasies, and fashionable nightclubs featured the ragtime pianist. It was in St. Louis that Tom Turpin, a ragtime pianist, opened several nightclubs and called them 'ragtime clubs'. In Sedalia, the Williams' Brothers opened the Maple Leaf Club which inspired Scott Joplin's composition "The Maple Leaf Rag," the most popular of all rags. These ragtime pianists were the forerunners of today's 'piano singles' in which a solo pianist is employed to play either as a featured soloist or plays 'cocktail piano' as background music for dining or drinking. Unfortunately, the complicated syncopations and cross rhythms were quite difficult for the amateur pianists and ragtime quickly lost its popularity with them. The piano rolls, recorded by the leading artists were very popular and enjoyed excellent sales.

The Chicago Exposition (world's fair) of 1893 assisted in spreading ragtime music to the rest of the world. People attending the Exposition heard ragtime pianists performing along the midway. Others heard the music in the many Chicago clubs featuring ragtime.

During the St. Louis Fair of 1904, also known as the Louisiana Purchase Exposition, the Turpins sponsored a ragtime contest. The winner was a New Orleans pianist named Alfred Wilson. Following this event St. Louis began to lose its influence on ragtime as the pianists slowly drifted to other parts of the country; Chicago, Kansas City, and New York.

During its peak, European composers tried their hand at composing this style of 'black folk music' and to Europeanize it. Claude Debussy, a French impressionistic composer, wrote "The Golliwogs Cakewalk" a rather conservative and subdued example. Other European composers who composed ragtime were Igor Stravinsky and Darius Milhaud. Their compositions never achieved the popularity of the American composers.

Cakewalk Contests

The musical craze of ragtime enjoyed several variations. It was possible to dance to the music played by solo pianists or ragtime bands. Many of the descriptions printed on the cover of the published rags outlined as a march, a 'two step', or 'waltz' suggesting that they were composed for dancing. The popular dance at the time was the cakewalk, a dance originating during the work song period on plantations. There were 'cakewalk contests' in which contestants improvised steps to the syncopated rhythm of ragtime. Often these dance contests were coupled with 'ragtime piano contests', in which pianists were required to improvise songs in a ragtime style.

Ragtime Schools

For anyone wanting to learn to play ragtime, schools of instruction in the art were opened and instruction books were published. Scott Joplin wrote a set of six exercises and published them as "School of Ragtime" in 1908. The publication included explanations and warnings (Joplin indicated ragtime was never to be played at a rapid tempo). Music studios advertised ragtime instruction in area newspapers.

Published Rags

The composing and playing of rags was not restricted to the black pianist alone. Many white pianists joined the fad with a great deal of success both as pianists and composers. While the music of Dixieland bands was in a large part memorized (head arrangements) the music of ragtime was more sophisticated and because of the interest to the amateur pianist, had tremendous sales potential. Publishers realizing this potential were quick to print rags in the form of sheet music for the consuming public. Writers noted that many families both black and white had pianos in their possession and made their children study the instrument through private instruction.

The first published rag was the "Mississippi Rag" by white composer/bandleader, **William H. Krell** in January 1897. The first published rag by a black composer was "Harlem Rag" by **Tom Turpin,** December

Sheet Music Cover: Harlem Rag.

1897. Scott Joplin's "The Maple Leaf Rag" was not published until 1899. Its structure is based upon the march with several themes:

Theme A:	16 measures repeated
Theme B:	16 measures repeated
Theme A:	16 measures (not repeated)
Theme C:	16 measures repeated (in new key)
Theme D:	16 measures repeated.

At the time of its writing and subsequent publishing, Joplin boasted, and rightly so, that "The Maple Leaf Rag" would get him crowned 'king of ragtime'.

Fortunately for Joplin he encountered a music dealer named **John Stillwell Stark** in Sedalia, who became one of the leading ragtime publishers. John Stark came from a farming family in Missouri. An entrepreneur, he developed an ice cream delivery service. He did quite well and decided to expand his peddling. Stark began selling Jesse French Cabinet Organs, harassing customers until they finally purchased an instrument. He then sold pianos and when he had inundated the Chillicothe area with pianos he moved to Sedalia. Here he opened a music store. Sedalia was a railroad center and offered ample employment opportunities to the citizenry. The same opportunities also drew a varied and sordid populace whose primary occupations were associated with the illicit activities of society. Bordellos, honky tonks, and gambling establishments thrived, many of which employed musicians. It was in Sedalia that Stark met the then itinerant pianist Scott Joplin. They formed a liaison which lasted for a number of years, during which Stark became Joplin's music publisher. Stark bought "The Maple Leaf Rag" for 50 dollars and royalties. This was somewhat unusual at that time since most ragtime composers would sell a composition for a specific fee ($10.00 was a normal price) without a royalty clause. "The Maple Leaf Rag" sold hundreds of thousands of copies and established Stark as a publisher, whereupon he moved to St. Louis, which was becoming firmly established as a 'ragtime center'. Other publishers around the country soon followed suit and as the ragtime craze took over, publishers geared up for the explosion and were not disappointed. Stark moved east and continued his publishing

Sheet Music Cover: Maple Leaf Rag.

65

MAPLE LEAF RAG.

BY SCOTT JOPLIN.

Tempo di marcia.
THEME 'A'

Sheet Music: Maple Leaf Rag.

THEME 'B'

THEME 'A'

M. L. R.

THEME 'C'

TRIO.

THEME 'D'

M. L. R.

68

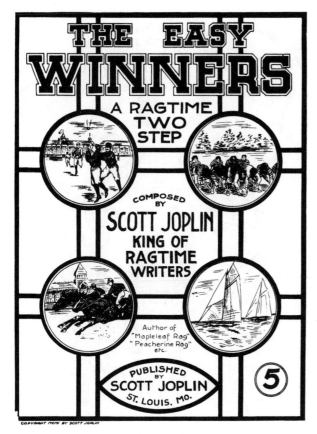

Sheet Music Cover: "The Easy Winners."

Sheet Music Cover: "Peacherine Rag."

business, but in 1910, following the death of his wife and failing in his efforts to compete with the 'big business' scheme of 'tin pan alley', he returned to St. Louis. During his publishing days, Stark published numerous works by Joplin. He did hesitate to publish Joplin's operas however, much to the disappointment of the composer. A partial listing of Scott Joplin's works as published by John Stark and Sons Publishing Co. includes: "The Maple Leaf Rag", "Swipsey Cakewalk", "Peacherine Rag", "The Cascades", "Augustan Club Waltz", "A Breeze From Alabama", "The Entertainer", and "March Majestic".

Early Recordings

In 1877, **Thomas Alva Edison** became involved in inventing a machine that would capture the sound of the human voice. Originally intended as a dictaphone machine for use by office secretaries, it soon became evident that this had much greater value to the music industry. His first machine employed the use of what appeared to be foil covered cylinders. In subsequent years, other inventors joined in and contributed to its development. In time it changed from a cylinder recorder to one utilizing the flat disc. In 1877, Emile Berliner invented a machine known as the gramophone, which utilized the flat lateral-cut discs rather than the vertical cut cylinders. In a short time, recording companies emerged to produce recordings both instrumental and vocal, jazz and classical. Victor Talking Machine Company, Columbia Phonograph Company and Edison Record Company were the pioneers in the field.

In 1921, black musicians made the first recordings on piano rolls for the QRS (Quality Reigns Supreme) company. With the design and manufacture of the upright "player piano", ragtime was brought into the home along with the published sheet music. Home entertainment took on a whole new dimension.

The Players/Composers

As there were hundreds of ragtime pianists in this country and abroad, it would be an exercise in futility to list them all along with biographical sketches of their lives. There are, however, a number of them

Sheet Music Cover: "The Entertainer."

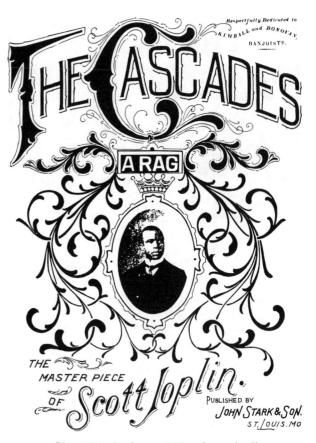

Sheet Music Cover: "The Cascades."

whose names seem to be mentioned in the various books dealing with ragtime. Some were performers while others, seemingly the majority, were also composers. Rudi Blesh and Harriet Janis in THEY ALL PLAYED RAGTIME go into great detail on the lives of these artists. For the devotee of ragtime, this book is a must! Listed here is but a sampling of those men who made ragtime an important event in the development of jazz.

Scott Joplin (1868–1917) was born in Texarkana, Texas. He became the best known of all ragtime pianists/composers, and was considered the leader in the field. He was an accomplished musician. As a child he studied piano, cornet, theory, and harmony. At the age of seventeen he migrated to St. Louis and began working in the various honky tonks and sporting houses. He also played the various 'houses' in Hannibal, Columbia, Jefferson City, and Sedalia. In 1893 he went to Chicago to perform at the World's Fair. After the fair Joplin returned to St. Louis and again played in the 'tenderloin' district. He later moved to Sedalia where he played and toured with the Queen City Concert Band as a cornetist. He became a friend and teacher to a number of young ragtime pianists including Arthur Marshall, with whom he collaborated with on "Swipsey Cakewalk". Often assuming the role of instructor, he would list suggestions at the beginning of his compositions as to how ragtime should be played. Unfortunately, for increased saleability, Joplin along with other ragtime composers, simplified their music so the amateur pianist could play it. The idea met with limited success. Ragtime, built in large part around syncopation, was and is, one of the most difficult styles of music attempted by the pianist.

A partial listing of Joplin's work follows, not including those listed in the biographical sketch of John Stark, music publisher.

Rags: Original Rag, 1899
The Chrysanthemum, 1904
Gladeolus Rag, 1907
Wall Street Rag, 1909

Operas: A Guest of Honor, 1903
          Treemonisha, 1911

Recordings (Piano Rolls): Magnetic Rag
                            Maple Leaf Rag
                            Pleasant Moments
                            Weeping Willow

Scott Joplin Rags, Genius Brought No Riches—Just a New Art Form

Mike Flanagan

Scott Joplin (Courtesy of the Institute of Jazz Studies, Rutgers University).

Scott Joplin's effect on American music cannot be underestimated. In a time before the music business was radio, stereo, or compact disc, he composed a body of work that elevated popular music to an art form.

The ragtime Mozart was a Westerner, born in Texas thirty-two years after the fall of the Alamo and nurtured in the home state of Jesse James. His accomplishments are all the more remarkable when we consider his bumpy personal life and the bigoted times in which he lived.

Joplin was born Nov. 24, 1868, on the Texas side of the town that would become Texarkana, where his father was working as a railroad laborer. He was the second of six children.

Giles Joplin, his father, was a former slave from North Carolina who had obtained legal freedom around 1863. His Kentucky mother, Florence Givens Joplin, was born free. The family was far from rich: Florence cursed the bags of laundry she took in. But they loved music.

Giles was an accomplished "plantation violinist," having played everything from waltzes to polkas in the finest mansions. Florence sang in the Sunday choir and played the banjo. She could see that Scott was the most musically adept of the family band, jamming away on a hollow guitar.

When a neighbor heard him play her piano, she gave him open access to the instrument. For his seventh birthday (and Christmas and the next birthday, insisted Giles), Scott was given a used piano, on which he spent all his free time.

By eleven, Joplin had caught the attention of an elderly German music teacher. In three years of study with him, Joplin received a classical background, learned to read music, improved his technique, and began composing.

His training was cut short at age fourteen, when his mother died. Joplin left home soon after, possibly because his father thought he was spending too much time on his music.

His teens were spent playing in bars, brothels, cafes, steamboats, wherever the tinkling of a piano was required atmosphere. From Texas to Nebraska and back, he provided the sound track in a variety of houses, from Scar Face Mary's in Oklahoma City to Chicago's plush Everleigh Club.

The kind of music he played was an early version of ragtime, an evolving joyful noise with roots in Africa. Music had come over on the slave galleys, but white owners often forbade the folk sounds. By blending the African rhythms with European musical discipline and counterpoint, the syncopated melodies were made "acceptable."

Original American music development. Plantation reviews beget minstrel shows, which introduced the country to new dance music that included the two-step and the cakewalk.

In 1983, Joplin and other itinerant "ticklers" congregated at the Chicago World's Columbian Exposition. Heartened by the crowd response, he moved to Sedalia, Mo, to compose. Musical horizons expanded further at the George R. Smith College for Negroes. He played and arranged for the Queen City Concert Band and the Texas Medley Quartet.

Joplin had penned his first rags by 1897, but publishers were reluctant to accept them. After rejection in Sedalia, his first sale of the new music was "Original Rags" to the Carl Hoffman house in Kansas City. Reflecting the predominate ugly racial atmosphere of the day, the sheet music cover depicted an old black rag picker in front of a dilapidated shack.

At Sedalia's Maple Leaf Club, the new sounds rocked the rafters. Here, Joplin met music publisher John Stark, forming the team that would change musical history. In September 1899, Stark published Joplin's "Maple Leaf Rag." Sales were phenomenal; fifty thousands copies sold in the first few months.

The song brought Joplin international attention as it became the first sheet music in history to sell more than a million copies. He and Stark, sharing royalties, moved to St. Louis, setting up a hit factory that produced "The Entertainer," "Peacherine Rag," and "Fig Leaf Rag." Later that year, he staged an ambitious ballet, "The Ragtime Dance," in Sedalia.

Ragtime became an immensely popular, forbidden rage. Because of its bawdy origins, "respectability" was a major issue in turn-of-the-century America, one that never really resolved itself. The racist climate of the day figured heavily in the uproar, as white and black music styles intertwined. "The country is awakening to the real harm these 'coon songs' and 'ragtime' are doing," spouted one editorial. An official statement from the American Federation of Musicians, meeting in Denver in 1901, called ragtime "musical rot."

Despite the controversy, his music was in demand. Joplin became obsessed with giving ragtime a place of honor. Thanks to modern technology, he could be heard across the country. The Pianola (player piano) offered a crude playback system from piano rolls. Joplin recorded many of his famous pieces in New York. By putting the paper roll inside the piano cabinet and pushing the foot pedals, one could hear Scott Joplin's ragtime in the parlor.

Joplin's personal life was not nearly as bright. At thirty-one, he had achieved enough financial success to wed Belle Hayden, the sister-in-law of one of his music pupils; but the marriage was one of turmoil and problems. Belle had little understanding of her husband's genius—as their funds dropped while he composed the ragtime opera "A Guest of Honor," so did her patience.

A child died in infancy in 1903. Their marriage fell apart soon after, and Belle died suddenly in 1905. Haunted but still driven, Scott Joplin again became a nomadic "professor."

Always the womanizer, Joplin's torrid romances now found their way into compositions such as "The Antoinette march," and "Leola." One of his most brilliant rags was "The Cascades," a rolling, flowing piece inspired by the Cascade Gardens at the 1904 St. Louis World's Fair.

In 1907 he moved to New York, married Lottie Stokes, and stabilized for a while. Lottie ran a rooming house for performers, allowing her husband freedom and the time to compose works such as "Rose Leaf" and "Sugar Cane." He also penned "The School of Ragtime," six exercises for the serious student. But his consuming passion was the creation of an Afro-American folk opera, "Treemonisha."

The last ten years of his life were spent on the project, a moralistic tale of what education could do for the black race. In 1911, he paid to have the 270-page vocal/piano score published.

Popular music tastes were again changing, something Joplin had failed to notice in his operatic trance. Attempts to find a producer for the show failed. In 1915, Joplin gave a solo performance of the work in Harlem to an invited audience.

Depression from the failure of "Treemonisha" along with an advancing case of syphilis contracted during his early years on the road slowly unraveled his sanity. By 1916, his condition had so deteriorated that Lottie was forced to commit him to the Manhattan State Hospital on Ward's Island.

Cause of death, April 1, 1917, was listed as "dementia paralytica." He was forty-nine. "You know," said Lottie, "he would often say that he'd never be appreciated until after he was dead."

Director George Hill heard a Joplin recording by Joshua Rifkin while working on his 1973 film, "The Sting."

The motion picture, starring Paul Newman and Robert Redford, took place in the Chicago of the Twenties, but Hill thought the Joplin humor and style would make the perfect sound track. "The Entertainer" became "The Sting's" theme song.

In addition to the film's winning the best-picture Oscar the following year, the theme and score won Academy Awards.

By the end of 1974, the Scott Joplin sound track had sold more than two million copies and a full-scale revival was under way. In Sedalia, they held the Scott Joplin Ragtime Festival. "Treemonisha" enjoyed a Broadway revival in 1975. Its composer was awarded a posthumous Pulitzer Prize in 1975.

For years, Joplin had shared an unmarked pauper's grave with two others at St. Michael's Cemetery in Astoria, Queens. The "rediscovery" earned him a bronze marker. During the ceremonies conducted by the American Society of Composers, Authors and Publishers, a gentle breeze blew maple leaves over the grave. Historical vindication had come for "The King of the Ragtime Composers." His genius had come full circle.

James Sylvester Scott (1886–1938) was born in Neosha, Missouri. Though not as prolific a writer as Joplin, Scott made valuable contributions to the music of ragtime. An accomplished musician, he spent some time in Kansas City as a music teacher and theater organist. He formed his own band, playing in theater pits for silent films in the Kansas City area. He had his first rag, "A Summer Breeze—March and Two Step", published at the age of seventeen. He spent his early years working as a handyman in a music store until the proprietor heard him play the piano after which Scott demonstrated sheet music to the customers.

His compositions were works of musical art—complicated harmonies which included five note treble chords with varied bass lines, called 'black scores'. Most of Scott's compositions were beyond the capabilities of all but the accomplished pianist. The advent of 'talking pictures' put him as well as hundreds of other 'theater' musicians/composers/arrangers out of work. He spent his final years composing and playing.

A partial listing of Scott's work are given below:

Rags: A Summer Breeze—March and Two Step, 1903
       The Fascinator—March, 1903
       Frog Legs Rag, 1906
       Kansas City Rag, 1907
       Great Scott Rag, 1909
       Sunburst, 1909

Songs: She's My Girl from Anaconda, 1909
       Take Me Out to Lakeside, 1914
       The Shimmie Shake, 1920

Waltzes: Hearts Longing Waltzes
       Suffragette Waltz

Thomas Million Turpin (1873–1922) who was to become one of the most colorful of ragtime pianists was born in Savannah. Georgia. He is established in jazz history as one of the major proponents of the art of ragtime. In addition to his compositions and his playing ability, he assisted in the development of the era by being the proprietor of one of the most famous of all ragtime clubs, The Rosebud, in St. Louis, in which any pianist who was anybody, performed. He and his father, John (Honest John), became proprietors of several clubs, in essence 'sporting houses', but in relation to ragtime, were the hub of the musical activity in Missouri. Until ragtime moved east, these clubs were the places in which all the giants of ragtime met, performed, and occasionally competed. Turpin was given the honorary title of 'Father of St. Louis Ragtime'. He published some of his own rags. Possibly his greatest claim to fame was that he was the first black to have a rag published, "Harlem Rag" in 1897 by Joseph Stern and Co. in New York. While his list of compositions is relatively short, his major contribution was in fostering ragtime and assisting pianists to gain the needed exposure to become known. His works include the following rags:

Harlem Rag, 1897
Bowery Buck, 1899
Ragtime Nightmare, 1900
St. Louis Rag, 1903
Buffalo Rag, 1904

James Price Johnson (1891–1955), recognized for his competitive spirit, was born in New Brunswick, New Jersey. Johnson, an accomplished ragtime pianist, engaged in 'cutting contests' in which he would implement 'tricks' during the breaks in the melodic line of a composition. These embellishments, such as glissandos and tremulos, gave the music new sounds from its original context. Johnson studied classical piano music in order to put concert efforts into his playing. He began his career playing in a Long Island resort and later worked the 'district' on Manhattan's west side. While ragtime was his favorite musical activity both in performance and composition, Johnson also composed music for symphony orchestras. Here he found limited success compared to 'white' composers. Even though he had his works performed by major symphony orchestras, it was classed as Negro music, and as such, it never achieved the popularity with white audiences who were the majority of concert goers. His classical works included: "Symphonic Harlem", "Symphony in Brown", "Symphonic Suite on the St. Louis Blues", and his Negro rhapsody, "Yamekraw". Many of his ragtime compositions were never published, but those that were became favorites of not only ragtime pianists but also of the later jazz pianists.

Among Johnson's other compositions were:

Rags: Caprice Rag, 1914, also recorded as a piano roll and disc
       Harlem Strut, 1917
       Carolina Shout, 1925, also recorded as a piano roll and disc

Songs: Old Fashioned Love, 1923
       Charleston, 1923, also recorded as a piano roll and disc
       If I Could Be with You One Hour Tonite, 1926

Jelly Roll Morton (1885–1942) was born Ferdinand La Menthe in New Orleans, Louisiana. Following the death of his father, his mother remarried a man names Morton and gave the boy his name. He was to become a composer, performer, and jazz historian. In 1938, Alan Lomax, then curator of the Music Division of the Library of Congress, interviewed and recorded Morton's version of the history of jazz. This recording of Morton talking, playing, and singing is preserved in the American Folksong Archives. It must be noted that these interviews gave Morton's version of jazz history and not necessarily the true historic picture. Morton was an egotist, who, in the course of his musical career claimed to be the 'inventor of jazz' . . . there never was a New Orleans style, Kansas City style, or Chicago style, only a Jelly Roll Morton style.

Egotist though he may have been, his abilities were tremendous. Morton's career encompassed three of the major eras in jazz, ragtime, Dixieland and swing. He began his musical career playing guitar in a 'strolling' quartet, playing spirituals at funerals. By fifteen he was playing piano in the brothels of New Orleans. Morton was considered a blues player and singer. He was a gambler, pimp, poker shark, and hustler. But beyond this, he was one of this country's finest pianists.

Morton traveled extensively from coast to coast and became known as one of the top 'professors', of the piano. His piano style was a bridge between ragtime and jazz. An interesting study is his treatment of Joplin's "Maple Leaf Rag" (contained in the Smithsonian Collection) compared to Joplin's recording (in the same collection). Jelly Roll was a superb improvisor. Much of his playing and composing was based on the blues but it was orchestral in nature. He was one of the first to notate the music for his players, a forerunner of today's arrangers. He was considered the best classic jazz pianist. He was a most welcome addition to the development of jazz.

A partial listing of his compositions includes:

Rags: Superior Rag, 1925
       Kansas City Stomp, 1923
       King Porter Stomp, 1924
       Milenberg Joys, 1925
       Chicago Breakdown, 1926
       Black Bottom Stomp, 1926

Instrumental Blues: The Jelly Roll Blues, 1915
Wolverine Blues, 1939
New Orleans Blues, 1925

Vocal Blues: The Winin' Boy, 1939
Buddy Bolden's Blues, 1939
Mamie's Blues, 1948

Instrumental Tangos: Spanish Swat, 1948
Mama 'nita, 1949

Songs: Mr. Jelly Lord, 1923
I'm Alabama Bound, 1939

Recordings (Piano Rolls): Dead Man Blues
Shreveport Stomp
Midnight Mama
Tom Cat Blues
Tin Roof Blues (with the New Orleans Rhythm Kings)

There were a large number of other ragtime artists who made significant contributions to the development of ragtime. To list them all would take a volume in itself. Here are just a few of these, with an apology to the rest.

Joseph Lamb (1887–1960), self taught composer/pianist, was born in Montclair, New Jersey. A student of and collaborator with Scott Joplin he composed several rags: "Sensation Rag", "American Beauty Rag", "Cleopatra Rag", "Ethiopia Rag", and "Champagne Rag—March and Two Step".

Louis Chauvin (1883–1908), Born in St. Louis, became known for his improvisation. Known as a 'boy wonder', he traveled with music shows working as a singer and dancer. Collaborated with Joplin on "Heliotrope Bouquet" and the musical revue "Dandy Coon".

James Hubert "Eubie" Blake (1883–1983) was born in Baltimore, Maryland. His first job was in a Baltimore sportin' house at the age of sixteen. Worked with singer/bandleader **Noble Sissle** on the musical "Shuffle Along". Became a ragtime legend, playing until just prior to his death. Blake's other compositions include:

Rags: Chevy Chase, 1915
Fizz Water, 1914
Bugle Call Rag, 1926
Eubies Boogie, unknown
Black Keys on Parade, 1935

Songs: I'm Just Wild About Harry, 1921
Love Will Find A Way, 1921

Other renowned ragtime pianists/composers include: **Charles Luckeyeth "Lucky" Roberts** (1895–1965); **Scott Hayden** (1882–1915); **Arthur Marshall** (1881–1956); **Willie "The Lion" Smith** (1897–1973).

It is only fitting to end the list of ragtime 'stars' with a brief biography of **Thomas "Fats" Waller** (1904–1943). In his book THE STORY OF RAGTIME, Marshall Stearns cites a conversation Waller had with an elderly lady in which she asked him, "What is jazz, Mr. Waller?" to which he supposedly replied, "Madam, if you don't know by now, don't mess with it!"

"Fats" became a classic ragtime composer who also loved to play the music. He spent a good deal of his early years adapting jazz piano style to the pipe organ. He worked for a time playing the organ at the Lincoln Theater in Harlem.

He became a student of James P. Johnson in his studies of jazz piano. Waller toured Europe as both a piano soloist and orchestra pianist. Besides his rags, Waller also made the transition into the composition of popular songs, which had been the domain of white 'tin pan alley' composers. Several of his songs have become well known 'standards'.

Following is a partial list of Waller's compositions:

Rags: Wildcat Blues, 1923
       St. Louis Shuffle, 1927
       Valentine Shuffle, 1929
       Smashing Thirds, unknown

Organ Solos: Rusty Pail, 1927
               Lenox Avenue Blues, 1927

Songs: Squeeze Me, 1925
       Ain't Misbehavin', 1929
       Honeysuckle Rose, 1929

Ragtime Songs

The Irving Berlin song, "Alexander's Ragtime Band," in 1911, seemed to signal the end of the era. The style of the music was fast fading. The recordings were still quite popular, but the nation wanted something new to listen to and dance to. The opinion that "If you've heard one rag, you've heard them all," became the death knell. Ragtime continued to be played and taught but not on the scale it once knew. Ragtime songs began to utilize the syncopation found in the piano music. The music found in minstrelsy had limited syncopation associated with it. Stephen Foster's songs were basic straight-ahead-time compositions. When ragtime engulfed the nation, songwriters began experimenting with basic syncopations in their melodies. Both black and white songwriters composed ragtime songs. The long list of writers includes; Chris Smith, Irving Jones, Fred Stone, Fats Waller, George M. Cohan and Irving Berlin.

A number of the early black songwriters had no formal musical training and played piano by ear. they would play their songs on the piano for tin pan alley arrangers who would write the music as fast as the composer could play it.

Examples of ragtime songs utilizing simple but effective syncopation are; "Hello Ma Baby," "Give My Regards to Broadway," "Alexander's Ragtime Band," "Sweet Georgia Brown," and "Waitin' for the Robert E. Lee."

Like many of the jazz eras, ragtime was short lived. Its peak came during the turn of the century, and began to fade from popularity by the end of World War I. The complexity of the sheet music eventually made it unpopular with the amateur pianist, who turned to the music of tin pan alley. It did however, set the stage for the jazz pianist and instrumentalist in later eras. It had a short resurgence in recent years when the nation turned to 'nostalgia' and the movie THE STING used ragtime as its background music. Unfortunately the ragtime revival was brief. A few clubs still feature ragtime pianists such as Ralph Sutton. A native of Missouri (born 1926) he still travels and performs extensively. His recordings are classics.

Discussion Topics

1. On hearing the two most popular players of ragtime, Scott Joplin and Jelly Roll Morton, one detects a vast difference in style. How do you compare the styles of these two men and which would be most appealing to audiences during the era?
2. Of what benefit to the development of jazz were the compositions in the style of ragtime of prominent European composers? How did their style of ragtime differ from that of the American composers?
3. Several ragtime composers wrote music that was classical in nature; opera, musicals and orchestral works. None ever achieved any fame in that area. Why was their music not popular with audiences of the time?

Louis Armstrong (Ed Dwight, Sculptor).

CHAPTER 8

Dixieland

The jazz form known as Dixieland takes its name from the location of its birth. The Mason-Dixon Line, named after the surveyors/astronomers who established the boundary, was established in 1767 to end a bitter colonial dispute over territory. It later became a symbolic dividing line between Union and Confederate states during the Civil War. Land south of the boundary was referred to as Dixon's Land. After continued use, the slang form of Dixieland was adopted and later used to designate the jazz style which found its roots south of the boundary, in New Orleans.

Its Beginnings

The music of Dixieland originated with the military bands of the South. Post-Civil War military bands used wind and percussion instruments and, until the turn of the century, provided the New Orleans area with music through various parades and concerts. The band generated interest in would-be musicians who followed the bands in every parade. The band members gave their young followers their first music lessons and, in some cases, provided them with instruments. It was not uncommon for a band member to give a youngster an instrument and then report it as lost or stolen to the commander. Some black families were also willing and able to provide instruments and proper training for their children. Many offspring of former slaves were sent to France for musical training, but upon their return to New Orleans found the classical training unmarketable in the 'white classical' music world. So they searched for other outlets for the skills they had developed.

Since the original interest had been generated by the military bands, it was only natural that these new musicians develop similarly. The marching bands played outdoors, and Dixieland bands performed outdoors at neighborhood parades, funerals, jam sessions, and on street corners. After the turn of the century, Dixieland bands found another area in which to perform, when nightclubs were opened.

Lodges and Secret Societies

The New Orleans' black community was honeycombed with lodges and secret societies which were the core of social life. Similarly structured to white fraternal organizations, each lodge was organized for the betterment of its members. The belief was that the more lodges a man belonged to, the better his funeral and the better care his survivors received.

Each lodge had enough musicians to organize a band. The lodge helped the musicians acquire instruments and, whenever possible, receive proper musical training, all for the enhancement of lodge functions. The lodge band was required to play for various events including concerts, dances, and members' funerals.

Funerals

For funerals, the bands played hymns sung by the lodge members from their repertoire. Not all members of the New Orleans black community were lodge members. Friends of the deceased, whether a member or not, made sure of a proper burial which included the presence of a band. The band was made up of friends organized for the occasion or was a professional group. Each neighborhood sported several professional groups. Indeed, a principal source of income for the early Dixieland bands came from funeral performances.

The funeral was traditional. The deceased's coffin was placed upon a mule-drawn wagon, followed by the immediate family on foot with the band directly behind, playing the various hymns sung by the church family in a dirge tempo. If the deceased belonged to several lodges, each lodge would be represented by a band. At the grave site, the band would play a hymn following the eulogy. After the funeral, the band was placed upon the wagon which led relatives and friends to the home of the deceased. During the procession from the cemetery, the band would play the funeral hymns in an entirely different fashion, 'jazzing them up', to indicate that a celebration was at hand. The trombone player was allowed to sit on the tailgate of the wagon allowing freedom of movement of the slide. This practice brought the term tailgate trombone playing into being and inspired the composition of a Dixieland standard entitled "Tailgate Ramble".

The traditions which began with funerals and other lodge functions played an important role in the development of later jazz phases. Many of the famous jazz soloists of the 'big band' days either graduated from these early New Orleans organizations or were so strongly influenced by them in their formative years that the features of the New Orleans style were a great factor in the development of individual styles. Men, like Louis Armstrong, clarinetist Barney Bigard, and Jack Teagarden, highly regarded trombonist of the big band days, as well as numerous other top musicians, attributed their success to early emulation of New Orleans style.

Influences

Although Dixieland was a direct offshoot and most influenced by the military bands, there were similarities with other phases of music which preceded it. Minstrel shows used instrumental accompaniment known as 'pit orchestras'. These orchestras varied in size from four to 30 players, depending on the size and prominence of the show. The shows allowed the musicians an opportunity to perform independently between acts and, as 'flagwavers', before and after the main performance. Dixieland used the varying size of the minstrel pit orchestras and expanded the techniques.

Dixieland and ragtime both incorporated the march style, using multiple themes of 16 measures. Both were designed for the instrumentalist and allowed creativity in performance. While the ragtime pianist was relegated to performing at the piano's location, the Dixieland band was mobile and could perform equally well indoors or out. The piano was a self-contained ensemble and could provide melody and harmony simultaneously with its own rhythmic accompaniment. The Dixieland band, on the other hand, needed the full ensemble to produce the music, because a single wind instrument was ineffective. The musicians needed each other while the pianist was independent. The advantage of the ensemble was the ability to create a variety of sounds while the pianist was limited to the sound of the hammers on the strings of the instrument.

In Dixieland's early days, the music was taken from the martial music. Since there were no composers writing specifically for the Dixie style, the musicians heard the music and improvised their own arrangements. Since the music was not set down on paper, the themes were memorized and then 'jazzed up' in each performer's style.

Instruments

Instrumentation was according to availability. All instruments had to project without amplification and, because most performances were in the open, the sound had to carry some distance. The fiddle and cello were seldom used. For the same reason, the guitar, because of its inability to project, was rarely used.

The instruments were put into two classifications—melody/harmony and rhythm. While today we use sections of instruments such as brass, reed, or rhythm, Dixieland categorized the sections as frontline and backline. Instruments capable of producing a linear or melodic sound, such as the trumpet/cornet, clarinet, trombone, and saxophone, were considered the frontline. In addition, there were the upright altos of the military bands (mellophone/French horn) and the strings (fiddles).

The backline consisted of the rhythm instruments, like drums, which provided the beat. The banjo provided chord progressions and, at times, was also used for a melodic line. The banjo, which used a drum head, had enough projection that it could cut through the full ensemble without amplification. The favorite

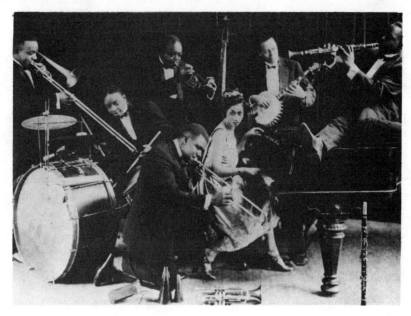

"King" Oliver's Creole Jazz Band (early 1920's)
Kneeling in foreground playing slide trumpet is Louis Armstrong. Others, l–r: Honore Dutrey, Baby Dodds, King Oliver, Lillian Hardin, Bill Johnson, and Johnny Dodds. (Courtesy: William Ransom Hogan Jazz Archive, Tulane University Library).

Jelly Roll Morton and His Red Hot Peppers
L–R: Omer Simeon, Andrew Hillaire, Johnny Lindsay, Johnny St. Cyr, Kid Ory, George Mitchell. Seated Jelly Roll. (Courtesy: William Ransom Hogan Jazz Archive, Tulane University Library).

Louis Armstrong (Courtesy: William Ransom Jazz Archive, Tulane University Library).

Sidney Bechet (Courtesy: William Ransom Jazz Archive, Tulane University Library).

instrument of the old plantation days, the banjo, had already achieved popularity and so it was a natural member of the instrumental ensemble. The tuba could play a rhythmic figure while playing specific notes of the chord, giving the frontline the chord changes and assisting the drummer in providing a beat. When the Dixieland bands moved inside, the string bass, with its more subtle sound, replaced the tuba. Yet, the Dixieland tuba is by no means a lost instrument as many Dixieland enthusiasts claim its presence is indispensable.

The Music

The frontline gave the listener a variety of sounds and the combination of the various instruments produced a texture similar to that of the military bands. While the frontline played the melody, harmony, countermelody, and obligato in the arrangements, the backline was not without its soloists. The drummer was allowed 'breaks' which were short solo interludes, and the banjoist and bassist were given full solo choruses. This, of course, did not happen in each selection, but was used sparingly for a change of pace. Dixieland bands were imbued with the thought that each member of the group was a soloist and should be featured in various selections. The music was patterned after the format of the march beginning with a short introduction, usually four measures in length. The introduction was followed first by two themes (A and B), then a trio section (theme C), followed by an interlude (break strain, theme D) and the ending, which is a repeat of the trio (theme C). The basic length of each theme was 16 measures or, sometimes, eight measures played twice.

Early instrumentalists were, for the most part, untrained in music fundamentals and 'played by ear'. They memorized a theme and then extemporized upon it. Many themes were copies of marches played by the military bands. One player would teach a melody to another who in turn improvised and rephrased the melody so that, in time, the melody became vastly removed from its original form. The young musicians probably did not know the original title of the melody, so they would rename it. Soon they began composing their own melodies. Since most could not read or write music, they relied on memorization. As a band worked on a melody and its harmonies, the selection became their particular composition and arrangement. These memorized compositions became known as 'head' arrangements with each part being memorized by a player. Parts of the selection were 'opened up' for improvisational solos. The opened sections were played by the soloist with accompaniment by the rhythm section or the frontline instruments.

As the era progressed, more and more selections were composed. 'Top Tunes' were created and played by the bands, with each developing its own particular arrangement of the tunes. Dixieland was instrumental in nature, therefore, the composers ignored the voice. The compositions were created for the demonstration of the instrumentalists' ability to improvise on a given melody. Each musician wanted to expose his virtuosity so that instruments would not be thought of as only vocal accompaniment. Even today, singers rarely perform with Dixieland bands.

Dixieland in New Orleans

Although Dixieland's beginnings were most influenced by the marching bands, factors outside the music world helped shape its growth and development. Unfortunately, Dixieland has been associated with periods of crime and corruption. New Orleans, itself, was labeled the 'wickedest city in the country'. New Orleans was established by real estate entrepreneurs whose motives were to make money quickly. They sold land to unsuspecting people in France, Spain, and Germany by billing the city as an area of immense beauty, rich in minerals, and full of monetary opportunities. The original developer, a Scotsman named John Law, was involved in a company with the French Regent Louis Phillipe, the duc d'Orleans. Phillipe approved naming the city Nouvelle-Orleans. For a relatively short time, Antoine de la Mothe Cadillac, founder of Detroit, was the colonial governor.

The advertising brought the dregs of Europe to New Orleans looking for wealth and prosperity. Instead, they found swamps, mosquitos, snakes, alligators, and a very wet climate.

Racial segregation codes were enacted to keep the slaves in specific areas of the city. While they could work in all parts of New Orleans, they were forced to live in the western part. New Orleans was separated into two cities by Canal Street. The affluent European sector with citizens of all nationalities, lived on the east side. The blacks lived west of Canal Street in the American sector.

Blacks were categorized according to skin pigmentation. Those of mixed (white and black) parents were classified according to the amount of black parentage. Quadroons were one-fourth black and three-fourths white; an octaroon was one-eighth black. Others were labeled mullato or creole. The darkness or lightness of skin determined the person's employment opportunities. The black population was subdivided within itself. Light-skinned blacks were allowed to work and own property in the European sector until the Civil War when their businesses and homes were closed because total residential segregation forced them to move to the western part of New Orleans.

Musicians were also segregated by skin color. East of Canal Street, 'downtown', black musicians were allowed to perform for social affairs and dances. Their music was quite sedate; easy to dance to, and acceptable as background music while dining and conversing. The downtown musicians were required to dress in a fashionable manner with tuxedos being standard. The west side or 'uptown' section was just the opposite. Dark-skinned musicians performed in the various clubs and sporting houses. Their music was different in style because it 'swung' and was loud. Compared to the downtown style, the music was raucous. Often the downtown musicians, having finished their high-society engagement, would go uptown and 'sit in'.

Prostitution was sanctioned by the city with prostitutes being required to register with the government. Good money was available for the black woman who could attract a white man as a patron. The best way to attract the wealthy client was through the 'quadroon balls'. Henry Kmen in his book *Music in New Orleans: The Formative Years, 1791–1841,* stated:

> The Colored Creoles with the richest opportunity for upward social mobility . . . were the female quadroons. And the arena in which they competed for what might be the good life (or at any rate a better life than they had known) were the bals de Cordon Bleu, commonly called 'quadroon balls'. The earliest balls were open to all—white, free black, mixed, male, and female. The first true quadroon ball was held in 1805, when Auguste Tessier, a professional actor and dancer, advertised "a plan to give two balls a week for the free women of color at which all colored men would be excluded." Black male musicians, however, were permitted to supply the dance music. . . . Interest in the balls was so lively and participation so keen that, before long, quadroon balls took place regularly, at least six nights a week in as many as eight different ballrooms, many of which were just around the corner from each other in the French Quarter.

In *Jazz City,* Leon Ostransky also wrote of the popularity of the balls:

> White New Orleans gentlemen with an eye for the ladies given the choice of attending all-white balls or quadroon balls, invariably chose the latter. The white balls may have had their 'flirtation walk', but most of the quadroon balls emphasized the excitement of promiscuous sexual indulgence.

The liaisons formulated through the quadroon balls led to the keeping of mistresses by the white 'gentlemen'. In many cases, the offspring of these situations received good educations, which included the study of music. Many of these European trained musicians returned to the United States to share their training with their less fortunate associates.

The quadroon balls gave encouragement not only to prostitutes, but also to the development of bordellos, gambling joints, saloons, and cabarets. As more establishments opened, more musicians were employed as entertainers and accompanists. Ostransky wrote on the effects of prostitution on a city:

> Where there is easy prostitution, the spirit of crime and corruption is generally not far behind. In New Orleans, from the early 19th century onward, the elements necessary to the development of an environment in which jazz would readily take root was already clearly evident. Easy prostitution means easy money, and easy money attracts both criminals and corrupt men in positions of power; easy money also gives rise to those establishments that thrive on easy money: bordellos, gambling joints, saloons, cabarets and dance halls, to name only a few. And it was in this atmosphere and ambience of places catering to the illicit fancies of their pleasure-seeking clientele that the popular music antecedent to jazz, which showed some of early jazz characteristics, was encouraged to grow and flourish.

Riverboats like this traveled up and down the Mississippi and Missouri rivers, carrying cargo and passengers from New Orleans to St. Louis and Kansas City. Dixieland bands would play for the passengers, and in so doing, helped spread the sound and style of jazz to the rest of the country. (Photo courtesy Bob Dunham, St. Louis, Mo.)

In 1898, the city government adopted an ordinance proposed by alderman Sidney Story which eliminated all prostitutes from the European sector. Since prostitution seemed synonymous with crime and corruption, Story and his associates intended to control these activities in an area where it would be least exposed to the general public. The confinement area, 38 city blocks square, was a concentrated area of brothels, dance halls, saloons, and cribs. Possibly out of hostility to the ordinance and its author, residents named the area **Storyville.**

In 1901, **Tom Anderson,** the legendary mayor of Storyville and subsequently a state legislator, opened a saloon on the edge of town and published the "Blue Book", a descriptive guide to the sporting houses in the district. (In later years, other cities, including Chicago, Kansas City, New York, and Denver, had similar publications.)

Storyville's sporting houses were not, for the most part, quick dollar brothels. They were often elaborate and ornate dwellings. The wealthy customers were expected to spend the entire evening in the house of pleasure. To attract the desired clientele, the 'madames' created nightclub-restaurant atmospheres complete with dining and dancing where a patron (many of whom were regulars) could come and spend the evening with the lady of his choice: enjoying dinner, cocktails, dancing, and finally sex. Not all 'houses' could afford live entertainment nightly, but those who could hired the finest jazz musicians in New Orleans. King Oliver, Kid Ory, and Jelly Roll Morton were 'top billings' in the district. The earnings of the musicians varied in two manners. The piano players, called 'professors', worked as singles and were paid primarily by tips augmented with a guarantee from the 'madam'. Their weekly earnings were often as high as 1,000 dollars. The bands earned much less because the tips were divided among the band members, with the leader receiving twice as much as the sidemen. The leaders earned about 75 dollars a week while the sidemen earned approximately 35 dollars. In comparison to other vocations in the black community, the income was very good.

A history of prostitution in the United States and Storyville, was in essence an integral part of jazz history. The New Orleans style of Dixieland was derived directly from the music in Storyville. The music was called 'whorehouse music'.

Storyville was closed in 1917 by the United States Navy under the premise that the Navy personnel spent too much time frequenting the houses and had contracted various forms of venereal disease, posing a health hazard to the military.

During Storyville's 20 year existence, about 200 musicians worked in the various establishments. Although this does not seem like a large number of people (most major college marching bands today exceed that number), they provided the impetus for things to come in jazz.

Dixieland in Kansas City

The closing of Storyville put many musicians out of jobs, a blessing in disguise for music in general. The musicians began to move to new places, providing the rest of the country with this new style of music. The Mississippi River was a natural route from New Orleans to the North. Upriver, the Missouri moving in a westerly direction connected New Orleans with the West. The common form of river transportation was the riverboats, and just as these riverboats provided jobs for ragtime pianists they also hired Dixieland bands. These bands performed not only during the voyage, but also for the embarking and disembarking passengers which attracted the attention of the local citizens. News of the new music spread the popularity of Dixieland. Many dance hall and saloon owners hired the bands off of the riverboats to entertain ashore.

Kansas City, a major port on the Missouri River, was a jumping off place to the West. The political and entertainment aspects of Kansas City were controlled by the 'Pendergast Machine', formed by Tom and Jim Pendergast. Kansas City soon became host to one of the largest 'sin industries' in the world, with gambling being one of the more popular forms of entertainment.

Aside from or because of the crime and corruption, Kansas City became noteworthy in the development of jazz. At the beginning of the 20th century, the Jenkins Music Store was founded and became a major manufacturer and supplier of mandolins and guitars. Kansas City was also a regular concert stop for the touring bands of John Philip Sousa and Patrick Gilmore. Numerous local brass bands, similar to those found in New Orleans, joined together in band contests. While playing in Kansas City in 1914, noted concert band leader Arthur Pryor composed "Heart of America March". Sousa heard it and began performing it worldwide with his band. Since Pryor had dedicated it to E. J. Shanahan, member of the Pendergast machine, Kansas City became known as the 'Heart of America'.

Three Kansas City nightclubs played a significant part in the development of jazz: the Reno Club, Subway Club, and Sunset Club. All were controlled by the Pendergasts. They were favorite places for jazz musicians to hold 'jam sessions'. A jam session was a welcome event for a club owner because the best musicians came to perform. Tenor saxophonist Lester Young, regarded by jazz historians as one of the finest jazz musicians, would appear with Ben Webster and, in later years, Charlie Parker. Clarinetist Benny Goodman, saxophonist Coleman Hawkins, and Jimmy and Tommy Dorsey would 'sit in' when in Kansas City.

The Reno Club was the favorite of the musicians. It catered to blacks and whites, although separate facilities and dance floors were provided. The club, exempt from police raids, was a favorite night spot for local citizens. It featured such players as Andy Kirk, Walter Page, and William "Count" Basie. Basie, originally from Redbank, New Jersey was stranded in Kansas City when the show he traveled with folded. He was hired by the Eblon Theater to play background music for silent movies and later joined the Benny Moten Band. After Moten's death, Basie became the leader. He later organized another band and worked at the Reno Club.

For band members, hours were long and pay was minimal—18 dollars per week. Bands played from nine in the evening to six in the morning, seven nights a week. Still, the musicians were grateful for the opportunity to jam. In later years, jam sessions became illegal because club owners were profiting from musicians who were playing for free. The Musicians' Union prohibited members from playing such sessions without pay.

Instruments

Jam sessions were an important factor in introducing new instruments to Dixieland. While the principal wind/melody instruments to Dixieland were the trumpet, clarinet, and trombone, the saxophone later worked its way into the ensemble. Sidney Bechet was one of the first to use the sax in a Dixieland band. The saxophone family consists of several instruments varying in size and tone quality: the soprano (smallest), alto, tenor, baritone, and bass. (The baritone and bass saxes did not achieve their real potential until the swing/big band era.) While few saxophones were used in New Orleans bands, in Kansas City the instrument came into prominence and established itself as an important component of Dixieland bands of the Roaring Twenties. "Buster" Smith, "Budd" Johnson, Lester Young, Ben Webster, and Coleman Hawkins would appear together in Kansas City in informal 'cutting contests.' These contests, which pitted skill against skill, were invaluable in establishing the instrument in jazz bands.

The sax was only one of the instruments that was introduced during this era. Early Dixieland bands used the tuba as the bass instrument because it had the power of projection required for playing outdoors. But with the bands appearing in clubs and dance halls, the tuba's sound was too heavy an accompaniment for wind instruments. So, Kansas City string bass player, Walter Page, introduced a new concept to the bands. Instead of using the heavy sound the tuba produced, Page played the string bass in what was termed a 'walking' manner. He plucked the strings in a scalewise pattern in beats one, two, three, and four of the measure, giving the music a smooth forward flow which in turn influenced the rest of the rhythm section and gave the music a swinging feel.

String Bass

The rhythm section was also affected by other aspects that dealt with percussion instruments. Drummers in early bands were restricted because of the limitations of their instruments. Unlike today's drummers, who have virtually an entire percussion section at their disposal, early drummers played on drums similar to early military models that used rope tension. Humidity was always a factor affecting the tautness of the heads. Since the cities were in areas of high humidity, sound consistency was a never ending problem. Some of the drums had fixed heads that were put on the shell with a form of tack which would not allow any method of tuning once manufactured. Early cymbals lacked the tone and ringing quality

Illustrator: Pat Dietemann

Trap Drum Set:

of today's models. As a result, the percussionist was only there to supply a steady beat. It is ironic that the drum, which was the basic instrument of jazz, was the last to be changed by technological advances. The present hi-hat cymbal used by drummers to emphasize the second and fourth beats of a measure was not developed until the 30's. Until that time, the drummer used sticks on the snare drum to give the rhythm section a strong 'backbeat' in beats two and four.

Cymbals were much smaller in diameter and thinner than later ones. Today's percussionist relies heavily on the cymbal's ability to project over the intense amplification of contemporary bands. They now use large, 20 inch, ride cymbals to play 'time'. The bass drum is used for accents (bombs and fills) and solo work. In early bands, the bass drum also provided the beat as well as accents and solos. The continual 'thumping' of the bass drum gave the beat a drone-like pulsation which, rather than enhance

Illustrator: Pat Dietemann

Illustrator: Pat Dietemann

Early Hi-Hat:

Modern Hi-Hat:

the 'swing' or flow of the band, could, sometimes bog it down. With the development of the modern trap set, the drummer became a musical entity which enhanced the overall sound of the band.

Even with changes in instrumentation, the music was very similar between Kansas City and New Orleans. The music remained four-beat in nature. After Dixieland arrived in Chicago, the rhythmic concepts changed to a two-beat version with the emphasis on the first and third beats of a measure. This change eliminated the drone-thumping sound of the continuous four beats provided by the drummer in each measure. The two-beat style gave the music a new rhythmic flavor. The development of the hi-hat or sock cymbal provided the drummer a new sound so that the music gave more of a 'laid back' feeling in place of the continual forward rush.

The Riff

Kansas City was a mecca for jazz musicians. Musicians came from all parts of the country because abundant work was available. The creativity they brought with them helped the art develop more quickly than in any other city up to that time. As musicians experimented with style, a cornerstone was laid for the big band era which followed. The jam sessions in the various clubs allowed musicians to develop their improvisational skills. Improvisational ideas were exchanged continually and, as new musicians continued to arrive on the scene, more interaction took place.

One of the characteristics of Kansas City style was the invention and development of the 'riff'. The riff was a simple phrase or figure repeated over and over throughout a chorus. Initially, it was used as background for an improvised solo or as a call and response device between instruments (reeds and brass). The riff was adopted by the big bands in many arrangements and more fully developed during the be-bop era.

Illustrator: Pat Dietemann

Dixieland Drummer

Along with the riff, Kansas City was credited with formulating the 12 bar blues. The 32 bar song form was making its way into jazz. The eight bar blues was used by instrumentalists in both Kansas City and New Orleans. The repeat of the eight bar phrase made up the 16 bar march style from which the music originated. The vocalists; like Bessie Smith, Ma Rainey, Mamie Smith, and Alberta Hunter, sang the 12 bar blues by breaking it down into three four-bar segments or phrases with the words repeating themselves. An example is "North Bound Blues":

Goin' North, chile, where I can be free (four bars)
Goin' North, chile, where I can be free (four bars)
Where there's no hardship, like in Tennessee (four bars)

Second verse:

Goin' where they don't have no Jim Crow laws (four bars)
Goin' where they don't have no Jim Crow laws (four bars)
Don't have to work there like in Arkansas (four bars).

Although Kansas City has not been noted as a leading jazz city by historians, it was a major contributor to its development. It also served as a springboard for the movement of jazz into the Southwest. Oklahoma and Texas became active in the promotion of jazz because the bands leaving Kansas City often migrated to these states and developed the 'territory bands' of the Southwest.

Dixieland in Chicago

While many of the New Orleans jazzmen went to Kansas City after the closing of Storyville, a large number also moved to Chicago. Prior to 1911, Chicago had very little jazz, but when the New Orleans musicians arrived, the city was receptive. Chicago had been favorably exposed to jazz through ragtime during the Exposition of 1893. The populace had enjoyed the music and was ready for something new. Chicago was already the major stop for road shows of the T. O. B. A. (Theater Owners Booking Association) circuit and the Orpheum circuit.

Chicago was larger than either New Orleans or Kansas City and could accommodate more musicians. A large number of minor musical figures arrived in the city hoping to be discovered and 'hit big'. These minor names had played in the shadows of the musical giants of New Orleans and hoped that, with the country's focus turned to Chicago, they would get the chance they did not have in New Orleans.

The first emigrants from New Orleans found Chicago receptive to their music and notified others in New Orleans, who in turn moved north. In a short period of time, many big names from New Orleans made their way to Chicago. Some of these were Sidney Bechet, Jelly Roll Morton, Joe "King" Oliver, Johnny Dodds, and Louis Armstrong.

While the majority of jazz immigrants to Chicago were black, a number of whites tried their music in the Windy City, also. The most notable of these was a group called Stein's band from Dixie. Booked at Shiller's Cafe, they were billed as Stein's Dixie Jazz Band. Shortly after, Stein's sidemen left him and formed the Original Dixieland Jazz Band. This band was important in jazz history, not because of their musical ability, but because they were the first band to make a jazz recording for public sale. Previously, most recordings were of the 'race-recording' type limited to sales in black communities.

The invasion of jazz musicians into Chicago, along with their interaction with local musicians developed Dixieland into a new style, and made Chicago the jazz center of the world. Other factors also helped this development. Chicago was an industrial and agricultural hub, a lake shipping port, and rail center. It was also becoming one of the major meat-packing centers. Drawing citizens from all over the world, it was truly a 'house for all people'.

As in other major cities, the influx of people brought vice, corruption, and crime. The Levee in Chicago was the counterpart of Storyville in New Orleans. Like Storyville, the Levee included brothels, saloons, dance halls, and clubs. When a dance hall was combined with a saloon and eating place it became a 'cabaret'. The south side of the city, called the black belt, supported the opening of a number of cabarets which catered to black and white customers. These clubs became known as 'black and tan'.

As the city grew, the number of musicians increased. In the 1920's, Chicago had 3,400 whites and 730 blacks whose occupations were listed as musician. Of the 730 black musicians 200 were women.

The influx of musicians was also affected by the National Prohibition Act of 1919, which closed the breweries and distilleries. Bootleg whiskey arrived Chicago and the underworld found a new leader in Al Capone. The time for Chicago was set and the jazz musicians felt they had found Utopia, because the number of cabarets quickly multiplied. Outside the city limits, the underworld opened 'roadhouses'. As the popularity of the automobile increased so did the mobility of the people who could leave Chicago to visit the roadhouses. Even in the city, most of the nightclubs were controlled by gangsters. The north side of Chicago was the domain of "Bugs" Moran and the south side belonged to Al Capone. The musicians had little choice as to where they worked and pay was low, but, at least, they had work.

The best paying jobs went to white musicians, although some black musicians found work outside the black belt. At one time or another, most of the jazz greats played somewhere in the city—Benny Goodman at the Rendezvous Cafe, clarinetist Jimmy Noone and vocalist Bessie Smith at the Paradise, the New Orleans Rhythm Kings at the Friar's Inn, cornetist Bix Biederbecke at the Rendezvous, guitarist Eddie Condon at the Alcazar, trumpeter Muggsy Spanier at Sig Myer's Druids, "King" Oliver and Sidney Bechet at the Dreamland, pianists Jelly Roll Morton and Earl Hines at the Elite #2, and Louis Armstrong at the Pekin. There always was an impressive selection of clubs and artists from which to choose.

The new Orleans musicians brought their own style to Chicago, it was still based on the structure of the march with its numerous themes and phrases. The music had four heavy beats to a bar and an overall driving sound. The Chicago musicians and listeners were given a new insight into jazz. A compromise was developed between the New Orleans style and the sweet, melodic sounds of the Chicago style, resulting in Chicago style Dixieland. Instead of the driving four beats to the bar, the second and fourth beats were emphasized and became known as backbeats. With the development of the hi-hat cymbal, the hi-hat was played on beats two and four, and the bass drum was played on one and three. The fusion of the two styles gave jazz a new direction.

Dixieland in New York

Dixieland and its composers/leaders were well-established before New York actually opened its doors to the jazz scene. While New Orleans and Chicago were the major development areas for Dixieland, Kansas City had it's influence and input. New York, on the other hand, had only given this musical form tacit approval. Although New York was seemingly aloof to jazz, its citizens enjoyed the music of Paul Whiteman, the dancing of Fred Astaire, Rudy Vallee's band, and the floor shows which included entertainers like Jimmy Durante.

New York did not fully come into focus as a jazz city until the advent of tin pan alley and the big band/swing eras. It was, however, the time of 30,000 speakeasies, many of which provided live music. The major area for music in New York was Harlem, the black belt of New York. Harlem had many nightclubs where the top bands performed. The three most notable were the Cotton Club, Small's Paradise, and Connie's Inn. Strangely enough, these three clubs were in business for the city's 'white thrill-seekers'. Even though members of the black community of Harlem were barred from entrance as patrons, black leaders were thrilled with the existence of these clubs. They provided employment for a large number of blacks as musicians, waiters, cooks, and doormen. The prices in these clubs were quite high with the average cost per person ranging from $12–15 for an evenings entertainment. This price range kept out the average working man. After some resistance to the black barrier, blacks were allowed to enter but, the prices were a deterrent to their patronage. The music found in these clubs (Connie's, Small's, and the Cotton) was, in reality, musical revues including chorus lines, stand-up comics, and small musical productions. Following the floor show, dancing to local bands led by men such as "Duke" Ellington and Fletcher Henderson became part of the evening.

Opened in 1926, the Savoy Ballroom became a major Harlem attraction. A dance hall for blacks with music provided by black jazz bands, it was given the nickname, 'the home of the happy feet'. The Savoy was large enough to handle 1,500 dancers and had stage facilities to hold two complete bands. A top name band alternated sets with a house band with each playing approximately one-hour sets.

Citizens of Harlem enjoyed musical entertainment and would listen to jazz at every opportunity. The leaders of the "Harlem Renaissance" were trying to elevate the cultural level of Harlem. They felt that whites should take black artists seriously. The black leaders promoted performers like Marian Anderson, Paul Robeson, Roland Hayes, and composer, William Grant Still. The music performed by Jelly Roll Morton, Duke Ellington, Louis Armstrong, and Fats Waller was neglected by Harlem's social and artistic elite. While leaders worked to upgrade the culture of the community, one fact stood out, the blacks in Harlem were as poor as the blacks in any other major city. Employment for blacks was mainly limited to low paying unskilled labor and domestic service jobs. As a result, entertainment activities were limited. The local clubs which catered to the average black were much of the same as those found in Kansas City and Chicago. The main difference was the kind of music Harlem citizens enjoyed. Dixieland was not as popular as it was in the other cities. New York's Dixieland bands were the predecessors of the big bands and were larger, using multiples of the same instruments. Their music was conducive to dancing and Harlemites loved to dance.

Dixieland Composers

Throughout Dixieland's development, music was composed and passed on through the musicians and groups. Many of these numbers became 'standards', a composition that has become a permanent part of an era's music.

The compositions that have endured share common criteria: a combination of melodic line and rhythmic simplicity. If the listener can easily sing or hum the melody in its proper rhythmic structure, it has a chance of becoming a standard. If the composition has words (lyrics) that can easily be remembered, so

"Big Butter and Egg Man"

Joe "King" Oliver: Dippermouth Blues
Alligator Hop
Just Gone
Weatherbird Rag

much the better. Many Dixieland compositions were written without lyrics and, so, their melodic lines were the factors in determining if they would become standards. If the melodic line and the rhythmic structure were complicated and included intervals too difficult to sing or hum, the song was usually forgotten.

The composers that stand out in history have had the creative ability to produce a never ending stream of compositions which have become standards in jazz literature. People like Scott Joplin, W. C. Handy, Louis Armstrong, Irving Berlin, George Gershwin, Johnny Mercer, Cole Porter, Lorenz Hart and Richard Rogers top the list. Similarly, classical music had its outstanding composers who produced volumes of work within their lifetimes.

Louis Armstrong seems to be the most prolific composer of Dixieland. His compositions are a basic part of Dixieland literature and, although, there were many fine composers, Armstrong tops the list. Following is a list of Dixieland composers and their most popular compositions.

"Struttin' with Some Barbeque"   *Lil Hardin Armstrong*

Louis Armstrong: S. O. L. Blues
                  Potatoe Head Blues
                  Weather Bird
                  Big Butter & Egg Man
                  Someday
                  Canal Street Blues (Written with Joe Oliver)

Jelly Roll Morton: Dead Man Blues
Black Bottom Stomp
Milenberg Joys
King Porter Stomp

"Milenberg Joys"

Jelly Roll Morton

"When the Saints Go Marching In", is often referred to as the national anthem of Dixieland.

"The Saints Go Marching In"
Traditional

One Dixieland standard which was most often used for funeral parades is "Just a Closer Walk With Thee." It represents the eight and 16 bar phrases used in Dixieland compositions.

"Just a Closer Walk with Thee"
Traditional hymn

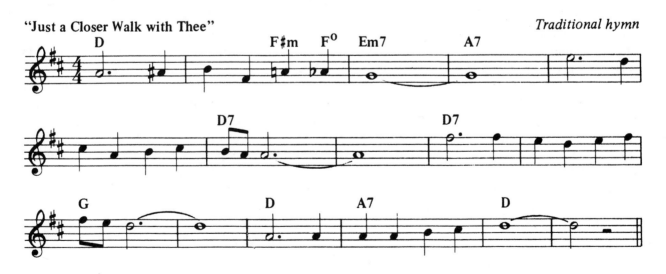

There are many traditional Dixieland standards. Here is a partial listing:

Jazz Me Blues	Ballin' the Jack
South Rampart Street Parade	Royal Garden Blues
Magnolia Street Parade	Jada
Muskrat Ramble	Back Home in Indiana
High Society	Wabash Blues
Sugar Foot Stomp	Wang Wang Blues
That's a Plenty	Tailgate Ramble
Tiger Rag	Bye Bye Blues
Basin Street Blues	Beale Street Blues
Sister Kate	When the Saints Go Marching In
South	

Dixieland Performers

In the Dixieland era, numerous individuals left their mark and assumed a rightful place in the jazz history hall of fame. Ragtime pianists laid the groundwork for improvisation, and during Dixieland, the wind players developed it even further. If Dixieland's originators could have heard the final product, they would have been amazed at its development. The people that played the first funerals, performed the first concerts, and participated in the first jam sessions in Place Congo would, no doubt, have felt great satisfaction in knowing their contributions laid the foundations for an original American art form.

When we think of Dixieland, we automatically think of the likes of Louis Armstrong, Joe Oliver, "Kid" Ory, and "Bunk" Johnson. But, prior to these stars we have to look at the early brass bands. We have to consider the instrumentation and literature with which they had to work. Their instruments were technically simple. It is also true that early classical composers were limited in their work because they had to write for wind and percussion instruments that had not yet undergone mechanical refinements. In the majority of cases, learning was either by rote or individual experimentation. Improvision was not the invention of jazz musicians. Centuries before jazz was invented, European performers/composers performed 'theme and variations'. Dixieland's inventors, however, helped refine the art of improvisation.

In Dixieland's beginnings, about 200 working musicians participated, but as jazz spread throughout the country, thousands of musicians were involved. To list all, or even a major portion of the people credited with its development would again take volumes. It is more appropriate to list the people whose names appear most often in works of jazz history.

Louis "Satchmo" Armstrong became the best known jazz musician of all time. Born in New Orleans in 1900, Armstrong was labeled Satchmo, because of his thick lips (short for Satchel Mouth). Raised in a black waif's home in New Orleans, he had few rivals as the greatest of all instrumental soloists. Although Armstrong's active performing years spanned six decades, he stayed with the basic Dixieland style. Beginning with the street bands in New Orleans, he later became the Ambassador of Jazz. As a vocalist, his talent is somewhat questionable although some historians feel he was the greatest jazz singer and an inspiration to singers like Billie Holiday. His big break came when he was called to Chicago to join King Oliver's band as a featured soloist. He met and married Lil Hardin, one of the first female instrumentalists (piano). Armstrong was well known for his compositions but his forte was his improvisational skills. His joy and inspiration came from the Guy Lombardo Band although the two were musically opposite in style. He worked with the bands of "Kid" Ory, "King" Oliver, Clarence Williams, and Fletcher Henderson. He made recordings with singers Bessie Smith and Ella Fitzgerald.

Historians feel Armstrong's greatest musical contributions were prior to 1940 even though he continued to perform until his death in 1971. Armstrong's warm personality endeared him to millions of fans, and his world travels, even behind the Iron Curtain, were tremendously successful. He once remarked that nations had bestowed medals and awards upon him but his own country gave him only money.

Born in 1897 in New Orleans, **Sidney Bechet** began his career as a clarinetist in the early marching bands of New Orleans. He worked in a shoeshine stand and a tailor shop. He later became a virtuoso of the soprano sax and introduced it as an important Dixieland instrument. Bechet played in the bands of Oliver, Morton, and Ellington. After playing in England and France for some time, he organized his own group called the New Orleans Feetwarmers.

Leon Bix Biederbecke was born in Davenport, Iowa in 1903. He became a legend over a very short span of time. Making jazz history with his cornet, he was featured with the "Wolverines" and the Paul Whiteman Band. Unlike the New Orleans musicians who started as members of the marching bands, Bix learned his music in the school music program. He played on riverboats, with various Chicago area bands, and formed his own "Rhythm Jugglers." Rated along with Armstrong as one of the leading trumpet players of the 1920's he was known as a very creative player. Beiderbecke played neither New Orleans or Chicago style of Dixieland. Unlike most Dixieland trumpeters he played with a lighter, less-brassy sound. He composed "In a Mist" and was the inspiration for Dorothy Baker's novel *Young Man with a Horn*. Plagued by alcoholism, Beiderbecke died at age 28 of pneumonia.

Buddy Bolden, a cornet player, influenced both trumpet players and bands. Born in New Orleans in 1868, Bolden as a young man ran a barber shop, his 'daytime job' that allowed him to exist. Bolden's band was comprised of cornet, clarinet, trombone, violin, guitar, string bass, and drums. He played the cornet with a rather coarse sound and, so, the band played in a very 'rough' fashion. He is credited with forming the first so-called 'jazz band'. Bolden spent his playing years in New Orleans and was the first jazz musician to earn the title 'king' as he reportedly never lost a cutting contest with other cornet players. In 1907, he jumped off the bandstand while performing and ran drunk down the street blowing his horn as loud and hard as possible. Shortly after, he was committed to an institution where he died in 1931.

Johnny Dodds, rated as the greatest clarinetist of the Dixieland era, was born in 1892 in New Orleans. He was known for the warmth and passion of his music, a quality lacking in most clarinetists. He played in marching bands and on riverboats in his early years. An outstanding soloist as well as ensemble player, Dodds, like brother "Baby" was in great demand for recordings and performances. During his short lifetime (48 years) he formed his own band "Chicago Boys", and collaborated with Kid Ory in a group called "New Orleans Bootblacks and Wanderers." During his career he worked with "King" Oliver, Armstrong, and "Jelly Roll" Morton.

Warren "Baby" Dodds, nicknamed "Baby" because of his older brother, Johnny, was born in New Orleans in 1898. "Baby" was the first real 'trap' drummer in jazz history and the style setter for drummers who followed. A factory worker, he got his early musical experience playing with the brass bands. Famous for his steady beat, press rolls, and overall flexibility, Dodds played on drumsets that were antiquated by today's standards. Despite this, he demonstrated an unique ability to 'kick' a band and was in great demand with the best musicians/leaders in the country.

Born in Mobile, Alabama in 1881, **James Reese Europe** played an important role in the development of jazz. Though not known as a great musician, he contributed by helping to spread jazz to the European continent and to improve the working conditions of musicians. As a military bandleader during World War I, he directed bands in Europe. Styled after American jazz bands, though larger in size, Europe's bands gave Europeans a feel for this American musical style. After the war, Europe formed a band, the "Clef Club Orchestra", in New York. In 1910, he organized the first musicians' union (for black members). It became known as "The Clef Club".

William Geary "Bunk" Johnson, born in 1879, became a legendary trumpet player with the distinction of never having made a recording. Known as a fine ensemble player, he played with circus bands, minstrel shows, and in theaters in the Louisiana territory. Not a typical New Orleans hardblowing trumpeter, Johnson was known for his teaching ability. He worked as a truck driver, caretaker, and later formed several bands: "Bunk Johnson Band", "Bunk Johnson's Street Paraders", and "Bunk Johnson's Original Superior Orchestra".

"Jelly Roll" Morton, a leading figure in the ragtime era, made the transition to Dixieland with ease. He is credited with the development of the 'break' in a composition. Morton believed that if the music did not have a break in it, it was not jazz. Morton's band, the "Red Hot Peppers", was known for its classic recordings of the New Orleans style of Dixieland. His composition, "King Porter Stomp," was later recorded by Benny Goodman, making it a swing era hit.

Joe "King" Oliver, born in 1885 in New Orleans, spent his early years playing in the "Onward Brass Band." He formed the "Creole Jazz Band" in New Orleans which later moved to Chicago and added trumpeter Louis Armstrong and pianist Lil Hardin. Oliver's band made a number of memorable recordings.

Credited with the New Orleans style of Dixieland, Oliver's band was a sensation at the Lincoln Gardens in Chicago, where it was named the "Best Band in the Land". In his early years, Oliver was a butler and played music as a sideline. Later, he lost his teeth and being unable to play the cornet he dropped from the spotlight. He spent his later years working in a pool hall.

Trombonist **Edward "Kid" Ory,** born 1886 in La Place, Louisiana, was also proficient on clarinet, drums, string bass, alto sax and valve trombone. The 'king' of tailgate trombonists, Ory was an outstanding ensemble player. His fame came from his ability to help make an ensemble swing. As a young man, Ory worked on a chicken farm with his brother. Later, he relocated in California and organized the first black band to make a recording (1922). Ory played with all the notable Dixieland bands, and with Johnny Dodds formed their own band. His last band was the "Kid Ory's Creole Jazz Band." His recording of "Muskrat Ramble" became a classic. In later years, he acted and performed in the movie, *The Benny Goodman Story.*

String bass player **Walter Page** was born in 1900 in Gallatin, Missouri. He developed the walking bass style in which the string bass was used instead of the tuba. Rather than playing roots and fifths on beats one and three, the bass player would play scalewise patterns on each beat of the measure as well as mixing in tuba style roots and fifths on beats one and three. A well-schooled musician, he graduated from Lincoln High School in Kansas City and attended Kansas State Teachers College majoring in music. After three years of college, he joined a road show traveling throughout the Southwest. Page organized and led 'Page's Blue Devils' which featured Oran "Hot Lips" Page on trumpet, Jimmy Rushing vocalist, saxophonist Lester Young, and Bill "Count" Basie on piano. A battle-of-the-bands enthusiast, he conquered all the bands in the Kansas City area including the great Benny Moten. The riffs in Page's music became the basis of music used by Moten and Basie.

Johnny St. Cyr, birthdate unknown, appears most frequently among names of banjo players in early jazz. In addition to the banjo, St. Cyr was also adept at the guitar, and, no doubt, played it more frequently as the era developed. He played with a number of the bands including Morton's "Red Hot Peppers", and recording groups (Hot Five and Hot Seven) of Louis Armstrong.

There were vast numbers of bands and individuals that made a definite mark upon the development of Dixieland. The "Austin High Gang," circa 1925, had its beginnings in Austin High School, Chicago. Bud Freeman, Jim Lanigan, Dick McPartland, Jimmy McPartland, and Frank Teschemacher are five of its alumni that became jazz giants. They all attended Austin High at about the same time and were influenced by the immigrant jazz artists from New Orleans. The "New Orleans Rhythm Kings" served as their inspiration .

Other bands of this period included the "Georgia Jazz Band" with Ma Rainey as leader, the first woman bandleader; the "New Orleans Rhythm Kings" led by Paul Mares, originally named "Friar's Society Orchestra"; and Papa Celestin's "Original Tuxedo Orchestra".

"Muskat Ramble"

Recordings

While New York was not that receptive to Dixieland, it was the home of the major recording companies and so bands were drawn to the city. Following the advent of radio in 1922, recordings became popular nationally furthering the spread of jazz.

In 1917, the "Original Dixieland Jazz Band" made its first recording and the results were phenomenal. Record companies were formed quickly and their promotions became nationwide. Black artists were still relegated to 'race recordings'. W. C. Handy and Harry Pace formed a publishing firm and recording company named Pace-Black Swan. Other companies were Edison Records, Okeh, Victor, Columbia, Gennett, Aeolian, Vocalion, Paramount, and Brunswick. The recording industry blossomed and record sales in America, in 1929, were listed at 150 million. For the musicians, the records proved a boon. They could hear recordings of established artists and copy their favorites. They would, in essence, take lessons from their favorite performers and often, exceed their musical heroes with their own performances.

By modern standards, early recordings were very crude. Electronics was still in its infancy and the recording industry had to bide its time as progress was being made. Fortunately for America's musical audiences and students of jazz history, many of the early recordings have been re-released and have, in fact, been given an electronic 'shot in the arm' to enhance their quality.

Early artists recorded into a series of megaphones. The performers were placed in different locations in the studio depending on the projection power of their instruments and/or voices. Today's recording studios use multi-track recording. Each individual at a recording session can have his or her own microphone and record on an individual track. These individual tracks are then assembled by an engineer into a well balanced performance.

Rent Parties

With recordings, jazz popularity grew. New York musicians, while they may have sacrificed meals, wearing apparel, and many other necessities, were faced with one major unrelenting need. They had to pay the rent. While many musicians had relatively stable employment, there were others who had to devise a way to pay for the monthly housing or be evicted. The rent party was born and, as the name implies, it was a party to help tenants raise money to pay the rent. Jazz musicians found the idea of a rent party to their liking because it had a twofold purpose. First, it helped earn money to keep a roof over their heads and, second, it was free advertising for their musical talent. Musicians placed ads in area newspapers indicating time, place, and the admission charge. The rent parties were a tremendous success with some of the top jazz names performing. A counterpart to the rent party was the 'house hop' which included dancing if space permitted.

Dances

America enjoyed the fact that the music of Dixieland allowed the listener to participate physically. Three major dances emerged during the era: the Black Bottom, the Charleston, and the Lindy Hop (names after the trans-Atlantic flight of Charles Lindbergh). With Dixieland and the audience's excitement over dancing, ballrooms and dance halls cropped up nationwide. These later became major performance arenas of jazz bands during the swing era. This enthusiasm fostered the late-night, live broadcast by various bands of that era.

Musicians Unions

The first unions designed to better the working conditions and salaries of professional musicians were formed during this period. The American Federation of Musicians was the first, which in turn was followed by the Musicians Protection Union, the New Amsterdam Musical Association, and the Clef Club. The Musicians Protective Union, the New Amsterdam Musical Association and the Clef Club were organized because the American Federation of Musicians would not allow black musicians into their membership. The Clef Club was organized and administered by a bandleader named James Reese Europe, who had been a military bandleader in Europe during World War I. The union also acted as a booking agent for bands in the New York area. The American Federation of Musicians finally allowed membership to black musicians. The other unions eventually disbanded and today the American Federation of Musicians is a subsidiary of the American Federation of Labor.

The Decline

While Dixieland did not die abruptly, it began to fade as the popular music form after several decades. The Armstrongs, Bechets, and Bigards continued to maintain their popularity as Dixieland performers. Other performers made the transition to the big bands. Paul Whiteman organized a jazz orchestra, which, with the aid of recordings and radio, became a popular sound for American audiences. "Duke" Ellington and Fletcher Henderson enlarged the instrumentation of their bands, giving the listeners new and fuller sounds. Those musicians that were able to read music easily made the transition from bands that memorized music to ones which read music. Musicians who had never learned to read music either had to give up performing or remain in their old style. Bands did tolerate a few nonreaders, however. Bix Biederbecke had difficultly reading music but was hired by Whiteman as a soloist. Armstrong was forced to learn to read music when he joined Henderson's band. But most of the Dixieland musicians were left behind.

The Music Staff at the Arizona Jazz Festival. Left to right: Glenn Shull, trombone; Larry Lashley, bass; Gil Garcia, trumpet; Bob Nisbett, piano; Mic Hardin, reeds; Otto Werner, drums.

The real demise of the era came with the stock market crash in 1929, and the beginnings of the depression. The general public could no longer afford to spend nights on the town, dining and dancing. The demand for live entertainment became limited. Although some people could afford luxuries, the general public, black and white alike, faced a time of financial disaster. Entertainment was the first item cut from the family budget.

The period of financial recovery was slow and the reentry of the general public into entertainment circles was equally slow. By the time the nation had moved back into economic solvency, a new style of music had emerged and was forging ahead. Dixieland, like ragtime, would continue to be played and listened to, but never again with the force it had during the roaring 20s.

Jazz Festivals

Americans seem obsessed with nostalgia. Parades throughout the summer months include vintage automobiles that have been refurbished to look like new. Homeowners fill their homes with antiques. Homebuyers want older homes to remodel. And clothiers sell items that were popular during the flapper era. Men return to wearing suspenders and children must wear bib overalls to be in vogue with their peers.

So, too, has the music industry been effected. Dixieland and ragtime are in demand, so much so that jazz festival organizers feel assured that a traditional jazz format including an abundance of Dixieland and ragtime, along with an ample amount of solo banjo pickin', will assure the festivals success in attendance and revenue. European festival promoters likewise include this style of music. The media assists in the advertisements because it draws spectators and jazz lovers from all over the country, and in the summer tourist season, visitors bring dollars.

Discussion Topics

1. Why did Dixieland, which had its beginnings at about the same time as ragtime, outlast it chronologically?
2. New Orleans, Kansas City, Chicago and many other large cities in both the North and South enjoyed the music of Dixieland. Why did the largest of all American cities, New York, neglect it so?
3. Why does Dixieland enjoy popularity today by audiences both young and old when it seemed to have faded out of existence during the big band era?

W.C. Handy (Ed Dwight, Sculptor).

CHAPTER 9

Tin Pan Alley

Some jazz purists and historians tend to feel that 'tin pan alley' and its products have no real significance to the development of jazz. The writers of popular songs of the era had very little regard for jazz as an American art form. Their primary interest was in producing 'hits' that helped establish them as composers of popular music and would bring them economic rewards.

Tin pan alley, its people; the composers, arrangers, and publishers were concentrated in New York. The majority had never heard jazz performed in Storyville, Kansas City, or even Chicago. They were concerned with New York City and after the development of the 'talking pictures,' with Los Angeles. Geographically, what occurred in music between these two cities was of little or no interest or importance to them with the exception of a very few such as George Gershwin. Gershwin was genuinely interested in the blacks and their music; his compositions reflected it.

The era of tin pan alley, if it can be called an era, spanned the period from 1900–1950, and also the eras of ragtime, Dixieland, and the big bands. In itself, tin pan alley did not develop a new jazz style. But its products were and still are being used by jazz musicians worldwide. Jazz historians refer to tin pan alley as the 'song or tune factories,' giving the implication that it was a 'mass production' method of composing songs. Though true, the songs written during tin pan alley became the standards of popular music. Today many of them are still being performed by instrumentalists and vocalists. Each new jazz or rock style that comes upon the musical scene, utilizes the products of the song factories. The harmonies, the tempos, and the rhythms used as accompaniment may be changed but the melodies and lyrics remain the same. Tin pan alley has become a valuable storehouse of material. In this respect it has made a very major contribution to the development of jazz. Many of the songs have in a sense been plagiarized to fit a particular need. Examples include the melody to "Whispering" by John Shonberger which was changed (utilizing the basic chord progressions) to "Groovin' High" by Dizzy Gillespie; "How High the Moon" written for "Two for the Show," by Morgan Lewis, 1940, was changed by Charlie Parker to "Ornithology" during the be-bop era.

The writers of tin pan alley were in some cases also guilty of plagiarism by taking classical compositions and rewriting them as popular songs. A segment of the "Polivetsian Dances" became "Stranger in Paradise." The theme of the last movement of Beethoven's Ninth Symphony became a popular rock version of the "Ode to Joy." "Yankee Doodle" has the same basic chord progressions as does "Silent Night".

Songwriting in the United States did not begin with tin pan alley. Songwriters have been plying their trade since the Revolutionary War. Of course, the style was different then, but the same concept was there. Songs are written to be sung by individuals or groups and to entertain audiences, whether it be at a recital, minstrel show, vaudeville, a Broadway musical, movie, nightclub performance, or on a recording.

This country's early songwriters were primarily immigrants from Europe, the majority coming from England. The melodic and harmonic style of their compositions was European in nature. They were adept at all forms of musical composition. They wrote keyboard compositions, orchestral works, concertos, and light opera. It must be pointed out that these musical immigrants were not 'top of the line' composers, but usually persons who were looking for a 'break' in the field of composition. If fame meant writing songs, then write songs they would. In addition to songwriting, some became involved in music publishing. It assured that their compositions would be published. This was also true during the time of the tin pan alley composers.

It is important to note that while tin pan alley was a New York entity, early American songwriters were located in several Eastern cities; Baltimore, Boston, Columbus, Hartford, New York, and Philadelphia. These cities were considered 'cultural centers' and musical 'havens' for composers.

While it was no doubt difficult for a songwriter/composer to earn a living from compositional efforts, many supplemented their incomes by tutoring, conducting church choirs, playing the church organ, performing accompaniments for vocalists, and/or song plugging. Tin pan alley composers found themselves in similar situations. For a time, George Gershwin played accompaniments and worked in a music store playing sheet music, a standard practice at the time.

The Songs

The settings (lyrics) for early songs were based upon poems and stories. The form of the early songs was primarily strophic; verse upon verse, similar to church hymns. Besides poetry and stories, the lyrics were also based on ethnic songs (Irish melodies), nostalgia (life in the Old World), the beauty of the new land, and other subjects pertaining to life in America.

Early Composers

Benjamin Carr (1768–1831), with his brother, Joseph, and father, Joseph, formed Carr and Company music publishers in Philadelphia. He wrote "The Little Sailor Boy".

James Hewitt (1770–1827), was an orchestra conductor and opera composer. He published music and composed:

The Wounded Hussar
The Primrose Girl
How Happy Was My Humble Lot

Thomas Moore (1779–1852) was a composer, poet, and singer. He is best known for his "Irish Melodies".

Of all the early American songwriters, perhaps the most popular was **Stephen Collins Foster.** Born in Pittsburgh in 1826, he is regarded as a genius songwriter. Many of his songs were written for minstrel shows. By 1850, he was supporting himself fully on his songwriting. He was one of the first composers to be paid royalties by publishers (2¢ per copy). He was also able to draw 'advances' from publishers for songs yet unwritten. Though low by today's standards, the royalties he received were considered quite good for the time. For a while he was under contract to Firth, Pond and Co., music publishers from which he was to receive a ten percent royalty.

The following illustrates some of Foster's songs, the royalties he received, and the number of copies (if known) as taken from Hamm's book *Yesterdays.* This information is through 1857.

Songs	Royalties	Copies
Old Folks at Home	$1,647.46	130,000 (by 1854)
My Old Kentucky Home	1,372.06	90,000
Massa's in de Cold Ground	1,080.25	74,000
Nelly Bly	564.37	
Jeannie With the Light Brown Hair	217.80	
Camptown Races	101.25	
Ring de Banjo	35.24	

Nationalism in Songs

It is not unique to this country to have songs written concerning patriotism. Every nation has songs written about its attributes, songs designed to elicit a feeling of national pride from its citizenry. It is rather unique to find songs written of the inner conflict of a nation. This was the case during the Civil War. During this time, songwriters in both the North and South, composed songs designed to stimulate the citizens and the military. This was also a practice during World Wars I and II, the peak years for tin pan alley.

Songs written during the Civil War dealt with slavery (pro and anti), political rallies, specific battles and campaigns. A list of songs and their authors follows:

John Browns Body: William Steffe
Kingdom Coming: Henry C. Work
Marching Through Georgia: Henry C. Work
Battle Hymn of the Republic: Julia Ward Howe
Battle Cry of Freedom: George Root

Tin Pan Alley—Its Birth

In his book, *After the Ball: Forty Years of Melody,* songwriter Charles K. Harris writes of the philosophy of the songwriter:

When writing popular songs always bear in mind that it is to the masses, the untrained musical public, that you must largely look for support and popularity. Therefore, do not offer them anything which in subject matter or melody does not appeal to their ears. To do so is just so much time thrown away.

Other suggestions for the potential success of a song:

State your theme in the first eight bars, which should include the title.
Amplify in the next eight bars.
Build further in your next eight bars.
Then come in strong with a punch line and title again.

During tin pan alley, the sheet music publishers played as important a role as the composers. It was through the publishers that the public was exposed to the music itself. Early recordings did not have a very large market until the development of the disc recording in 1904. Radio did not become popular until the 1920s. Up to this time, performances and sheet music sales were the major methods by which popular music was spread throughout the country. **Charles Harris'** publication of "After the Ball" really got things moving by selling five million copies.

Each publishing firm had its 'stable' of composers, much like today's booking agencies have their 'stable' of artists. The leading publishers at the turn of the century included:

New York: T. B. Harms
M. Witmark & Sons
Charles Harris

Boston: Oliver-Ditson

Chicago: Root & Cady

Philadelphia: Lee & Walker

Cincinnati: John Church Co.

Baltimore: Willig Publishing

Later sheet music publishers that formed in New York were: Shapiro & Bernstein, Jerome Remick & Co., and Leo Feist Publishing Co.

Location

The first location for tin pan alley was in the Union Square section of New York, on East Fourteenth Street, the heart of the theater district. Guy Lombardo in his autobiography *Auld Acquaintance* places the location in a row of buildings along Twenty-third Street in Manhattan, later moving to the Brill Building on Forty-ninth Street. Regardless of the exact location, tin pan alley was a collection of offices dominated by the publishing firms, agents, composers, and the performers (songpluggers) in New York City.

Name

There is some question of who actually created the name 'tin pan alley'. Guy Lombardo gives credit to composer/publisher **Harry von Tilzer**, while Charles Hamm in *Yesterdays*, credits composer **Monroe H. Rosenfeld** with the name. In Lombardo's description the name was coined when a newspaper reporter visiting Tilzer's office commented on the strange sounds of Tilzer's piano. Tilzer explained that the sound was created by stuffing newspapers behind the strings in an effort to mute the piano (evidently, offices and studios in the building were not acoustically treated) thereby giving it a 'tinny' sound. In his article the reporter called the area 'Tin Pan Alley' and the name stuck.

Tin Pan Alley and Vaudeville

The beginning of tin pan alley coincided with the end of minstrelsy and the beginning of vaudeville. Evidently people were tired of the entertainment of minstrelsy that mocked blacks. They were tuned for something new and vaudeville seemed to fill their needs. Vaudeville was a potpourri of entertainment. An evening of vaudeville included singers, dancers, jugglers, magicians, instrumental performers, and trained animals. It also included stand-up comics.

The effect on tin pan alley was in the need for material for the singers. There was a continual demand for new songs. When a vaudeville troupe returned from a road tour, the singers and instrumentalists would converge on tin pan alley's writers and request new songs and arrangements for the next tour. Vaudeville was a tremendous hit with the public and a major contributor to the spread of 'popular songs'. Entertainers such as **Lillian Russell** and **George M. Cohan** were members of vaudeville troupes.

The Songplugger

The 'songplugger' became an important member of the musical world. It was the songplugger's job to promote the new songs. At times the methods could be considered rather devious and became the forerunner of a similar action, 'payola'. Financial rewards (in one form or another) were given performers and disc jockeys for plugging a song, either by performing it or playing the recording, in the hopes that the song would gain popularity and become a 'hit'. Charles Harris, in his book *After the Ball: Forty Years of Melody*, cites an example of the efforts of songpluggers:

> Daily in Tin Pan Alley, the song pluggers, from early morning until late at night, stood in front of their respective publishing houses waiting for singers to come along, when they would grab them by the arm and hoist them into the music studios. There was no escape. Once the singers entered the block, they left it with a dozen songs crammed into their pockets. . . . It was a common sight any night to see these pluggers, with pockets full of professional copies, stop the singers on the street and lead them to the first lamppost, where the plugger would sing a song from a professional copy. It mattered not how many people were passing at the time. . . . They (the singers) certainly had a good time of it, as the pluggers and publishers fed them up with cigars, drinks, and food of all kind gratis. In order that a firm's song might be heard in different cities, many a singers board bill was paid and many a new trunk, together with a railroad ticket, was purchased by the particular firm whose song the singer was exploiting. The publishers spent their money freely, their slogan being, "Anything and everything to land a hit."

Sheet music of song To-morrow as sung by singer, Eddie Cantor

Sheet music for Gershwin's Swanee as sung by Al Jolson.

The 'trunks' to which Harris refers were the Hartman Trunks, which could hold a performer's complete wardrobe. If a performer had a Hartman Trunk (value approximately $400), it was an indication of 'star' status in the music industry. Guy Lombardo cited a typical evening when his band was playing the Roosevelt Grill in New York. Each evening the songpluggers would gather at a rear table in the Grill, and at intermissions, would descend upon him with the new songs they were plugging. They hoped that Lombardo would have an arrangement made of the song and then play it both in the Hotel and during their remote radio broadcasts.

It was a publisher's heyday! There was demand for material. An unofficial guide for songwriters was:

1. In the lyrics, avoid slang and vulgarity;
2. Keep the melody simple (for quick memorization by the public)
3. Avoid lyrics with many syllable words and consonants
4. Make a point with the lyrics
5. Be aware of public demand

The Lyricist

The lyrics to a song very often are the reason for a song's success. It is with the words that the listener identifies. The melodic line in songwriting is often repetitious and serves as an aid to the lyrics. However, in the publishing field, melody, harmony, and rhythm are important. The lyricist was of a lower status than the composer in that without a 'catchy' melody, the lyrics are wasted. As a result, songwriting teams formed (Rodgers and Hammerstein, Gershwin and Gershwin), in which the composer and the lyricist worked well together and both the music and the lyrics contributed to make a 'hit'. The lyricist decided (perhaps in collaboration with the composer) upon the subject matter of a song. In 'musicals' *(Porgy and Bess; Oklahoma; South Pacific; Jesus Christ, Super Star)*, the script determined a central theme around which the music was written (similar to opera). The lyricist then concentrated on the central theme of the

107

show. For independent songs (not associated with a musical production) the lyricist selected the theme (i.e. love, national issues, fantasy) for the lyrics. On occasion, a singer would determine the type of song he/she needed for performance and would in effect, suggest lyrics.

Early Songs, Their Composer and Lyricist

Song	Composer	Lyricist
A Bird in a Gilded Cage	Harry Von Tilzer	Arthur J. Lamb
Wait 'til the Sun Shines Nellie	Harry Von Tilzer	Andrew B. Sterling
In the Good Old Summertime	George Evans	Ren Shields
The Band Played On	Charles B. Ward	John E. Palmer

Ragtime Songs

Not to be confused with the ragtime of Joplin and Jelly Roll Morton (Chapter 7). Tin pan alley composers had heard of ragtime but probably had not studied the style or the performers. The ragtime songs of tin pan alley were composed because of the national interest in ragtime. Jumping 'on the bandwagon' so to speak, tin pan alley composers began composing ragtime. There is very little comparison between the complex syncopation of piano rags and tin pan alley's version. The songs merely touched on syncopation. It must be remembered that ragtime songs had to have a simple rhythmic, melodic line in order to meet the criteria for success. A number of composers delved into ragtime songs because they were 'selling' at the time. The lyrics were often humorous and the tempo was spirited. The melodies had simple rhythmic syncopations. Some ragtime songs and their composers include:

Alexanders Ragtime Band: Irving Berlin
Bill Bailey, Won't You Please Come Home: Hughie Cannon
Good Bye, My Lady Love: Joe Howard
Waiting for the Robert E. Lee: Lewis F. Muir
Hello! Ma Baby: Joe Howard

The Leaders

As with any jazz era, there are those people who are looked upon as the 'headliners' or leaders in the field. Tin pan alley was no exception. While there are innumerable songwriters, some have written only a few songs, while others seem to have a talent for continuous creation. Classical composers such as Haydn, over 100 symphonies; Mozart, over 30 symphonies; Beethoven, nine symphonies; and Schubert, innumerable songs and symphonies; are well known for their productivity. Tin pan alley had many songwriters who are well known for the quantity and quality of their songs. **Irving Berlin, George Gershwin, Richard Rodgers, Jerome Kern, Harold Arlen,** and **Hoagy Carmichael** are a few of the songwriters who wrote numerous hits.

An entire volume could be written about the songwriters of tin pan alley, their lives and music. Here are a few whose names consistently appear in books on the history of American music.

George M. Cohan (1878–1942) wrote over 700 songs during his career. He was involved in all aspects of the entertainment industry; acting, dancing, singing, directing, and musical plays. Most of his songs were marchlike in style and tempo. His life was portrayed in the 1942 movie, *Yankee Doodle Dandy.* A few of his songs are listed below:

Over There
You're a Grand Old Flag
The Yankee Doodle Boy
Give My Regards to Broadway
Mary's a Grand Old Name

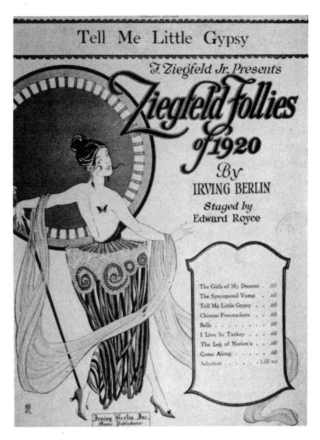

Sheet music covers for the songs "Mandy" and "Tell Me Little Gypsy." Irving Berlin compositions for the 1919 and 1920 Ziegfield Follies. Published by Irving Berlin's publishing company. Berlin wrote extensively for both Ziegfield's Follies and George White's Scandals.

"Over There" written during World War I, won for Cohan a medal from the United States Congress in 1940. His musical productions include *The Governors Song* and *Little Johnny Jones.*

Irving Berlin was born **Israel Baline** in Russia in 1888. Probably the best known American songwriter. His ragtime songs earned him the title of the 'father of ragtime' in England. Credited with creation of the 'ballad', Berlin wrote musical comedies, and music for movies, and the "Ziegfeld Follies." Considered by many to be a pioneer of modern jazz, many of his songs sold over a million copies (records and sheet music).

His friend Jerome Kern described Berlin's place in American popular music by saying: "Irving Berlin has no place in American music. Irving Berlin *is* American Music." His fellow Tin Pan Alley composer George M. Cohan said the following in describing the man and his music, "Berlin writes a song with a good lyric, lyrics that rhyme, good music, music you don't have to dress up to listen to. He is uptown, but he is there with old downtown hard sell."

His lifetime production numbers in excess of 1500 songs, show tunes, ragtimes songs, ballads, waltzes, two steps, reveries and reviles ("Oh How I Hate To Get Up In The Morning").

He offered nine rules for songwriters:

1. Write for the average voice, for either sex to sing.
2. The title should be strong.
3. The lyrics euphonious.
4. It should have "heart interest."
5. Words and music should be original in idea.
6. Keep it simple.
7. Songwriting is not for amateurs.
8. Songwriters must look upon their work as business.
9. To be a success he must work, Work, WORK!! Always.

Perhaps his upbringing and early musical experiences had something to do with his attitude about the music consuming public. He guarded his copyrights with great care even though some of them had run out. A recluse for his last several decades, he spent his time at the piano composing. His last musical, *Mr. President,* written in 1962, was a flop. His best is no doubt *Annie Get Your Gun,* starring **Ethel Merman,** who in her autobiography *I Got Rhythm,* relates tales about composers that would have "piano bench music", songs that were written some time in their past but were unused either as solo songs or songs that just did not fit in a particular show. When writing music for a new show, the composer would then go to his storage area (piano bench), and rewrite the lyrics of a song and try to make it fit the new show. Merman wanted originals for all her shows, tailored for her voice, style, range and personality. Berlin tried to pass off one of his oldies, but was discovered by Merman and after a heated discussion, the old tune was discarded and Berlin returned to the piano to write a new song. This practice of rewriting songs was standard procedure for Tin Pan Alley composers.

Unable to read music, Berlin employed assistants to help with the notation and the harmony. He was, himself, an expert lyricist, seldom using anyone to help with the lyrics of his songs.

His best known works, "White Christmas" and "Easter Parade", were written for movies. His song, "God Bless America," made singer **Kate Smith** a national legend. The song is described as the second national anthem. All the royalties from it go directly to the Boy & Girl Scouts of America.

Michael Walsh, a writer for *Time Magazine* paid tribute to Berlin by incorporating the titles of his songs:

"So, here's to you Irving Berlin; at 100, you keep coming back like a song. For you, a pretty girl is like a melody; for you your melodies are like a pretty girl—irresistible. On May 9 (1988) you'll be home, probably painting or picking out a new tune on the piano. But you can't brush us off: we'll be singing. Maybe we don't have to dress up, but just this once we can be forgiven for puttin' on the ritz; they say it's wonderful, so let's break out the top hat and white tie. Let's face the music and dance."

Movies: *The Jazz Singer*
           Holiday Inn
           Easter Parade

Musicals: *Annie Get Your Gun*
            This Is the Army
            Music Box Revue

Hit Songs: White Christmas
              Easter Parade
              God Bless America
              Blue Skies
              How Deep is the Ocean
              Cheek to Cheek
              Oh How I Hate to Get Up in the Morning

Music: "When My Dreams Come True." Copyright 1929.

Sheet Music Cover: "Waiting at the End of the Road." Copyright 1929.

George Gershwin (1898–1937) began his career as a songplugger for Remick Music Co., and as an accompanist for singers. "Swanee" written by Gershwin and sung by **Al Jolson** became an overnight 'hit'. The premiere of Gershwin's *Rhapsody in Blue,* commissioned and performed by the Paul Whiteman orchestra, in 1924, in New York City, was considered the first orchestral jazz. His music was a fusion of European and Negro elements. His brother, Ira, wrote lyrics for many of his compositions.

Following is a list of but a few of his compositions:

Orchestral works: *American in Paris*
        Concerto in F
        Second Rhapsody

Music Theater: *Porgy and Bess*
        Of Thee I Sing
        Strike Up the Band

Movie scores: *Delicious*
        Damsel in Distress
        Goldwyn Follies

Songs: I Got Rhythm   Summertime
       Strike up the Band   But Not for Me
       A Foggy Day   Somebody Loves Me
       Loved Walked In

George Gershwin (Photo courtesy Institute of Jazz
Studies, Rutgers University)

George Gershwin was one of the giants of tin pan alley. A prolific composer who passed away in the prime of his life, he no doubt would have continued on for many years giving the nation the very best in popular songs and musicals. Many tin pan alley as well as ragtime composers attempted to stray from their best areas of composition and enter the area of classical music. Some have met with limited success. Popular music composers seem obsessed with the dream of composing something classical akin to men such as Tchaikovsky, Beethoven, Bach or Brahms. George Gershwin did that with much success. His amount of productivity in that area was all too small and no doubt would have been enlarged had he lived.

In 1987, in a Warner Brothers warehouse in Secaucus, New Jersey, eighty boxes of sheet music were discovered. Among the contents were unpublished works of Gershwin. The following article by Rocky Mountain News Staff Writer Jackie Campbell describes this musical treasure.

Treasure Trove in Secaucus

Experts differ on impact of sheet-music 'discovery'

by Jackie Campbell, Rocky Mountain News Staff Writer

From the Great White Way to the Great Plains, the American theater community is talking about last week's "discovery" of a reasure trove of original music manuscripts and sheet music, "some previously unknown," in 80 boxes stored in a Warner Bros. warehouse in Secaucus, N.J.

In the boxes are songs—some in the composer's handwriting—by George Gershwin, Jerome Kern, Victor Herbert, Richard Rodgers and Cole Porter.

Among the reported discoveries are about 70 heretofore "lost" songs by George Gershwin as well as missing original scores to his musicals *Primrose* (1924), *Tiptoes* (1925) and *Pardon my English* (1933).

Also found were complete scores for Kern's most important shows, including *Very Good Eddie* (1915), *Leave It to Jane* (1917), *Sitting Pretty* (1924), and *Sunny* (1925). In addition, there are 30 Cole Porter manuscripts and the long-lost piano score to the Rodgers and Hart 1920's musical *Peggy-Ann.*

The experts sifting through the material expect to take at least two years to complete their tasks of cataloging every item.

At the moment, nobody seems able to identify the really "unknown" items. But that may not be the point. The value of the collection seems to lie in its uniqueness as an original source.

Jule Styne, 81, the extraordinary prolific (more than 1,000 songs) composer of Broadway musicals like *High Button Shoes, Gentlemen Prefer Blondes, Peter Pan, Bells Are Ringing, Gypsy,* and *Funny Girl,* commented on the Secaucus discovery in a telephone call from New York City.

"The Gershwin is new, but everything else is from the trunk," Styne said. "Every composer has a trunk. When you write a score, you write maybe 40 songs and use 14. The rest go in the trunk and they aren't always the best. If you thought they were great, you'd use them. *The Man I Love* (by Kern) was a trunk song, and it was finally used after six shows.

"(The Secaucus collection) is not valuable because of its greatness," he said. "It's value

lies in the original manuscripts. I have 10 original manuscripts for every song I write. There are changes in harmonics.

"What is the original—the lead sheet or the first version? Original manuscripts have an historical value, not a playing value. Everything they found has been known."

Gerald Schoenfeld, chairman of the Shubert Organization, which owns 17 New York City theaters, wondered why he was getting calls about the Secaucus collection. For a man who oversees many of the theaters where Broadway musicals are performed, he seemed surprisingly calm about the discovery.

"That library they found?" he said from New York City. "A lot of people are calling me about that. I've never seen it. I think it would be more appropriate to talk to a songwriter about it."

Denver producer Kirby Lewellen can't believe there are undocumented Cole Porter songs. Lewellen's skepticism is understandable. For his latest musical revue, *Uncommon Cole,* Lewellen researched obscure sources and dredged up a handful of rare Porter songs.

Lewellen's incredulity aside, Patrick Smith of the National Endowment for the Arts said there are indeed unknown Porter songs in the Secaucus collection.

Smith, whose organization is funding a project charged with cataloging American musical theater, said: "The find in Secaucus is absolutely amazing. You have to understand how shows were written. When a song didn't fit, it was discarded. In some cases a show opened and closed in one night and the material was lost. Suddenly, we find the material at Secaucus."

Surprisingly, Michael Price, producer at Goodspeed Opera House in Connecticut, says he has "already been using" some of the Secaucus material.

Price was in a unique position to use material from the Secaucus find, according to John M. Ludwig, executive director of the National Institute for Music Theater in Washington, D.C.

Edward Jablonski

Ira (left) and George Gershwin (Courtesy of ASCAP, Ed Jablonski).

An old anecdote has George Gershwin in his favorite spot, at the piano. He had just finished playing an extended medley of his songs. In the brief hush that invariably followed his performances, he was heard to muse, "I wonder if my music will be played a hundred years from now."

"Yes," quipped his friend Newman Levy, "if you're around to play it."

It is a snappy Jazz Age retort. Still, half that time has passed since the composer's death at the age of 38—and his music is heard more than ever. No doubt it will be played a hundred years from now.

George Gershwin was born in Brooklyn on September 26, 1898. Six weeks later the family was back in Manhattan, where his brother, Ira, had been born on December 6, 1896. It was there that the brothers grew up, learned their respective trades, and would make musical history.

The Gershwin collaboration was unique—and inevitable, not because they shared the same quarters for virtually all of their professional lives, but because their talents were singularly attuned and complementary. Yet as personalities they were opposites: George was dynamic, quick-moving, gregarious: Ira phlegmatic, a slow-working polisher and a homebody.

As a boy Ira was bookish, his tastes running from dime novels through A. Conan Doyle to the classics. George was not. He did his running in the streets, roller skated (champion of Seventh Street on the Lower East Side), and skipped school. When an interviewer asked, "Didn't you play anything when you were a youngster?" the answer was, "Yes. Hooky."

George's initial study of the piano began at the ripe age of 12. Three years later he took a job playing in Tin Pin Alley, where music publishers would hawk their wares to performers and sheet-music retailers. There his desire to compose was nurtured, inspired by the suave melodies of Jerome Kern and the earthy rhythms of Irving Berlin, as well as the music he heard in concert and recital halls. He would begin to fuse these two worlds and eventually create his own signature. By the time he was 20, George had written a number of solo piano "novelettes" as well as a *Lullaby* for string quartet, and had filled several "tune books" with ideas for songs and instruments.

Ira's progress was synchronous, though still bookish. He attended Townsend Harris Hall for exceptional students. There he attracted attention as an artist and contributed drawings to the *Academic Herald,* the school paper on which he served as an art editor. He also collaborated on a column, "Much Ado," with a Lower East Side friend, Isidore Hochberg (later to be better known as lyricist E. Y. "Yip" Harburg). Ira's later mentor was the renowned satirist P. G. Wodehouse, one of Kern's early lyricists.

The outpouring of inspired songs from George began with the innocuous though charming "When You Want 'Em You Can't Get 'Em, When You've Got 'Em You Don't Want 'Em" (lyric by Murray Roth), his first published song, written when he was about 17. Just four years later, in 1919, George took a giant step with "Swanee" (lyric by Irving Caeser), which led to his being hired to write for a series of revues, the *George White Scandals.*

The Gershwin collection began in earnest when the brothers managed to place a song, "The Real American Folk Song (Is a Rag)," in *Ladies First* (1918). (Ira was then known as "Arthur Francis," because he did not want to make his way into the business on his brother's name. The pen name was concocted from the names of their younger brother and sister.) Contrary to legend, George brought a solid musical background to his work, whether applied to a 32-bar song or a half-hour concerto. Ira too worked from a near academic base. While rejecting the idea that a lyric was a poem, he labored over his words as if it were. The wry wit, adroit rhymes, the often arresting and unexpected but right word, all of which seems so true and so effortless—were the result of hard work.

George's creations—melodies, rhythms that frequently laughed, and harmonies that enriched those spare melodies—came easier, although he admitted that making music could be "nerve-racking" and "mentally arduous." He had technique to burn, but he relied as much on instinct—"ideas" and "feeling" were most important to him; no one could have taught him to do what he did.

The Gershwin brothers hit their stride in 1924 with the epochal *Lady, Be Good!,* one of the earliest of what were called smart shows at the time, a turning away from European operetta and toward more modern American themes and settings, with songs to match: "Fascinating Rhythm," the title song, and the torch classic "The Man I Love." The show's pace was swift; it was urbane and funny. And it started a great team, Fred and Adele Astaire, in their first American smash. Incidentally, while the book was merest fluff, many of the songs were "integrated" into it—a rare occurrence at the time. *Lady* set the tone for most of he Gershwin musicals throughout the Twenties and into the Thirties. The music was sophisticated, unsentimental. (Not that the Gershwins ignored the romantic ballad. They merely approached it differently, with tongue, often, in cheek.) The scores that followed produced more of the same: *Oh, Kay!* 1926; (Someone to Watch Over Me," Clap Yo' Hands," "Do, Do, Do") and *Funny Face* 1927; (" 'S Wonderful," "My One and Only," "How Long Has This Been Going On?"). *Strike Up the Band* was the first of the three political operettas and marked their transition away from the 1920's musical comedy. A great success, it produced such standards as the title song as well as "Soon" and "I Got a Crush on You," a characteristic adaptation of a current slang phrase and oblique declaration of affection.

The Gershwins closed the year of the successful *Strike Up the Band*—1930—with a return to the fatuous Twenties-like libretto of *Girl Crazy,* despite which they created one of their richest scores. The book may have been forgettable, but the songs remain: "I Got Rhythm," "Embraceable You," "But Not for Me," and more. The sound and the language of this score left the Jazz Age behind.

This was further demonstrated by *Of Thee I Sing* (1931), the first musical to be awarded a Pulitzer Prize. Like their earlier political operetta, this satire was thoroughly integrated, though its title song, as well as "Wintergreen for President," "Who Cares?" and "Love is Sweeping the Country," did well on their own. *Sing's* sequel, *Let 'Em Eat Cake* (1933), one of the Gershwin's most significant scores, failed miserably. Ira believed that this was so because its book was down on everything (including the government); George felt it had failed because it had no love story (but it did have their wonderful contrapuntal "Mine").

All during the prolific years working on Broadway with Ira, George was branching out into the "serious" world of classical music. Most American critics were not in Gershwin's corner when his symphonic music debuted; he was taken seriously in Europe long before musicologists and critics rediscovered him at home. During his lifetime critics kept hoping he would turn out to be an American Bach, Beethoven, or some other imported luminary. Instead, he turned out to be the American Gershwin. Once *Rhapsody in Blue* (1924) established him in the concert world, it was followed by the more traditional *Concerto in F* (1925) and the exceptionally orchestrated *An American in Paris* (1928). Since their inception, these compositions have been played and recorded all over the world. Although not instant hits as were the big three, the *Second Rhapsody, Cuban Overture,* and *Variations on "I Got Rhythm"* would eventually come into their own in concert performances and recordings.

Each of these works, in its own genre, was a harbinger. In his first rhapsody, George set out, and succeeded, in composing with an American accent. This disturbed many critics, who preferred their serious music, no matter who wrote it, with a German, or if one were really "modern," French accent. The critics, too, had a problem with his Tin Pan Alley roots and found it perturbing that a mere songwriter could write rhapsodies, concertos, preludes, and heavens to Betsy, an opera. Another factor bothered them: his popularity.

But it was if the general music-loving public didn't read the pundits. If the wide popularity of his songs was disturbing, the popularity of the concert works, especially the big three—*Rhapsody in Blue, Concerto in F;* and *An American in Paris*—rendered critics superfluous. This is not to suggest that Gershwin did not have his champions among the critics. He did. In addition, some of his greatest "fans" were men of musical grandeur: composer-pianist Sergi Rachmaninoff, composers Maurice Ravel and Bela Bartok, violinist Jascha Heifetz, and many others.

Not all of George's more serious work, however, was immediately appreciated by audiences. The now classic *Porgy and Bess* was a commercial failure when introduced by the Theatre Guild in 1935. But the American-inflected richness of the score and the humanity of the play have made it, over the years, a prodigiously loved work. *Porgy and Bess* has found its place in the repertoire of the New York Metropolitan Opera, La Scala, and other world-class companies, and has even been cheered by audiences throughout the Eastern Bloc.

But after *Porgy's* initial "failure," the Gershwins turned toward Hollywood, then at the peak of the Astaire and Rogers film-musical renaissance. Alas, the front-office types feared that George had gone "highbrow." George denied it, saying that he was "out to write hits"—an assertion he proved once he and Ira had settled into Beverly Hills in the summer of 1936.

There they created the evergreens for *Shall We Dance*—"They Can't Take That Away From Me" and "Slap That Bass"—and for *A Damsel in Distress*—"A Foggy Day," "Nice Work If You Can Get It." They were working on *The Goldwyn Follies* when George began to manifest the symptoms of what was revealed to be a brain tumor. Surgery proved unsuccessful, and George Gershwin died, aged 38, on July 11, 1937.

The death of his brother did not end **Ira Gershwin's** career. After some time off, he began working on songs with **Jerome Kern** and **Harry Warren.** Then came a major Broadway offer resulting in a remarkable success, *Lady in the Dark* (1941), with music by **Kurt Weill.** Ira proceeded to work with Weill on a couple of film scores and a beautifully scored flop, *The Firebrand of Florence.*

He did even better in Hollywood, whose relative serenity he treasured. With Harry Warren he did the score that reunited Astaire and Rogers, *The Barkleys of Broadway* (1949); with **Burton Lane** he collaborated on good songs for a bad movie, *Give a Girl a Break* (1953). The next year he worked with **Harold Arlen** on the **Judy Garland** classic, *A Star is Born* (1954), with its unforgettable, "The Man That Got Away."

He took time out to write his book *Lyrics on Several Occasions* (1959), and then quietly retired to prepare and annotate the papers of the brothers Gershwin for preservation in the Library of Congress. Ira's peaceful death on August 17, 1983, closed an extraordinary era in the history of American music and song, one that endowed us with a rich—and unmistakably Gershwinesque—legacy.

Music: "My Buddy." Copyright 1920.

Sheet Music Cover: "Somebody Loves Me."
Copyright 1924.

Sheet Music Cover: "If You Knew Susie."
Copyright 1925.

Sheet Music Cover: "Sweet Indiana Home."
Copyright 1920.

Mostly remembered for his compositions for the musical theater, **Jerome Kern** (1885–1945) had his start as a songplugger and rehearsal pianist. He worked with lyricists; **Buddy DeSylva, P. G. Wodehouse,** and **Oscar Hammerstein II.** An artist at writing melodies, Kern's songs were considered lyric ballads. His musical theater hits and the shows for which they were written follow:

Can't Help Lovin' Dat Man *(Showboat)*
A Fine Romance *(High, Wide and Handsome)*
The Last Time I Saw Paris *(You Were Never Lovelier)*
Dearly Beloved *(Cover Girl)*
Smoke Gets in Your Eyes *(Roberta)*
All the Things You Are *(Very Warm for May)*
Ol' Man River *(Showboat)*

Richard Rodgers was born in 1902 in Long Island, New York. He is well known for his partnerships with lyricists, **Lorenz Hart,** and after Hart's death, **Oscar Hammerstein II. Stephen Sondheim** also was a lyricist for Rodgers. His best known musicals and hit songs are listed below:

Musicals: *A Connecticut Yankee* (1927)
    Babes in Arms (1937)
    Oklahoma (1943), Pulitzer Prize winner
    Carousel (1945)
    South Pacific (1949), Pulitzer Prize winner
    The King and I (1951)

Songs: Blue Moon   Some Enchanted Evening
   With a Song in My Heart Bali Ha'i
   This Can't Be Love   Lover
   Oh What a Beautiful Morning My Funny Valentine
   People Will Say We're in Love You'll Never Walk Alone
   If I Loved You
   It Might as Well Be Spring

Harold Arlen, born in 1905, was a student of black musicians and their music. Many of his songs were written specifically for the black vocalist, and/or instrumentalist. Arlen's hits include:

Stormy Weather   Over the Rainbow
Blues in the Night   Come Rain or Come Shine
It's Only a Paper Moon   Old Black Magic
St. Louis Woman (musical)

Other songwriters associated with tin pan alley and some of their better known works:

Songwriter	Songs
Harry Warren	Lullaby of Broadway
	Chattanooga Choo Choo
	You'll Never Know
Vincent Youmans	Tea for Two
	Great Day
Hoagy Carmichael	Star Dust
	Old Rockin' Chair
	The Nearness of You
Walter Donaldson	Love Me or Leave Me
	My Blue Heaven
Arthur Johnson	Pennies From Heaven

It should be noted that while a number of the composers of the tin pan alley era also wrote the words to their songs, many depended on lyricists. The two prominent exceptions were Irving Berlin and Cole Porter, both of whom had the ability to create their own lyrics and melodies. Classical composers utilized librettos by popular writers such as Schiller and Goethe and, of course the Bible provided them with ready made lyrics (*The Messiah* by Handel). The tin pan alley composers relied in a large part on the lyricists. The lyrics had to fit the melody or the melody the lyrics. In tin pan alley it is interesting to note that a composer might use several lyricists during his career, while others would collaborate with only one. Following is a list of the better known lyricists and the composers with which they wrote.

Lyricist	Composers
Ira Gershwin	George Gershwin
	Jerome Kern
Oscar Hammerstein II	Richard Rodgers
	Sigmund Romberg
	Jerome Kern
Mitchell Parish	Hoagy Carmichael
Buddy De Sylva	George Gershwin
Lorenz Hart	Richard Rodgers
Johnny Mercer	Harold Arlen
Otto Harbach	Jerome Kern
Gus Kahn	Walter Donaldson
Alan J. Lerner	Frederick Loewe

Standards

In popular music, the term 'standard' refers to a song which has endured the test of time. It has been used by instrumentalists and vocalists during the eras since its inception. Originally written for minstrelsy, vaudeville, or musical theater, the songs have undergone adaptations depending on the type of musical entity using them. The big bands performed them as instrumental arrangements for dancing, the be-boppers used them and in some cases built 'riffs' upon them which melodically hid the original melody line, and the rock musicians have continued using them with rock rhythms.

Form

However they were and are used, some of the popular songs written in tin pan alley have given jazz an enormous collection of material on which to draw. The form of the music was standardized into 32 bar choruses. As an introduction to the chorus, composers wrote a verse (used primarily in musicals or movies). Not all songs have a verse. It was the option of the composer whether or not to include a verse. The chorus was the main thrust of the song. The 32 bar choruses were segmented into four eight measure phrases either using two or three themes A, B, C, with repetitions. Generally speaking, the form was A—8 bars, A—8 bars (repeated but with different words), B—8 bars (called a bridge or interlude) and finishing with A—8 bars (again different words from the original A) making a total of 32 bars. While the composer decided upon a central tonality (key) and meter (2/4, 3/4, etc.), on occasion the bridge (theme B) was used to make a key change, to give the composition a 'shift', and create a new sound, even though it was a mere eight bar segment, returning to the original key for the last eight bars (theme A).

In his book *Yesterdays,* Charles Hamm has outlined the form of some of the standards written during tin pan alley.

Song	Composer	Themes
Smoke Gets in Your Eyes	Jerome Kern	AABA
Blue Moon	Richard Rodgers	AABA
Body and Soul	John W. Green	AABA
I'm Always Chasing Rainbows	Harry Carroll	ABCA
Tea for Two	Vincent Youmans	ABAC
My Blue Heaven	Walter Donaldson	AAAB
Embraceable You	George Gershwin	ABAC
White Christmas	Irving Berlin	ABAC
Easy to Love	Cole Porter	ABAC

The majority of the songs included the verse which in turn was followed by the chorus. It is the chorus of a song which is the most popular with audiences. The format would be as follows, verse, chorus, 2nd verse, chorus, 3rd verse, chorus, etc. The words of the verse at times were half-spoken and half-sung. The words of each verse were different, while the words of the chorus remained the same. While most of the music written in Tin Pan Alley was for music theater (musicals), the songs did not necessarily fit with the theme of the show. The musical, *Oklahoma,* while very entertaining and melodic, does not delve into the cultural features of the state. The music of Gershwin's *Porgy & Bess* does, however, envelop around a main theme with relationships of music to story.

The verse of the song told the story of the song and continued doing so with each additional verse. In his book, *Music in the New World,* Charles Hamm lists two examples of verse-chorus:"After the Ball" Charles Harris,

verse:

A little maiden climbed on old man's knee,
Begged for a story—"Do Uncle, please.
Why are you single; why live alone?
Have you no babies; have you no home?"
"I had a sweetheart, years, years ago;
Where she is now pet, you will soon know.
List to the story, I'll tell it all;
I believed her faithless after the ball."

chorus:

After the ball is over, after the break of morn,
After the dancers' leaving; after the stars are gone;

Many a heart is aching, if you could read them all
Many the hopes that have vanished after the ball.

This was followed by another verse and another chorus (same as above) and yet another verse and another chorus.

"Mary's A Grand Old Name" George M. Cohan

verse:

My mother's name was Mary, she was so good and true;
Because her name was Mary, she called me Mary too.
She wasn't gay or airy, but plain as she could be;
I hate to meet a fairy who calls herself Marie.

chorus:

For it was Mary, Mary, plain as any name could be;
But with propriety, society will say Marie;
But it was Mary, Mary, long before the fashions came,
And there is something there that sounds so square,
It's a grand old name.

followed by another verse and another chorus.

A problem surfaced when it became apparent that many of the songs with their continuation of verse-chorus upon verse chorus would become too lengthy to fit on a three minute, ten inch recording disc. The composer retrenched and either discarded the verses entirely or limited the song to one verse and two choruses, with the performer having the options on what to include and what to delete. Songwriters began composing with the three minute time limit as the norm. "Smoke Gets in your Eyes," (Jerome Kern & Otto Harbach) as well as "Stormy Weather," (Harold Arlen and Ted Koehler) are examples of songs which had only a chorus and no verse. Singers with the big bands when performing band arrangements did not include verses in any of the songs. They merely sang the chorus interspersed with instrumental phrases and then an "out-chorus" by the singer with band.

The spread of the music of tin pan alley was assisted by disc recordings in 1904. The disc playing phonograph now gave a customer two selections on a recording, replacing the cylinder recordings which preceded it. By 1920, recordings sold in the millions of copies surpassing the sales of sheet music. One song could be performed/recorded by several singers giving it additional exposure. Radio programmed music to 'fill' air time, and hotels and ballrooms put in 'wires' for live remote broadcasts by bands. Aired throughout the country, there was a constant need for new songs.

ASCAP-BMI

In 1914, the American Society of Composers, Authors and Publishers was formed to force establishments using live music to pay fees for the use of the music. Theaters, hotels, cabarets, ballrooms, and restaurants had to get an ASCAP license. Radio stations and movie studios also came under its jurisdiction. It was created to ensure monetary reimbursement to the composers for the use of their music. The recording industry was already paying a two cent per disc royalty under a copyright law.

Years later, another organization with similar goals was organized. Broadcast Music International (BMI) functions in the same manner as ASCAP. It was formed as a competitor to ASCAP when ASCAP showed little interest in Country and Western composers and arrangers. As the membership in BMI grew, other artists from other areas of music became interested and also joined. Today BMI is as strong as ASCAP. Composers have the option to join either organization.

Your Hit Parade

Today the music listener wanting to know the latest 'hits' has a weekly published guide, the 'top 40'. The top 40 songs on the 'charts' which are the most popular with the listening public for a particular week, based on record sales. Its predecessor was a radio program called "Your Hit Parade". It featured the top ten songs for any particular week. A barometer of success for a song was its ability to stay in the top ten for an extended period of time. The original radio show began in 1935, with the television show of the same name beginning in 1950. The television program ended in 1958.

Tin pan alley lasted for 50 years. The end coming with the beginning of Rock and Roll. The 'torch songs', the lyrics about love, moon, croon, June, and the life of fantasy became history. The youth of America liked the excitement of Bill Haley, and the gyrations of Elvis Presley. But the writers of tin pan alley had indeed left a tremendous legacy. Even today, regardless of the style, whether it is rock, swing, fusion, or country, artists dip into the music of tin pan alley for their materials.

It was an era that catapulted the vocalist into the spotlight. While other forms and styles of jazz continue to play 'push and shove' for the audiences attention, the singers still command the biggest share of the audience.

Discussion Topics

1. How have the composers in Tin Pan Alley contributed to the development of jazz when the music written by them was for another media, namely vaudeville, music theater, movies and shows (Zigfield Follies, George White Scandals)?
2. The end of Tin Pan Alley came at the beginning of the rock era. Why, when rock music was based upon the voice/singing, did the era come to such an abrupt halt?

Benny Goodman (Ed Dwight, Sculptor).

CHAPTER 10

The Big Bands

At times the name of the era is confusing. Then as now, several names were used. It was called the era of swing bands, name bands or dance bands. It was the same era. The bands were not referred to as 'jazz bands', because of the sexual implications of the word jazz (from Creole patois jass, sexual term applied to Conga dances). Radio was quite strict in its broadcasting rules prohibiting anything which had sexual connotations. So the word 'swing' was devised. It offended no one!

The word 'swing' described a group's ability. If the group measured up to all the criteria included in jazz, it was said to 'swing'. If it did not measure up it was called 'square'.

To some historians, the swing/big band era is the epitome of the development of jazz. In this era jazz received its greatest public exposure. Experimentation and expansion fostered the utmost in musical creativity. Though a short period in jazz history, the peak came rapidly with a less pronounced, yet dramatic decline. Like other eras, the decline was due more to socioeconomic conditions than to the music. As with other jazz eras, it continues today but with fewer bands and less broad based popularity.

The Beginnings

Following World War I, the Dixieland musicians wanted to expand their groups to play theaters, hotels and dances, instead of the 'speakeasies' of prohibition. The time was right and the American audiences wanted to dance! The time frame for the era is a matter of conjecture. It began about 1919–1920. It suffered a slight setback during the depression when many people could not afford entertainment. The peak of the big bands was between 1935 and 1945. They were the boom years for the big bands. It was the period of their highest exposure to the American public. Bands prospered, grew in numbers and hundreds of them appeared throughout the country. Some were excellent, some were good, some were mediocre, and some were bad! It is impossible to list them all. With apologies to the unnamed, a small number of the bands that helped promote the development of the era will be included.

The Early Bands

Two of the pioneers who set the standards for the bands are worth studying in depth. They were contrasts in style and concept, but, they had the same objective, to play for dancers. Each opened new vistas in the entertainment industry and became pacesetters for future bands. These bands were led by Fletcher Henderson and Paul Whiteman.

A piano player, Fletcher Henderson, formed a nine piece band, which was really an enlargement of the Dixieland band. While the Dixieland bands had a front line of wind instruments (trumpet, clarinet, saxophone, and trombone) plus a rhythm section (piano-banjo-guitar, drums and bass tuba or string bass), Henderson expanded the number of wind instruments into sections—brass and reeds, while keeping the same rhythm section. Saxophones became the dominant reed instrument although the three sax players were able to play clarinet upon demand. The brass section included two trumpets and one trombone.

The primary difference (besides the style of the music) was that in Dixieland, the musicians played head arrangements, while in Henderson's band, the musicians had to read music. No longer could players improvise a background to a melody played by the soloist or lead player. Each player in a section had to play specific notes at specific times. This gave rise to the use of the music arranger—an individual who determined who was to play what and when! Henderson (who became a leading arranger) hired a saxophone player named Don Redman, to be his arranger. Due credit should be given Redman as being the first big band arranger. Redman's arrangements for Henderson's band, while they seem rather conservative by today's standards, made the Henderson band 'swing' and propelled it to popularity. The arranger gave the band its own style, a sound that became identifiable with the band. Henderson went on to become the arranger for the Benny Goodman band.

Paul Whiteman (1891–1967), a violinist, was to gain the title 'king of jazz'. His band was a contrast to Henderson's. It was somewhat conservative, but Whiteman earned recognition for inventiveness and experimentation. Ferde Grofe (composer of "Grand Canyon Suite") was Whiteman's arranger. The band was enlarged to include a string section. Whiteman hired some outstanding musicians to perform in or with his band; Tommy Dorsey, trombone; Jimmy Dorsey, sax; Bix Beiderbecke, cornet; and a young singer, Bing Crosby. The group included 30–35 musicians and Whiteman was the first to use the phrase 'orchestral jazz' to describe the band's music. Whiteman's performance of Gershwin's *Rhapsody in Blue* was an important event in jazz history. Don Redman was hired by Whiteman to write some arrangements, to make the band swing. Unfortunately, the band's size and instrumentation, plus the limited ability of Whiteman's musicians to play jazz, made the task impossible. Whiteman had tremendous vision for the place of dance bands in popular entertainment. He formed his own booking agency, one of the first of the era. He had as many as 28 bands under his management. It is rumored that during the depression, Whiteman earned a million dollars from his bands' performances and his booking fees.

Henderson and Whiteman were the forerunners. Others who were active but less well known, in the early days of the big band era, included: Ben Bernie, Jan Garber, Jean Goldkette, Isham Jones, Kay Kyser, the Lombardo Brothers (fronted by Guy), Abe Lyman, Ray Miller, Dave Specht, and Charlie Straight.

There were several bands that were labeled co-op bands, in which everyone had a financial as well as musical interest. The Coon-Sanders band organized by Carlton Coon and Joe Sanders, the Bob Crosby band, the Casa Loma Band (led by Glen Gray), and the Lombardo band in which each of the Lombardo brothers—Guy, Victor, Leibert, and Carmen—were partners.

The Territory Bands

The early dance bands were relegated to playing in a specific territory or geographic region. This was dictated by the ranges of their popularity and the costs of travel. The Lawrence Welk band played the Dakota territory and ventured into neighboring states. Benny Moten played out of Kansas City and traveled as far as Oklahoma, while Charlie Straight had a Midwest band, headquartered in Chicago. Musicians salaries were quite low. Proprietors were hesitant to hire bands from other territories, risking their clienteles' acceptance, and having to pay expenses for long distance travel. Even during the peak of the era, some bands remained as territory bands while the big 'name bands' traveled nationwide. Personnel in the territory bands were content to stay within a territory with a reasonable amount of travel and were able to buy homes and raise families while pursuing full time musical careers.

Bands were placed in several categories, both by themselves and the public. They were labeled 'hot', 'sweet', and 'novelty-specialty' bands. The sweet bands became the territory bands. The sweet bands played 'on location' for extended periods of time, possibly the longest location date was by the Lombardo band at the Roosevelt Grill in New York City.

The sweet bands were stereotyped in a less than complimentary fashion, often called 'Micky Mouse bands', 'sissy bands', 'tenor bands' (in reference to their instrumentation of the sax section, the tenor having a subtle, sedate sound compared to the brilliance of the alto), 'commercial bands' and 'hotel bands' (indicating they were primarily used for background music for diners in addition to playing for dancing).

Lee Barron Orchestra. Photo Courtesy Bunny Lee Barron Collection.

Based on either coast, the hot bands gained fame nationwide through performances, recordings and movies. The sweet or territory bands were in most cases relegated to playing in a specific geographical area. The territory bands could be found throughout an entire geographic region such as the Midwest, Southwest, Far West, Central or Eastern States. None were more active than the bands of the Midwest territory. The late band leader Lee Barron, kept a journal of the bands working in Minnesota, the Dakotas, Nebraska, Kansas, Colorado, Iowa, and Missouri and wrote a book, THE ODYSSEY OF THE MID-NITE FLYER. He lists hundreds of bands and has included photographs of the various types and styles, including bands led by Lawrence Welk, John Cacavas (later to become a composer for TV and movie films), Hal Leonard (leading publisher of jazz band and jazz choir arrangements), Don Strickland, "Big Tiny" Little and the very popular Johnnie Kaye.

The bands traveled in the same general territory working as many as 250 to 300 dates a year. The schedule would consist of a series of "one nighters" followed by a day of long travel in the sleeper trailers or busses to the next engagement. In his book, Barron describes the construction of the sleeper busses used not only by territory bands but also by some of the hot "name" bands.

This extensive traveling necessitated the use of a band bus. Many times there would not be time to check into a hotel because of the mileage involved. The need for sleep and sufficient rest brought about the creation of the "Sleeper Bus." The Sleeper Bus was basically a semi-trailer rig complete with tractor and trailer. However, they were specifically designed for comfort and beauty. Their streamlined tops make them attractive and to save fuel by cutting down wind resistance. Their appearances were enhanced by the colorful way they were painted and lettered in order to make each bus distinctive in its identity.

Mid-Nite Flyer, Sleeper Bus. Lee Barron Orchestra. Photo Courtesy Bunny Lee Barron Collection.

The interiors of the bus contained bunks that were ingeniously designed to fold down while not being slept in, and formed into a studio couch type furniture. There was an area which contained a booth type table and cushioned seats for eating, writing or playing cards. Heat was provided by an oil heater. Water was available by means of a large water tank built into the rear of the trailer at an elevation that provided the gravity needed to force the water through the open taps. The busses also contained storage for wardrobes, instruments and personal belongings. In some cases, there was a special compartment to give privacy for the girl singer. These busses were an expensive luxury for the traveling bands. All had to be specially ordered.

The problem with the buses was the inability to comfortably accommodate more than perhaps 9–12 people. This made it a problem for the large hot bands which numbered from 17–20. Traveling bands not having sleeper busses had to seek other modes of travel, from airplanes, to trains to automobiles, usually the latter. As a mode of transportation for a band, airplane travel was too costly and job locations did not always have airports.

As the era began its decline, the bands were booked on weekends only and the musicians were forced to find day jobs to meet their financial obligations. It is interesting to note that at the peak of the big band or dance band era, a city such as New Ulm, Minnesota, was home to at least a dozen working bands. Omaha and Lincoln, Nebraska, seemed to be the center of the midwest territory and became the home base for large numbers of bands.

Following are some of the Midwest towns which were home bases with the band leaders listed: Huron, South Dakota, Mike Gibbs; McCook, Nebraska, Ralph Emerson; Waterloo, Iowa, Harvey Bourkland; Alden, Minnesota, Lloyd Allen; Ravenna, Nebraska, Clara Skala All Girl Polka Band; Fond Du Lac, Wisconsin, Harold Menning; Yankton, South Dakota, the Leo Terry Swing Band; and Cushing, Iowa, Bobby Beers (one time vocalist with Lawrence Welk and Blue Barron).

The various ethnic cultures found in these eight states enjoyed all forms of dancing. It was a major part of their cultural heritage and an important part of their social activity. It seemed that every town had a place which would serve as a dance hall. Also notable was the fact that not all the dance bands were composed of male musicians.

Women played an active role in the territories. Never to reach the fame of Ina Rae Hutton, they were major contributors to the style of the sweet bands. The Manthey Meadowlark Band, Ruth Coleman All Girls Band, The Harp Sisters, The Mary Ann Lesar Band, The Modernettes, and Dot Kay's All Girl Band were very popular with audiences throughout the territory. One of the major factors in their inability to attain a national reputation was the lack of recording contracts.

Sleeper Bus, Paul Moorhead Band. Photo Courtesy Shorty Vest Collection.

The territory band singers did perform on the remote radio broadcasts but were only heard and known as far as the local radio station had power to reach. They did not have the advantage of appearing on recordings since the bands did not have contracts with the various recording companies. Therefore, singers with the territory bands, nationwide, did not achieve the national popularity or fame of the vocalists with the top name bands. June Christy, Helen O'Connel, Ella Fitzgerald, Helen Forrest, Rosemary Clooney, Anita O'Day or Peggy Lee (real name; Norma Jean Egstrom from Fargo, North Dakota where she performed on radio sharing air time on station WDAY with the Fargo Red Jackets), were heard on recordings, coast to coast broadcasts, and appeared with the bands in movies.

The bands were of all sizes and styles. From traditional ballroom dance bands to polka bands, accordion bands and Dixieland bands. They would range in size from four players to as many as 11 plus leader and singer. The instrumentation was similar to the first bands of Fletcher Henderson, consisting of three or four brass (two or three, one trombone), three or four saxophones (combinations of alto, tenor, and baritone) and a rhythm section of piano, bass (tuba or string bass) and drums. The leader either played an instrument, sang or led (fronted) the band. Female vocalists were an important part of the personnel. They provided an important link among musicians and dancers. They provided the lyrics to the songs, which were based upon love and romance, always a popular topic with dancers.

The territory bands were for dancing. Whether in a service club (Elks Hall, Moose Lodge), American Legion Hall, Knights of Columbus Hall, firehouse, or school, dances were held on any night of the week year round. Winter blizzards, summer rains, and tornados took their toll on schedules. Salaries were not always paid on schedule. If a band did not draw a large enough audience, or weather forced a cancellation, the musicians were not paid. In some instances, dance hall managers would not pay the band at the end of an engagement. To avoid such a problem bands required monies to be paid "up front" or prior to starting the engagement.

The bands were in constant search for personnel to supplant those members that either tired of the arduous travel or to play a specific style of music. "Downbeat" magazine, a publication focusing on the big band era as a whole, listed locations (ballrooms, theaters, hotels, and nightclubs) where the top hot bands were scheduled as well as advertisements which included 'help wanted' or musicians 'at liberty.' Band leader Don Strickland from Omaha ran continuous musicians wanted advertisements for musicians of various band instruments. Some of the bands were what was to become known as cooperatives in which several or all members were shareholders.

Bob Crosby (Courtesy: Willard Alexander, Inc.).

The Hot Bands

Appearing throughout the country, the hot bands were called the 'swing' bands. Theirs was the true big band sound and style. They featured soloists with great improvisational skill. The hot bands were larger in size (15–18 musicians) and when the arrangement called for it, could play with tremendous force. In the hierarchy of a hot band (not unlike a military 'chain of command'), the 'ranks' were; the commander—the leader; the officers—lead men (whose responsibility it was to act as foremen for their section); the sergeants—the hot man, ride man, get off man (the improvising soloist, at least one in each section); and the corporals and privates—the sidemen, whose function it was to play the subordinate parts (3rd, 4th, and 5th trumpet parts, etc.). It was the hot bands who were best known as the 'name bands'. During the peak years, the hot bands settled into an instrumentation of five to eight brass, four to five reeds, and three to four rhythm instruments.

Forming a Band

As mentioned before some bands were cooperatives, but most were under a single leader, musically and financially. Starting a big band was not simple. As the leaders soon found, it was big business! Financial backing was the prime component. A 'book' had to be secured, often by hiring a player/arranger to write all the music in the style the leader wanted. The personnel and the arranger were to be paid for their services (rehearsals, arrangements), prior to the first performance. Advance fees were necessary for travel arrangements, property men (band boys), uniforms, music stands and in some cases, portable public address systems. Booking agencies were also involved in financing bands, if the bands would allow them to become their agent.

Competent personnel were needed. This brought about a bit of piracy on the part of new leaders in raiding established bands by offering more money to players. In some cases, players, who after playing with a band for some time, felt the urge to become leaders themselves. Harry James started his own band with financial assistance from his former boss, Benny Goodman. A number of others began their bands in the same manner.

130

It was an expensive undertaking, and while the ability to lead a band might be there, the business sense might be lacking. While they were excellent musicians, their abilities with business affairs may have left much to be desired. As a result, some of the bands became financial catastrophes. The leaders quickly found it more practical to hire a person to manage the financial affairs of the band, while the leader handled the musical matters. Today, we see the same approach by most professional athletes who have hired business managers/agents to handle their financial matters. Some bands had a home office with a band manager, who handled bookings, publicity, etc., as well as a 'road' manager. The road manager was often a band member, and handled matters such as travel, housing, payroll, collection of fees, and disbursement of funds.

The Early Bands

Early bands were comparatively small in size. The average number of players including the leader was nine or ten, not including vocalists. Partially due to the lack of adequate public address systems, instruments such as the banjo and bass tuba were found in the rhythm sections. These instruments were later replaced by the guitar and string bass. As bands expanded, often as financial conditions improved personnel were added to the sections. It gave the band a more complete sound and extended the possibilities for the arranger. Bands reached their optimum with the Stan Kenton Band which became known as the 'wall of brass'. Kenton's Band had five trumpets, five trombones, several French horns, five saxes, and four rhythm (including a Conga drum). As the economy changed in the mid 40's, band leaders were forced into reducing the number of musicians, without changing the sound and style of the band too drastically.

The Music

With the expansion of the instrumentation, arrangers had greater latitude in their orchestrations. Instead of the restrictions imposed by having four wind instruments (in Dixieland Bands) to play melody, harmony, and countermelody, arrangers could extend the harmonic possibilities by having like instruments (saxes, brass) harmonize with the same sound. Countermelodies could be played by an entire section either in unison or in harmony; this in effect replaced the 'tailgate' countermelody played by the trombone, or the 'obbligato' of the clarinet in Dixieland. As the instrumentation expanded to four or five like instruments, the arranger had the opportunity to expand the chordal structure by adding notes and creating what became known as 'lush' harmonies. The variety of saxophones (two altos, two tenors, one baritone) also gave the arranger a wide variety of tonal possibilities from brilliant to harsh to mellow.

Arrangers had three types of music at their disposal—music carried over from Dixieland; music produced in tin pan alley (the standards); and music composed for the specific band. Many of these were simply based on riffs, others were structured on the blues.

It would be futile to list the many bands, both hot and sweet, that appeared during the big band era. While the ragtime pianists and the Dixieland bands were themselves large in numbers, neither individually or collectively did they outnumber the big bands. Many notables will undoubtedly be left out on these pages. Those wanting to do in-depth reading about the various bands are urged to read George Simon's *The Big Bands* and/or *The Wonderful Era of the Great Dance Bands,* by Leo Walker. In addition, the Franklin Mint Record Society has produced a series of "The Greatest Recordings of the Big Band Era" which includes descriptive pamphlets of the leaders of the era. The *Readers Digest* has produced a series of recordings (rerecordings) on LP's of the big bands.

Following is a partial listing of the bands and their style of music; hot, sweet, and novelty-specialty.

Hot	*Sweet*	*Novelty-Specialty*	*Latin Bands*
Count Basie	Lawrence Welk	Spike Jones	Machito
Les Brown	Guy Lombardo	(novelty)	Perez Prado
Cab Calloway	Franki Carle	Phil Spitalny	Tito Puente
Tommy Dorsey	Blue Barron	(All girl)	Xavier Cugat
Woody Herman	Sammy Kay	Ina Rae Hutton	
Harry James	Kay Kyser	(Woman band leader)	
Stan Kenton	Dick Jurgens		
Duke Ellington	Wayne King		
Gene Krupa	Del Courtney		
Benny Goodman	Freddie Martin		
Charlie Barnet	Vaughn Monroe		
Fletcher Henderson	Ray Noble		
Artie Shaw	Fred Waring		
Glenn Miller	Tiny Hill		
Jimmy Dorsey	Henry Busse		
Buddy Rich	Russ Morgan		
Andy Kirk	Glen Gray		
Chick Webb			

The Arrangers

Arrangers became an integral part of the big band movement. The arrangers were the creators of the music the public heard. It was vastly different from the music of Dixieland, which was never written. The bands of Basie, Goodman, Ellington, and others were known for their individual styles and sounds, yet each one was considered a great band. The styles and sounds of the big bands fostered debates among the public as to which style was the finest and which band best executed their arrangements.

The unfortunate aspect of the arrangers efforts was that some of the musicians felt they were merely tools for the writer. The musicians were given little opportunity for individual expression and improvisation, everything including the dynamics and phrasings were dictated by the arranger. The only opportunities for any individuality was given to the soloists and these were for short periods at best.

A number of the bandleaders had the creative ability to write their own arrangements. Henderson, Glenn Miller, Duke Ellington, as well as Don Redman, Les Brown, Ray Noble, and Benny Carter wrote for their bands. For the most part, the leaders hired arrangers. The arrangers were paid well to assure maximum productivity and allegiance. Following the big band era, many of the arrangers went on to jobs in movies, television, studio writing (including commercials, 'jingles'), and writing accompaniments for leading song stylists.

The arrangers were in large part responsible for the direction jazz took during the big band era. They refined it and gave direction to the art. They made it a very disciplined form and yet, allowed the innovators to become a part of it. The arrangers did not do this alone. They had the help and guidance of the leaders. The following arrangers were associated with the top name bands. Many of these arrangers are still writing today, although in a different media.

Glenn Miller (Courtesy: Downbeat).

Glenn Miller (Glenn MILLER family collection)

The Glenn Miller Band (Courtesy: Downbeat).

Glenn Miller (Glenn MILLER family collection)

Sammy Kaye (Courtesy: Willard Alexander, Inc.).

Arranger	Band
Tutti Camarata	Jimmy Dorsey
Nelson Riddle	Charlie Spivak
Leibert Lombardo	Guy Lombardo
Sy Oliver	Tommy Dorsey
Henry Mancini	The Glenn Miller Band, Tex Beneke, leader
Ray Coniff	Artie Shaw
Gil Evans	Claude Thornhill
Rete Rugolo	Stan Kenton
Ralph Burns	Woody Herman
Gerry Mulligan	Gene Krupa
Fletcher Henderson	Benny Goodman
Frank DeVol	Horace Heidt
Gordon Jenkins	Isham Jones
Billy Strayhorn	Duke Ellington
Sam Nestico	Count Basie
Bob Haggart	Bob Crosby

The general rule governing arrangers was to keep the tempo the same throughout the arrangement (particularly for dancing) and show off the strengths of the group (sections and soloists). The arrangement was to be memorable to the public and the style identifiable with the band. There were some deviations, particularly concerning tempo changes. Stan Kenton, whose philosophy was to have a band for listening and not for dancing, allowed his arrangers the freedom necessary to make the band sound as though it were in a concert setting. This gave the arranger the opportunity to use drastic tempo changes, cadenzas, meter changes, and violent dynamic contrasts.

One restriction that faced the arranger was the length of the arrangement. Three minutes was the general rule in order to comply with the duration of ten inch recordings. Three minutes became the standard not only for recordings but also for dancing, so the dancers would not become tired or bored at the length of a selection.

Each band had one selection in their 'book' which was used as their theme song, which they played at the beginning and the end of an evening of dancing, or of a radio broadcast. It became their musical logo. In addition, some of the bands used descriptive superlatives as their advertising logos. Here are a few:

Band	Theme Song/Musical Logo	Advertising Name/Logo
Guy Lombardo		The Royal Canadians
Count Basie	One O'clock Jump	
Les Brown	Leap Frog	Band of Reknown
Cab Calloway	Hi De Hi—Hi De Ho	
Harry James		The Music Makers
Woody Herman	Blue Flame	The Thundering Herd
Benny Goodman	Let's Dance	The King of Swing
Lawrence Welk	Bubbles in the Wine	Champagne Music
Sammy Kaye		Swing & Sway
Spike Jones		The City Slikkers
Kay Kyser		The College of Musical Knowledge

a warm breeze

Music by SAMMY NESTICO

Instrumentalists—Lead Men, Soloists, Sidemen

The big band era should aptly be named 'the changing scene'. The patterns of the musicians' careers varied from those of stability to those of change. Most musicians frequently moved from one band to another. Some remained with one band for most of their career or until the band was disbanded. Guitarist Freddie Green had the longest tenure with the "Count" Basie Band. Others like the Lombardos have likewise spent their entire careers together. Some musicians rose from sidemen to lead men to leaders depending upon individual abilities, motivation and ambition.

The touring bands, those that traveled from coast to coast had the largest attrition rate. A musician would tire of the extensive travel, inadequate housing, poor food (Jimmie Lunceford died of food poisoning while on tour), racial discrimination, etc. After a period of this constant mobility the musician would return home, find a 'day' job and terminate fulltime musical endeavors. Still others, gave up the band business and continued their education, going into field quite diverse from music. Others gave up the road work and went into the studio as a musician. Even for those that remained in the bands there were periodic changes. Trumpet player 'A' might tire of the music in one band and join another. Trombone player 'B' will change bands due to a personality conflict. Another player may change for better money, or a better job as soloist instead

135

of sideman. Or as was the case with many, they left one band to form their own. Following is a list of musicians who left one band to form their own group.

Original Band	Player(s) Who Formed Their Own Group
Ben Pollack	Benny Goodman, Glenn Miller
Benny Goodman	Lionel Hampton, Harry James, Gene Krupa
Paul Whiteman	Jimmy and Tommy Dorsey, Henry Busse
Eddie Hill	Jay McShann
Gus Arnheim	Stan Kenton, Woody Herman
"Duke" Ellington	Charles "Cootie" Williams
Benny Moten	"Count" Basie
Tommy Dorsey	"Buddy" Rich
Harry James	Les Elgart
Billy Eckstine	"Dizzy' Gillespie
Fletcher Henderson	Don Redman
Jack Marshard	Vaughn Monroe

There were a number of sidemen who made major contributions to the big band style of jazz with their improvisational skills. They were outstanding lead men and featured soloists. Many are still practicing their musical art in America or Europe, which has become an appreciative haven for jazz musicians. Listed by instrument, these names represent just a few of the quality jazz performers.

Saxophone	Trumpet	Trombone
Coleman Hawkins	Roy Eldridge	Juan Tizol
Johnny Hodges	"Cat" Anderson	Kai Winding
Ben Webster	"Bunny" Berigan	Lawrence Brown
Benny Carter	"Sweets" Edison	"Trummy" Young
Chu Berry	Jonah Jones	J. C. Higgenbotham
Zoot Sims	Charlie Shavers	Bill Harris
Al Cohn	Jimmy Zito	Carl Fontana
Lester Young	Pete Condoli	Urbie Green
"Flip" Phillips	Conte Condoli	Frank Rosolino
Georgie Auld	Maynard Ferguson	
Vido Musso	Clark Terry	
Illinois Jacquet	Thad Jones	
Don Byas	"Snooky" Young	

Piano	Drums	Bass
Mel Powell	Shelly Manne	Walter Page
Jess Stacey	Dave Tough	Jimmy Blanton
Teddy Wilson	"Buddy Rich"	"Slam" Stewart
Mary Lou Williams	Gene Krupa	Oscar Pettiford
Bud Powell	"Cozy" Cole	Ray Brown
	Jo Jones	Eddie Safranski
	Max Roach	Milt Hinton
Guitar	Roy Haynes	
	Sid Catlett	
Freddie Green	Louis Bellson	
Tal Farlow		
Barney Kessel		
Johnny Smith		
Charlie Christian		

136

Al Cohn, tenor sax, Jake Hanna, drums.

Buddy Rich (Courtesy: Willard Alexander, Inc.).

Jo Jones (Courtesy: Avedis Zildjian Co.).

Coleman Hawkins (Courtesy: Downbeat).

137

Flip Phillips, tenor sax, Snooky Young, trumpet, Urbie Green, trombone.

Louis Bellson (Courtesy: Avedis Zildjian Co.).

Jay McShann, piano, Louis Bellson, drums.

Vocalists

Often the band leaders were not the Mr. Personality on stage. Although most were endowed with enough charm and charisma to captivate the audience with their introductions of selections, soloists, and singers. The singers—both female and male were the communicative link between the band and the audience. They had to sing all types of songs, many of the selections did little to enhance their musical ability or style. The top bands sometimes carried two vocalists, a female and a male, more often though they carried a female as their sole vocalist. Whether by design or accident, psychology worked in the band's favor. A female singer seemed to communicate with the men in the audience who fantasized that she was singing to them personally, the same was true of male singers and the women in the audience.

Female vocalists had the most difficult time being with a band. As the only female in the entourage, she was often the victim of advances by the members of the band. It was difficult to maintain feeling of being just one of the members of the group. Romances occurred and marriages took place. Leaders married

138

Singer Tony Bennett (Photo Courtesy ASCAP)   Frank Sinatra Photo Courtesy Shorty Vest Collection.

their singers, and singers married sidemen. For the female singer, unattached and unmarried, this was a hardship. They were a definite asset to the bands and go down in jazz history as contributors equal to that of many of the finest instrumentalists. Many of the singers 'paid their dues' as band vocalists and then went on to other careers in the entertainment field, movies, television, etc. Here then are some of the 'headliners' and the bands with which they sang.

Female Vocalists	*Male Vocalists*	*Band*
Billie Holiday	Jimmy Rushing, Joe Williams	"Count" Basie
Ella Fitzgerald		"Chick" Webb
Pearl Bailey		"Cootie" Williams
Peggy Lee, Martha Tilton, Helen Ward, Helen Forrest		Benny Goodman
Helen O'Connell	Bob Eberle	Jimmy Dorsey
Edythe Wright, Jo Stafford	Frank Sinatra	Tommy Dorsey
Kay Starr		Charlie Barnet
Helen Forrest (also with Artie Shaw Band)	Dick Haynes, Frank Sinatra	
Mildred Bailey (also with "Red" Norvo Band)	Bing Crosby	Paul Whiteman
Marion Hutton	Ray Eberle	Glenn Miller
Rosemary Clooney		Tony Pastor
Dale Evans		Anson Weeks
Ivie Anderson	Herb Jeffries	Duke Ellington
Betty Grable		Ted FioRito
Ginny Sims		Kay Kyser

Anita O'Day		Gene Krupa
June Christy		Stan Kenton
Doris Day	"Butch" Stone	Les Brown
Eydie Gorme		Tex Beneke
Sarah Vaughn		Earl Hines
Dinah Washington		Lionel Hampton
Lena Horne		Noble Sissle and Artie Shaw
	Merv Griffin	Freddy Martin
	Kenny Gardner	Guy Lombardo
	Perry Como	Ted Weems

Other familiar names who sang with the big bands include: Tony Martin; Dick Powell; Mel Torme; Tony Bennett; Ozzie Nelson; and even Art Carney.

There are also several vocal groups who gave the bands 'class'. Here are a few and the bands they sang with.

Vocal Group	*Band*
The Modernaires	Glenn Miller
The Three Waring Girls	Fred Waring
The Moon Maids	Vaughn Monroe
The Stardusters	Charlie Spivak
The Pied Pipers	Tommy Dorsey
The Rhythm Boys	Paul Whiteman
The King Sisters	Alvino Rey

Agents

Lawrence Welk in a discussion with fellow band leader Will Back, advised. "If you want to make it in the band business, get yourself a good agent!" That is precisely what most of the bandleaders did. An agent (also called 'booker' or 'booking agent') took much of the organizational details out of the hands of the leaders. For a fee (ranging from 10% to 15% of the band's earnings), the agents would handle all contractual negotiations, collect fees, pay salaries, handle bookkeeping (take care of the IRS taxes and Social Security withholding), and keep the public informed of the bands' availability. The agents handled publicity and determined routings whereby the band did not have long travel distances between engagements. They also assisted with recording and movie contracts.

Early agents worked from one-man offices. As the band business grew in volume, agents merged and formed agencies with a large clientele. Such was the case of **Joe Glaser,** Louis Armstrong's agent, who later formed an agency called the **Associated Booking Corporation.** It became one of the more prominent agencies, handling such bands as Lionel Hampton and Les Brown. **General Artists Corporation** was (GAC) founded by Tom Rockwell and Francis O'Keefe. GAC was the agent for Artie Shaw, Woody Herman, Glenn Miller, Jimmy Dorsey, and Claude Thornhill. **Jules Styne,** was the founder of **The Music Corporation of America.** It had an excellent 'stable' of talent including; Guy Lombardo, Xavier Cugat, Benny Goodman, Count Basie, and Tommy Dorsey. One of their salespersons, Sonny Werblin, later became associated with the New York Jets football team. **Willard Alexander** another of MCA's employees later joined the **William Morris Agency.** Alexander, as a representative of the William Morris Agency, was influential in signing the bands of "Duke" Ellington, "Dizzy" Gillespie, Charlie Spivak and Billy Eckstine. Alexander went on to form his own agency, the **Willard Alexander Agency** which at this time is considered one of the top booking agents for bands. There were numerous others including, the **National Orchestra Service,** the **Stanford Zucker Agency,** the **Harold Oxley Agency,** and the **General Amusement Corp.,** it is doubtful that without their assistance many of the bands would have survived as long as they did.

140

Joe Williams, singer (Courtesy: Willard Alexander, Inc.).

Singer-Bandleader Billy Eckstine (Photo Courtesy, Thomas Cassidy, Artist Management)

Lionel Hampton (Courtesy: Willard Alexander, Inc.).

Helen O'Connell (Courtesy: Willard Alexander, Inc.).

The Dorsey Brothers, Tommy, left and Jimmy, right (Courtesy: Downbeat).

Carmen McRae (Courtesy: Willard Alexander, Inc.).

Getting into the Spotlight

How did the big bands become known? There were several avenues available and most of the bands pursued all of them. Personal appearances were first and foremost. Playing to live audiences was the most effective way to achieve popularity. The public could see and hear their musical 'heroes'. Secondly, were the live broadcasts either from a well known location (ballrooms, casinos, hotels) or on weekly radio shows (often as accompaniment to leading personalities—Bob Hope, Jack Benny). Finally, the public heard the bands through recordings, in theaters as part of the stage shows, and in movies. Again, it was the agents who were responsible for getting the band in the spotlight.

The Wire

The telephone line was put into clubs, ballrooms, hotels, or casinos, to do 'remote' live broadcasts nationwide, similar to live broadcasts of athletic events. At that time radio needed 'fillers' for their broadcast days. Prime time, 6:00 P.M. to 10:00 P.M., was designated for weekly shows from mysteries (INNER SANCTUM) to celebrity shows (Bob Hope). Following the prime time slots, remote broadcasts of bands were nightly occurrences. On any given night, listeners could hear bands broadcasting live from coast to coast. Of course the various time zones had an effect on when a band could be heard. Bands broadcasting at midnight in New York would be heard at 9:00 P.M. in California, while a band broadcasting from California at midnight would be heard at 3:00 A.M. in New York. It was imperative for bands to get booked into places that had a 'wire', and gain additional regional or national exposure. It was during these 'air shots' that bands would play their latest recordings to encourage record sales.

Recordings

During the big band era, there were four companies that did the majority of the recordings; Decca, Victor, Brunswick, and Columbia. A recording contract was a necessity for the national popularity it generated. In 1942, **James Ceasar Petrillo,** then president of the musicians union, the American Federation of Musicians (AF of M), imposed a recording ban, forbidding instrumentalists from recording. It was a measure in part designed to improve the performers' royalties and salaries. It had an adverse effect and the instrumentalists were the losers. Vocalists did not belong to the AF of M and were not prevented from recording. They continued recording using vocal groups as accompaniment. The ban lasted two years. Historians feel the instrumentalists never regained the popularity they previously had. The recording companies and the public enjoyed the music of the singers and it set the stage for things to come in the popular music world.

Television

Television, during its formative years, utilized bands as part of its programming. As television became the major focus of entertainment, family oriented programs surfaced and became the bulk of the programming. On rare occasions big bands were given feature spots during 'specials'. The last holdout was the weekly Lawrence Welk Show which featured the band in 'production' numbers. Unfortunately, the show was not a true indicator of the big bands. The "Tonight Show" has the Doc Severinson band in residence, but it is used primarily for entertaining the studio audience during commercials, and as a backup for guest artists. This is unfortunate in that the band is comprised of some of the finest 'jazz' musicians in the country.

Gig-Jobs

A "gig" is a gathering of musicians for a session of jazz. Gigs have taken place in all locales—from the sporting houses of Storyville to the concert halls of our cities—from the speakeasies of Chicago to the movie lots of Hollywood. Jazz musicians have held gigs in the Reno Club in Kansas City, the Corn Palace in South Dakota, the Cotton Club in Harlem, a quonset hut in the Philippines, and on an aircraft carrier in the Pacific. Jazz of all types from ragtime to bop was heard throughout the country. The gig might be for one night or for several decades, depending on the proprietor, the audience, and/or the musicians.

There were several types of jobs available to musicians. For maximum exposure, the 'road' with its constant travel was the best, especially of the engagement was held where there was a 'wire'. Road bands were often required to do 'one nighters', an engagement that was booked for one night, then traveling a substantial distance to another 'one night stand'.

In the 30s, travel was by car caravans or chartered bus. It meant long distances and hours on the road. A distance of 400 to 500 miles between gigs was quite common. Eventually, the musicians' union ruled that bands could travel no more than 300 miles between engagements. The 'sleeper bus' became the musician's home. Train schedules did not always conform to the band's schedule, nor did they go to the 'out of the way' locations. Automobiles and buses were the only viable means of transportation. Travel was not without its problems; long hours, inclement weather, and accidents were some of the things the musicians faced on the road. During World War II, the rationing of gasoline imposed further restrictions on travel. Air travel was and, in many cases, still is too expensive for traveling bands.

The road took its toll on the bands. Most musicians preferred 'on location' engagements. It was not unusual for bands to secure engagements lasting several months, then moving on to another location for an extended period. Here again, it was the task of the agent to secure locations, with limited travel, and long term contracts.

The ideal gig for the musicians was "studio" work. Working daylight hours in radio, recording, or movie studio, and making it home in time for dinner. Weekly radio shows were another sought after gig. While radio gave the musician stability, it did take them out of the spotlight. An example of this bears mentioning. A former student of mine was a member of the 'house band' at the MGM Grand in Reno, Nevada. During his tenure there, he saw the stage show only on the video monitors piped into the band studio, located several floors below the stage. The audience never saw the band, nor did the musicians have any audience response. He went to work dressed in jeans, sweatshirt, and sandals. After several months of this, the urge to play for a 'live' audience overtook him and he left what some might feel was an ideal job.

Where Did the Big Bands Play?

During their peak, the bands were found from coast to coast and from north to south in theaters, hotels, dance halls, and casinos, the majority of which had remote broadcast capabilities. Most of these locations provided a dance floor, as dancing was very popular during the big band era.

One could easily trace the travels of the name bands by reading the issues of DOWNBEAT magazine which included the schedules of the various bands. Following were some of the popular locations in which one would find their favorite bands:

Where	Theaters	Hotels	Ballrooms
New York	Apollo Paramount Palace Strand	Park Central Astor Roosevelt St. Regis Waldorf	Playland Casino Roseland Savoy
Chicago	Chicago Oriental	Sherman Edgewater Beach	Trianon Aragon
Philadelphia	Earle		
Washington, D.C.	Capitol		
San Francisco	Golden Gate	Mark Hopkins	
Los Angeles		Ambassador	Palomar Palladium
New Jersey			Glen Island Casino Million Dollar Pier Steel Pier
Denver			Elitch Gardens Lakeside
Boston			Raymor
Dallas		Adolphus	
Kansas City		Muelbach	
New Orleans		Roosevelt	

Besides those listed the big bands were found in Chicago's Blackhawk Restaurant, and the Granada Cafe; the Corn Palace in Mitchell, South Dakota; and the Cotton Club in Harlem.

The big bands were usually found where there was a dance floor. The dances varied according to the band's music. The 'fox trot' was danced to the music with a slower tempo, if the tempo was fast, a new dance, the 'jitterbug' was popular. The waltz was also popular when bands played a set called 'waltz time'. Bands also played music with a Latin beat, and dancers did the 'rhumba' or 'tango'.

Large ballrooms, such as the Palladium, were capable of accommodating several thousand dancers. In an effort to maintain order, bands were discouraged from playing too many 'up-tempo' selections to which the jitterbug was danced. The dance itself was exciting and included moments when the dancers would separate from each other (taking up additional floor space) and do 'leaps' and 'jumps'. These caused collisions (on a crowded floor) among dancers and created tensions. Physical melees and expensive property damage to the premises were not uncommon. It was easy to understand why ballrooms hired 'bouncers' who floated among the dancers in an effort to maintain order. Dancers not following the house rules were evicted.

Chicago Theater.

Headliners

While there obviously were a large number of bands in existence during the big band era, the question asked most often is, "Which were the best?" This is a very difficult question to answer. Fans were adamant that their favorite band, leader, singer, or soloist was certainly the best.

A native of Red Bank, New Jersey, **William "Count" Basie** was a pianist. Stranded in Kansas City, he joined the **Benny Moten** Band and later formed his own band. His band followed the 'riff' style that came out of Kansas City. During his peak years, the band played a number of head arrangements based upon riffs invented by band members. The band had a loose 'laid back' style of playing but nevertheless contained a 'driving' forward momentum at all times. Noted for outstanding band personnel who had tremendous improvisational skills, he featured them on everything from ballads to uptempo arrangements. The Basie band had possibly the finest rhythm section of all the big bands. This was one of the primary reasons the band swung so well. They included Basie on piano; Freddie Green, guitar; Jo Jones, drums; and Walter Page, bass. This was the heart of the band. The soloists and sidemen included: Lester Young, Herschel Evans, Don Byas, and Buddy Tate on tenor sax; Buck Clayton, trumpet; Harry "Sweets" Edison, trumpet; and **Jimmy Rushing, Billie Holliday, Helen Humes,** and **Joe Williams** as vocalists.

Following the big band era, Basie cut the band to a sextet. Later, he again formed a big band which is still active today, playing the same musical style for which he was so well noted.

Edward Kennedy "Duke" Ellington (1899–1974) was born in Washington, D.C. He was truly a pioneer in the big band era. A pianist, he had a band before Goodman, Shaw, and the Dorseys. But, perhaps because he was black, he did not attract the national attention given the white bands. In later years the racial

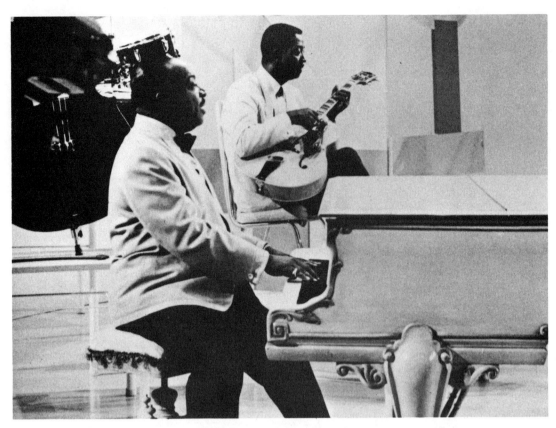

"Count" Basie, piano, Freddie Green, guitar (Courtesy: Downbeat).

"Count" Basie, left, and Arranger Sam Nestico (Courtesy: Kendor Music Inc.)

"Count" Basie (Courtesy: Willard Alexander, Inc.).

aspect was not a factor limiting his popularity, which exceeded the majority of the white bands. An ardent composer of popular songs—"Mood Indigo", "Sophisticated Lady", "I'm Beginning to See the Light", and "In a Sentimental Mood", he was involved in all aspects of jazz.

Ellington was the greatest contributor to the development of jazz. He used his band as a total instrument. Not having the large retinue of soloists found in the Basie band, Ellington proved his position in jazz by the sound and style of the band. He was regarded as a 'master painter', his music being his canvas. His compositional ability coupled with his fine musicianship gave the band a distinctive yet 'swinging' sound. He too surrounded himself with excellent musicians: Louis Bellson, drummer; Ray Nance, "Cat Anderson, and Sam Nanton, trumpets; Johnny Hodges, Harry Carney, and Ben Webster, saxophonists; Jimmy Blanton, bassist; and Sonny Greer, drummer. His band enjoyed a long engagement at the Cotton Club as well as tours of the United States and Europe. He was fortunate in having one of the finest big band arrangers in the talents of Billy Strayhorn, co-composer of his theme, "Satin Doll". On Ellington's death, his son Mercer took over as director and the band continues to perform. "Duke" Ellington must be credited with developing 'big band' history.

Born in Chicago, Illinois, in 1909, **Benjamin "Benny" Goodman** is known as the greatest perfectionist in jazz. A taskmaster, he left no room for error from his musicians. A driving force in the development of big band jazz, he began his music career as a sideman with Ben Pollak's band in which he played saxophone and clarinet. A clarinet virtuoso, he is adept at performing both classical music and jazz. He is to be given credit as the first bandleader to racially integrate a band with the hiring of pianist Teddy Wilson, and vibraphonist Lionel Hampton, with which he formed 'a band within a band' which included drummer Gene Krupa and called the Goodman Quartet. His bands performance at the Palomar Ballroom in 1935 marked the beginning of the 'big band era'. He was crowned "king of swing". His 1938 Carnegie Hall Jazz Concert was a high point of the era. He surrounded himself with excellent musicians: trumpeters Harry James and Ziggy Elman; drummer Gene Krupa; pianist Jess Stacy, and guitarist Charlie Christian. The band gained popularity when Fletcher henderson was hired as arranger. His arrangements made the band 'swing'.

The "Duke" Ellington Band (Courtesy: Downbeat).

Benny Goodman, clarinet (Courtesy: Downbeat).

Gene Krupa (Courtesy: Avedis Zildjian Co.).

The band had a weekly 'Nabisco' sponsored radio show which gave it additional exposure. Following the end of the big band era, he attempted 'bop' but was not successful. Today he is in constant demand as soloist with symphony orchestras. The movie, *The Benny Goodman Story,* was not really indicative of his life.

Harry Haag James is possibly the most underrated band leader of the era. It is appropo to begin his biography with a somewhat negative analysis as stated in *The Illustrated Encyclopedia of Jazz* by Brian Case and Stan Britt:

The Harry James Band (Courtesy: Downbeat).

Some folks have never forgiven Harry Haag James (born Albany, Georgia, 1916) for leaving Benny Goodman, starting his own band and playing schmaltzy trumpet on tunes like "Ciribiribin," "You Made Me Love You" and "Carnival in Venice". To the jazz lovers, it seems James had sold out and, to add insult to injury, he went and married a lady from Hollywood with the world's most famous legs.

As a result, jazz buff's disregarded him as a potent force in the big band era. He was a shining light as soloist with the Goodman band and while it seemed to many that when he formed his own band he became very commercial in trying to please the public, he was still an outstanding musician. True, his early recordings exemplified the commerciality for which he was accused: "I Had the Craziest Dream", "I've Heard that Song Before", and "I'm Beginning to See the Light", were all as Case and Britt said, 'schmaltzy' (the word is derived from the German word for lard). His marriage to World War II pin-up girl **Betty Grable,** gained him popularity with servicemen and the movie going public.

Nevertheless, his bands improved and even with the demise of the era and the advent of bop, he kept his band together, locating in the clubs of Las Vegas. He had new arrangements written by Neal Hefti, and it continued to move ahead musically approaching the style and sound of the Basie band. His own playing, in the 50's, equalled that of his days with Goodman. Harry James died of cancer on July 5, 1983.

Stan Kenton

Much has been written about this man. His style of music was a continual experiment. Where other big band leaders fell into the traditional mold, he always wanted to create something new. He is accused of ignoring the dancing public in lieu of concerts. He broke tradition and formed the neophobic (new sound) orchestra and at his own expense produced the recordings. When this phase passed, he created yet another style and sound. In order to achieve new sounds, he added instruments that had not been seen in jazz since the early days of Dixieland (mellophoniums). They are very prominent on his recordings of "West Side Story" and "The Christmas Album." He utilized a large number of arrangers in continually trying to find new sounds for the big band. His band was given the title, "The Wall of Brass," having the largest contingent of brass players ever found in a big band (five trumpet, five trombones, five mellophoniums).

He was one of the leaders in allowing school bands to have access to original big band arrangements. His publishing company "Creative World," was a windfall to school bands seeking to play original arrangements of the big bands. Soon to follow suit were leaders Count Basie, Duke Ellington, Maynard Ferguson and Woody Herman. His interest in America's young musicians encouraged him to develop the Stan Kenton Clinics/Camps, in which he and his band acted as the teachers, lecturers and performers. His efforts in this direction gave birth to a whole new area of school music. It gave former Kenton saxophonist Matt Betton the inspiration and drive to organize the National Association of Jazz Educators, one of the most active organizations associated with school music.

Dr. Frank Vattano, faculty member at Colorado State University, is a dedicated fan of Stan Kenton and his music. At the request of the author he has prepared the following piece on the life, the philosophy and the music of this giant of jazz.

The Kenton Era

Stanley Newcomb Kenton (1911–1986)

To say that Stan Kenton was one of the most influential figures in modern Jazz is perhaps the understatement of the century. He is considered by many to be one of the giants of the idiom. The impact that this tall, rather shy piano player from Wichita, Kansas, had on so many of the great modern school jazz musicians is legend. In his incredible career, which spanned more than fifty years, Stan Kenton discovered and nurtured some of the biggest names in modern jazz.

Many consider Stan Kenton a genius as composer, arranger, talent scout, and big band leader. His untiring commitment to the development of what was labeled "modern jazz" is illustrated by the number of albums issued as "new trend" music. Album titles with the words *Innovations, Contemporary, Modern, Improvisation* reflect both what Stan Kenton stood for and what he hoped to accomplish as a musical educator. Although Kenton had little formal education, he had an intense desire to bring people together through his view and what music should be. His evangelical spirit and untiring energy were demonstrated throughout his long and illustrious career. From 1933, when he began his musical career playing piano and arranging for Everett Hoagland, until his death in 1986, Stan Kenton arranged and composed some 246 works. His extensive tours on the band bus "Nowhere" to concerts, clinics, festivals, dance halls, dedications—all in the interest of promoting "his music" are exemplary of a man with a passion for his art.

Kenton experimented with many different sounds. He was one of the first to blend strings with brass bringing together classical and jazz idioms. His concert tour and album entitled "Innovations in Modern Music" is but one example of how far ahead he was of his contemporaries in his thinking and writing. Other big bands were swinging for the dance crowds while the Kenton band packed them in with musical arrangements, unusual instrumentations, and superb musicianship. Many of Kenton's featured musicians went on to form their own groups and make the recording scene under the Capitol Label called the Kenton Presents Series.

Kenton's unique arrangements of tunes like "The Peanut Vendor," "Artistry in Rhythm," "Artistry Jumps," "Opus in Pastels," "How High The Moon," "City of Glass," are illustrative examples of what have become "classics" in modern jazz. Stan Kenton had a real feeling for both his music and the musicians who made it all happen. He wanted others to know about his music, and in 1952 recorded a composition he enti-

The Stan Kenton band during the early 1970's. On floor, left to right: Chris Galuman, Dick Shearer, Roy Reynolds, Mike Jamieson, John Worster, Ray Brown. Seated on stage, left to right: Chuck Carter, Richard Torres, Jay Saunders, Mike Vax, Dennis Noday, Mike Snustead, Stan Kenton, Jerry McKenzie, Ramon Lopez, Mike Wallace, Fred Carter, Phil Herring and Quin Davis. (photo courtesy Mike Vax Collection Permission to reprint, Mike Vax)

tled *Prologue:* "This is an Orchestra." In this selection he introduces his band person by person, section by section, and reveals his feelings about the music and those who are committed to expressing their individuality, musical discipline, and corporate sound into what he calls an "orchestra".

Like many other band leaders, Kenton was not what you would consider a flashy piano player. He laid down massive chords and his penchant for compound, sometimes complicated sounds and rhythms literally drew people like magnets; those thirsty for expanding the limits of tempo, individuality of expressions and brilliance of brass sounds with an Afro-Cuban beat. The world of jazz will long remember Stanley Newcomb Kenton. He is gone, but his music lives on.

Dr. Herb Wong, one of the leading exponents on big band jazz, is also an independent record producer. Under the label of *Palo Alto Jazz Records,* Wong assembled musicians for record dates and produced recordings for the general public. This is a difficult task, considering the market for pure jazz compared to the various forms and artists of rock. In addition Wong is one of the most popular adjudicators at competitive jazz festivals. Past president of the National Association of Jazz Educators, Wong has been a driving force in the promotion of big bands in schools, one of the last frontiers of the big band jazz. A close friend and associate of the late Woody Herman, Wong has written a tribute to the jazz man, indicating Herman's willingness to help young musicians. The following article was written prior to the bandleader's passing.

Thundering from the Campuses:
Woody Herman's Herds and Jazz Education

Dr. Herbert Wong

Woody Herman's "Herds" have been extraordinary mobile jazz laboratories—universities on the road for young jazz players since the early days. However, in synch with the proliferation of jazz education programs, Woody's bands have been hospitable, coveted destinations/habitats for college-university and conservatory-trained musicians, especially in the last 25 years.

A true living legend, Woody has reached his 50th year as a jazz band leader and he occupies this amazing historical seat while he continues to blaze the road throughout most of the calendar year with his "Young Thundering Herd"—a joyful, relentlessly swinging band. Les Brown and Lionel Hampton are two other swing era band leaders who intermittently front their own groups—Hamp much more regularly than Brown. With the passing of Ellington, Basie, James, Kenton and Goodman—just a small handful of big bands still play the composite of contemporary venues such as festivals, theaters, hotels, country clubs, music camps, amusement parks, jazz clubs, shopping malls, casinos and loads of school/college campuses. Buddy Rich, Maynard Ferguson, Toshiko Akiyoshi and a few others along with Woody Herman fill the bulk of these pipelines.

The unique dynamics of the Herman band environment finds musicians gaining sustained musical/psychological support from Woody, reflecting his values on the growth and development of each musician in his band. Simply ask any of the many hundreds of graduates of "The Herds" and you'll get a confirmation of Woody's philosophy/system, told perhaps in numerous different ways but landing in convergent territory. In essence, they dig working with him and not just for him—the feelings couched in mutual respect and gratitude.

"Woody extracted the best of me, toward my personal and musical growth. I also learned how to be a sustaining musician on the road, preparing me for my professional future. It was an irreplaceable experience!" These are sentiments of pianist Andy LaVerne who was with Woody in the 70's before joining Stan Getz' band. I have interviewed scores of Woody's band members through the years and LaVerne's recent comments typify the general feedback. Trombonist Phil Wilson, a faculty member of the Berklee College of Music, made vital contributions to the 1962–65 Herds when his distinctive bone solos helped to characterize the sounds and energetic spirit of that great band. He told me several years ago another positive, common remembrance: "Woody had a way of cutting out the fat and getting right to the meat of an arrangement and to the audience." And his personality was the same—he allowed the guys to relax and be themselves musically and personally . . . until it got out of whack. Then "The Chopper" would come in and take care of business. He looked at everything that way—tolerant although not patient! Woody's band was the idol band—everyone wanted to be on it. About twelve of us who were at Berklee as students got on the band through our experience with Herb Pomeroy's band at Berklee and the NORAD "Commanders" Band (The North American Air Defense Command Orchestra). Bill Chase, Gordon Brisker, Jake Hanna, Chuck Andres, Paul Fountaine, Larry Cavalli, Jerry Lamy and Bob Rudolph were all hungry and wanted to be in the best big band in the land, and our dreams were answered with Woody."

Turning the clock back to the bands of the late forties and fifties, the majority of the alumni of Kenton and Herman bands got off the road and dominated the lucrative-based L.A. studios. Outstanding players in this migration included the likes of Joe Mondragon, Shelly Manne, Shorty Rogers, Bud Shank, Milt Bernhardt, the Condoli Brothers, Bob Cooper, Conrad Gozzo, Al Porcina, Larry Bunker and Jack Nimitz among many more in the New York, Chicago and Las Vegas circuits in addition to L.A. Yet others chose to become involved with leading their own groups: e.g., Stan Getz, Zoot Sims, Al Cohn, Urbie Green, Terry Gibbs and Gene Ammons.

By the late fifties and early sixties, this existing process depleted the rosters significantly, creating gaping spaces for replacements to fill. Overlapping perhaps in a providential way or at least via a vigorous twist of fate, a number of early maturing jazz education curricula/programs had coincidentally developed a ripe crop of young, well-schooled university students who began to filter into key roles of the Herman, Kenton and Rich big bands. These bright graduates were recruited from the highly reputed, powerful pioneer

152

Woody Herman (Courtesy: Ingrid Herman Reese Collection).

The Woody Herman Thundering Herd (Courtesy: Ingrid Herman Reese Collection).

Charlotte and Woody Herman (Courtesy: Ingrid Herman Reese Collection).

programs of North Texas State University and Berklee College in the main—precursors to the profluence of many dozens of sophisticated jazz studies departments and hundreds of jazz ensembles with a layered network of high school feeder programs.

In retrospect, the replacements comprised of many gifted performers and writers from rich campus resources, from many parts of the country, renewed a critical supply line of eager, fiery young talent, meeting the demands of the professional orchestras which virtually became the few true "post-grad" citadels in the idiom. In the opinion of most aspirants and alumni of Woody's band, his was a well-matched symbiotic relationship with the musicians.

In a recent discussion I had with Woody in September following his performance at a jazz festival in Palo Alto, California, he waxed enthusiastically over the state of the art linking his band specifically with jazz education over the years. In response to my query regarding his assessment of jazz education from his perspective, Woody said: "I'm asked very frequently around the world about how and where does the band get such talented musicians. I think there's no doubt about the successful job that's being done and we in the U.S.A are an object of admiration, and even some healthy envy.

"These young men come to the band with impressive chops, with well grounded musical theory and knowledge of the history of the music and can handle any style of playing. It wasn't always like this, you know. Over all, very seldom does any of them miss the reasons or meaning for our music . . . and I mean the future of the music. As for your question about their capabilities as I have seen them, I'm really blown away by the way they can, on one take, sight read the most complex charts, out in front of them for the first time. In the past, this high level of ability was not easy to find. Of course, there are more ways and people to help the young students than any past point in history—all sorts of wonderful books, charts, improv workshop techniques, records, tapes, videos, on and on. What a different scene it is today!"

Woody is known for his generous approach of providing extended time and space for each newcomer on the band, permitting him leeway to interpret the band's music in his own way. Former drummer with Woody—Ed Soph, a product of NTSU who has served the band on a number of segments, confirms Woody's tactic. Ed describes, "Woody will give you complete freedom to interpret the music, and since you're on his band, he feels you're musically mature for him to give you that freedom, and if you blow it, he'll say something. But he often doesn't say much, but when he does, it's always right on the button—right there, and it's like the clouds part and it's all clear. This applies to arrangements as well. A good example is when Frank Tiberi's chart for Coltrane's "Countdown" was rehearsed. Woody just sat there checking it out. After the first time it was played, he said nothing. We played it again. And he said, "Frank, the shout chorus

154

Martha Raye and Woody Herman (Courtesy: Ingrid Herman Reese Collection).

doesn't fit with the rest of the chart. It needs to be more syncopated like the sax solo." Woody hit it right on the head. Frank re-wrote that chorus and everything locked in perfectly! And there are dozens of other examples."

Frank Tiberi independently commented about the same incident, "Everyone who writes for the band as a band member grows with Woody. For instance, on "Countdown," he told me that the last part was great but it needed to be flashed up and, of course, now it's really exciting! Alan Broadbent and Gary Anderson who have written fine charts became really good writers, helped by Woody's keen ears and sense of editing. I think Woody is a patient man . . . he edits and corrects while he allows them to stay on the band to mature. I've been with the band about 18 years and I've seen him hold these values for a lot of guys. Nothing goes by him without him noticing it, but he seldom shows this in any demonstrable way. But he is incredibly on target. He helps to get people relaxed so they can get quality musicianship and quality presentation of a tune."

Woody has strong views about how jazz studies programs can help young players in their improvised solo work. "I firmly believe things would be much more improved if *guidance* were given to the players about alternative ideas and approaches. A wide variety of different ways to compensate what might turn out to be a narrow perspective for the players is a need, I think, that could be filled *before* they leave the campus searching for a professional endeavor.

"Of course, today we have professional jazz clinicians who are, in many cases, products of the jazz education movement, and they are familiar with what's needed out in the real music world and what would be effective in clinical situations. They are able to provide students and instructors with high quality guidance." Campus clinics are common educational fare for the Herman bands as they have presented practicums nearly every week for over 20 years, along with their concerts. Some of the finest pro clinicians incubated in the Herds—e.g., Ed Soph, Steve Houghton, Bobby Shew, Phil Wilson, Roger Pemberton and Willie Thomas come to mind.

Regarding the severe lack of professional playing opportunities for the disproportionately large number of excellent young jazz players, Woody recommended unhesitatingly, "I think these interested young men and women should be schooled in some solid alternative field such as computer science, get a steady day gig in the field, and then practice every night after work for a few years. Get a playing gig in town until the time and opportunity for the music is more receptive. Of course, there are always exceptions to the norm, in which case worthy players by some circumstantial quirk will find a viable niche in music within a reasonably short time."

L to R: Louis Armstrong, Woody Herman and Phil Wilson (Courtesy: Herb Wong Collection).

Returning to some thoughts about young arrangers—composers in the last dozen years or so, I mentioned pianists John Oddo and Alan Broadbent, trumpeters Tony Klatka and Bill Stapleton, saxophonist Gary Anderson and trombonist John Fedchock to Woody. He asserted, "Most of the budding writers arrive like rough diamonds. Gary Anderson, for instance, who has become a highly successful writer for a variety of media, started meagerly but matured dramatically. He worked very hard at it. I had asked him to arrange Aaron Copland's "Fanfare for the Common Man" after I heard the guys fooling around with its opening theme. It's become one of the most important staples in our book in the last decade. All of the writers you mentioned understood what the band needed simply because they were integrally involved with our music. John Oddo and, of course, John Fedchock, are the most recent major contributors and both are very special talents who have their undefinable spark." Speaking of Fedchock, who is a graduate of The Ohio State U. and its great jazz ensemble, and holds a Masters of Jazz from Eastman, he was inspired when he was in high school in Highland Heights, Ohio. "Of all the big bands, Woody's has always been my favorite. Ever since Woody came to play at my school in 1974, I had wanted to play in his band. As a matter of fact, that concert was one of the things that inspired me to go into music," reflects John. "In this day and age, without being on a band like this one, there would be very little opportunity for me to do the two things I love most—writing and playing jazz."

Woody Herman, a dynamic force in jazz and jazz education, creates a gang of thunder from the campuses, and in turn he coaches them to swing to the high heavens. We all dig you, Woody! Happy giant 50th!

From his beginnings in jazz at Ithaca Conservatory to Duke University, to New York and the professional world of dance bands, **Les Brown** has carved an undisputable niche in the development of the big bands. His band is one of the very, very few big bands still playing today. The Les Brown Band has earned the reputation as being one of the very finest of the big bands. He considers himself the leader of a "dance band," since this was the original concept of the big bands. A shrewd business man, Brown has kept his band together through turbulent years of economic setbacks, interest in other forms of music (such as rock), and diminishing activity in the recording industry in relation to big bands. His band is under the effective managership of his brother, trombonist, "Stumpy" Brown who handles the bands logistics, personnel, travel arrangements, and bookings.

In the following interview, Les Brown describes his personal career as well as the development and demise of the big bands. A very personal individual, he enjoys performing and has no plans for retirement.

156

February 13, 1988, Pacific Palisades, California

Q: When did you realize you wanted to become a band leader?

Les: I can't give you an exact answer to that, what year or anything, but it seemed like I had a band in high school, and another when I went to Ithaca conservatory. I had a band when I was in military school, and a band at Duke University. I came out of Duke University with a band, and I've been going ever since, so I guess I must have been kind of young.

Q: When you started, did you have any specific heroes that motivated you to say, "Hey, I want to be like him!"?

Les: Well, I admired certain bands that were extant at the time—Paul Whiteman, for one, Isham Jones, and then a little later the Casa Loma Band. I enjoyed them. Of course, I was also doing legitimate work. I played as a saxophone soloist in 1928 with Conway's band down at Wildwood, New Jersey. I don't know if anybody remembers Pat Conway, but he was sort of second to Sousa in the concert band field. Then, of course, when Benny Goodman, Tommy Dorsey and those came along, I changed my style a little with my Duke University Band.

Q: When you first organized your professional band, were there any special processes or procedures you used, such as getting an arranger, getting a book, getting an agent, things of that nature?

Les: Well, we came out of Duke University pretty well-organized. The band had been together under my leadership for two years. We had nothing but special arrangements. We didn't use stocks in those days, and that gave us more or less a style. And so we were pretty well-organized when we came out, and luckily we had a job up in New Jersey at Bud Lake. People from Decca Records found us, heard the band, and signed us to a record contract. We've been going ever since.

Q: Were you the leader of the Duke Blue Devils when you were at the University?

Les: Yes, I was the leader all four years I was there, but my name wasn't in front of the band until my junior year. The gentlemen who had the band encouraged me, in fact twisted my arm and got me down to Duke instead of the University of Pennsylvania. I had to rehearse the band, make arrangements and everything all the time I was at Duke, so I guess I became a leader my freshman year.

Q: In the music business, what percentage of being a band leader is being a musician, a businessman, a psychologist, a booking agent, and whatever else that has to be done?

Les: I couldn't give you an exact percentage, but you have to be a little of each. Psychologist, so you can get along with the fellows in the band and know how to treat them. It always helps to be a musician, although some of our most successful leaders don't know a note of music, but it helps. Businessman—I always had somebody to help me in that. I'm not the greatest businessman in the world, but I always had a good booking agent, especially when I got Joe Glaser, who was my "angel". He bankrolled the band for the first four or five years 'til we finally started making some money, and then we were partners for seven years. However, you've got to be a little of each.

Q: Of the two types of big bands that we have throughout jazz history, the "hot" and the "sweet," yours had the reputation of being one of the leading "hot" bands. Did you plan it that way? Were you satisfied with the results?

Les: Well, you know we weren't necessarily considered a "hot" band, unless you're saying the "Mickey Mouse" bands were the sweet bands, and the swing bands were the "hot" bands. We were strictly a dance band. I had a very nice compliment come in by way of Sweden the other day. We're working on a tour of Scandinavia for this coming summer. It hasn't been finalized yet, and we don't even know if we're going to make it, but the guy that we got in touch with said, "Oh, yeah. Your band is the greatest dance band in the world." And we said, "But no jazz." And he said, "No, you're not the greatest jazz band, but you're the greatest dance band." There's a difference, though. They're altogether different. Like, Woody Herman, to me, as far as I'm concerned, has had the greatest jazz band that I've ever heard. I went up and was his master of ceremonies in Ventura about two or three weeks before he passed away, and I emceed part of the show. I never heard a band like that. I don't care, Ellington, Basie, anybody. I never heard a band as good as that.

Q: Your band's toured extensively from coast to coast, playing theaters, hotels, ballrooms, college campuses, and special events such as Bob Hope's annual tours. Why do you feel that touring gave your band the recognition to be one of the top bands in the country, rather than, say, staying out here in the Los Angeles area?

Les: Well, I don't agree that touring does that. I think in one television show, you'll hit many more people. In radio, you're exposed to more people in one radio shot than in a year of touring, if you have a coast-to-coast hook-up, which we did all the time. The only reason we went on tour was to make money. We went on tour, and we hated it. That's why we don't do it any more. We just did it to capitalize on all the air time we had, and the television time, and the exposure we had with Bob Hope. See, we've been with him since '47, so we've done both television and radio. You go on tour to make up the money you lost while you were sitting down.

Q: Of all the vocalists that worked with your band during its tenure, which ones do you feel had the qualities to enhance the musicality of your performances?

Les: Well, we've been lucky that way. We've had a lot of good vocalists, starting way back with Miriam Shaw, then Doris Day, Betty Bonny, and then Doris Day again, after she got her divorce and came back with the band, and Lucy Ann Polk. And on the men's side, we had Ray Kellogg and Jack Haskell. Another one we lost to the Hit Parade was Eileen Wilson. We lost her to the Hit Parade, but with my blessing, because she was a great singer, and we still hear from her now and then. Now we have Joanne Greer and Butch Stone. Butch Stone does more or less comedy work, and brother Stumpy does rhythm work. I have my son singing with the band now, and he's sort of a Sinatra style. He phrases like Sinatra. I don't think he has his voice, but he sings in tune and he gets a lot of applause and recognition.

Q: What do you look for musically when you look for a singer?

Les: Well, voice first, and then intonation, which is very important. Without intonation you won't be there, that's all. I'd say that between Doris Day, Eileen Wilson, Joanne Greer and Lucy Ann Polk you had four different sounds but all of them good. They don't all have to sound like your favorite, whoever your favorite might be, whether it's Jo Stafford or Peggy Lee, or Doris Day, or whoever. There are different sounds, and they can all be good.

Q: What about the size of the bands? How have they changed during their development?

Les: When we started the Duke Blue Devils, we only had twelve pieces. We had one trombone, three trumpets and four saxes. Then we got five saxes and three trombones, and then four saxes and four trombones. Then we had a quartet, The Polka Dots. I was carrying about twenty-four people at one time. We're now back to a nice size of about seventeen.

Q: Regarding the instrumentation, what made you go from two trumpets to three, to four, etc.?

Les: The competition. All the other bands had four trumpets and four trombones. Stan Kenton had five of each.

Q: It's generally accepted that the big band as an era ended during the late forties. Why did you feel this happened?

Les: Well, everything has to come to an end, even rock and roll may. In fact it has gone down hill and it's changed a lot. When Petrillo wouldn't let us record, right in the middle of the forties, the vocalists went ahead and recorded without his permission, because they didn't belong to his union. That hurt us a lot. However, we're doing a new album right now. We don't sell as much as we used to, but enough to pay the freight. The singers took over. Of course, we made the singers. The bands made the singers. We put them in front of the band, made heroes or heroines out of them, featured them and we improved ourselves right out of business.

Q: It's been said that history repeats itself. Every once in awhile you see a bumper sticker on a car that says, "Big Bands Are Back." What's your theory on that?

Les: Everybody says, "The big bands are coming back!" And I say, "No, they're not. We don't have any ballrooms. That's where we played." There are no ballrooms left in the country worth talking about, maybe ten at the most, but only four or five would be major. We do concerts now and then. There's an interest in that. But, it's for people over forty-five, fifty, or sixty and seventy. Some of them are in their eighties.

Q: What is the style of your band today?

Les: I'd say ninety percent of our work is private parties. People say, "Where can we come to hear your band?" and I say, "Come to Disneyland next summer." That's open to the public. Now and then we play a concert that's open to the public, but most of our work is charity parties and weddings—not many weddings, maybe we play two or three a year. Because we play so many charity parties, we're putting some "yuppie" tunes in the books. I think they're good ones, tunes that they like, not necessarily the Chubby Checker type of thing, but good ballads, like "We've Only Just Begun," "If," and "Evergreen."

Q: How do you compare the big band recording techniques of today with that during the thirties and forties?

Les: The last album we did is digital, which means, when you put it on a compact disc, you don't have to use a needle. It's the best sound we've ever gotten. We don't record much differently. We go in and record it all at once. We don't do like the small groups, or the contemporary groups that go in and lay down the rhythm track, then come in and put some violins above that. If they don't like the violins, they cut those out and put in trumpets instead, or trombones. If they don't like that, then they'll put in a synthesizer. We record the whole band. The we get together and mix it. That's all. And we put a mike on every man in the band, which we didn't in the old days. We'd be lucky to have four mikes in the whole studio. We put a mike on every man in the band, and then when we mix it, if a guy hasn't played loud enough, we pull him up a little. If he played too loud, we pull him down a little. So, the final product will not be altogether the same as you heard on the "rough makes," as we call them.

Q: You hear a lot of live versus studio recordings by some of the bands. Have you been involved with live recordings?

Les: Probably our best album is a thing called "Concert at the Palladium," which was not a concert. That was the name of the album. We were at the Palladium for four weeks. We broadcast every night, and recorded every one of those broadcasts. Then we took the best of all those broadcasts and made an album out of them. It's not even stereo, because they didn't have stereo radio in those days. I think that's the best album we've ever done, and that's live, and non-stereo. That's when we had guys like Ronny Lang on alto sax, and Dave Pell on tenor. We had Ray Sims, Zoot's brother, on trombone, who played so beautifully. We had Don Fagerquist on trumpet, Jack Sperling, whom we still have on the drums, and Tony Reesie on guitar; Jeff Clarks on the piano. That was a great band, too. And that was never mixed, couldn't be mixed. The only thing we did if we had a bad broadcast, or a bad number on a broadcast, was to eliminate it.

Q: About recordings, were they influential in setting the styles of the big bands during the thirties and forties?

Les: Well, of course. If you didn't have records, you better forget it. And that's what's happening today. You know, there are probably more big bands around today than ever. Every college has one, and a lot of high schools have one, and damn good ones, too. But, they don't make records. I mean they don't make records that are open to the public, and you don't have a public that's buying that kind of record nowadays. So you might as well say they don't exist. It's like the tree that falls in the forest. If there's nobody around to hear it, it didn't fall. That's what happening. If you don't record, forget it.

Q: Regarding all the different names associated with bands, such as Guy Lombardo's Royal Canadians, Lawrence Welk's Champagne Music, Harry James' Music Makers. How did you get the name, "The Band of Renown"?

Les: In 1942 we were at the Hotel Roosevelt in Washington D.C., and we had a wire. We were supposed to broadcast at ten o'clock at night. Anyway, it came time for the broadcast, and we had a theme that had a trombone solo in it. Si Zentner, who was our first trombone player, wasn't on the bandstand. We sent Butch Dolman out and he looked around and found Si, got him by the ear, and pulled him on the bandstand. In the meantime, the announcer was stretching, and stretching, and stretching. When I finally gave him the signal to go, he said, "And here's the band of renown, Les Brown!" Thank God that Si was off the bandstand, because we picked that up, and have used it ever since.

Q: Your theme song is titled "Leap Frog." Who wrote it, where did you find it, and why did you adopt that as your musical logo?

Les: I guess it was at a two-week session at the Hotel Roosevelt. We had been carrying "Leap Frog" around in a suitcase for over a year before we had a chance to rehearse it. We finally had a rehearsal, because we were going to the Palladium right after that, in June of 1942. We had a rehearsal and tried "Leap Frog, " and we loved it so much we threw the old theme away. We used "Leap Frog" from then on. It was written by Joe Garland, who also wrote "In the Mood" for Glenn Miller.

Q: When you get a new arrangement, how do you decide its structure?

Les: I've had, at different times, different arrangers. Ben Holburn and I did the arranging back in the 40's. Then Frank Comstock joined us, and Skip Martin, and Jay Hill for the last 30 years. Skip, like Frank Comstock, played with the band, so he knew what I wanted. In the same way, Jay Hill played trombone with the band, and he knew what I wanted. They tailor-made them for the band we happened to have. We have arrangements that I can't use because the band I have now doesn't fit the arrangements that were made back in the forties and fifties. They just don't fit, so we don't use them.

Q: Has the style changed that much?

Les: Not so much the style as the men. Arrangements were tailor-made for the men we had at that time. The strengths and the weaknesses change. We have so many arrangements. We're up into the four thousand numbers now.

Q: What about guitars? Do you use a guitar in your rhythm section?

Les: Not anymore. However, we do when we record.

Q: Do both piano and guitar seem to perform the same basic functions?

Les: The piano isn't a rhythm instrument. Piano's a solo instrument.

Q: When you have a three-man rhythm section; piano, bass and drums, how then do you regard the piano?

Les: When you don't have the guitar, piano does help in the rhythm section. Like Basie—if he played a hundred notes a night, he got overtime, but he had a great guitarist in Freddy Green. When we record, the piano doesn't work as a rhythm instrument. It just plays solos and fills.

Q: Regarding the sidemen, soloists, and leadmen, what training, education, and experience do you expect of them before you hire them on your band?

Les: Just that they play well, that's all. Play well, play in tune, have a good tone, and keep their nose clean. Don't drink too much, and things like that. If we lose a man, we have to think of the arrangements that we are currently using, so we have to hire a man that fits the same category.

Q: How about high tech electronics? Has that affected style, performance, and the audience expectations of jazz, in relation to the big bands?

Les: Some big bands might use an electronic keyboard. In fact, we're thinking of doing that, because we hit too many pianos that are out of tune. You know, you go into a hotel and they say, "Well, we had it tuned last fall." They think that once a year is enough, or something like that. We play for so many private parties. We don't blow them out of the room, or they don't have us back. There are a few bands that have made that mistake, right here in L.A., and thanks to them, we're getting more work.

Q: How does the jazz style of your band compare with the overall big band style of some of the other bands? Do you try to make it distinctive, so they know this is the Les Brown sound, compared to the Basie sound or the Ellington sound?

Les: According to what people tell me, we have evolved some kind of a Les Brown sound. They say, "We can tell your band right away." I wish I could. We don't have anything that's instantaneously recognizable. For example, when Billy May came out with a band, you could tell right from the intro who it was. You could always tell when it was Guy Lombardo. They were identifiable. We don't have anything in our sound that does that. I think it takes a musician to tell whether it's our band or, say, Ray Anthony.

Q: What do you feel is the future for women instrumentalists in jazz?

Les: Great, if they can play. I don't know if there's any future in it. They have to really love it to want to travel like they do. If they can play and have the stamina, it would be fine. I've never had one that's asked for a job in my band. I never gave it a thought. I know Woody had a girl for awhile. I met a Japanese girl in

Tokyo back in 1950. Today she's a fine arranger and bandleader. Her name is Toshiko Akiyoshi. When I met her, she was in her teens. We were in Japan with Bob Hope during the Korean War. She was performing at the Deichi Hotel. We went in to hear her and one of our party asked her to sing something. She sang, note for note, one of Dizzy Gillispie's solos with perfect pitch. Then about eight or ten years later, I was in New York and I went to the Hickory House on Fifty-second Street. There's a Japanese girl playing piano, and playing very well, by the way. At the end of her set, she comes by and says, "Hello, Mr. Brown." I asked her how she knew me and she says, "I know you by your records and I met you at the Deichi Hotel in Tokyo." She had gone to Berklee in Boston. She is a great musician. Now, if I could find a few like that, I'd have them on the band anytime.

Q: What advice do you have for young jazz musicians wanting to make music a career?

Les: Well, again you'd better be the best or forget it. You've got to be right on top or love it that much that you can't be happy any other way, because it's pretty hard to make a living financially as a musician. Even the best men here in Los Angeles right now are having a hard time getting by, because like Petrillo said, "You're going to record yourself out of business." And I think we have.

Q: What personal satisfaction do you get from performing, both as an instrumentalist yourself, and as a leader?

Les: I haven't played enough to talk about in the last twenty, twenty-five years. I don't play solos or anything anymore. I do play with the saxophone section now and then, only because I have an instrument and I keep it in shape, and I guess I think it looks good, or something. But, I do enjoy conducting. I did ten years of conducting on the Dean Martin show, and that takes conducting. You don't just say "one, two, three, four," and go. And, of course, I've been with Bob Hope conducting for forty-one years. I get a good deal of satisfaction from that.

Q: What do you think has happened to jazz over the past forty years?

Les: Well, I don't think the big bands have changed that much, but of course it went into bop and then all kinds of jazz, from West coast, East coast, Latin. There's been some very interesting innovations, I'd say.

Q: What gave you the biggest satisfaction of being a big band leader over a long and illustrious career?

Les: Being successful, for one. Well, I got lucky. When I joined Bob Hope we settled down in California and we've been here ever since. What little traveling we've done since 1947 was minimal.

Q: Are the kids today better prepared on their instruments than was the case thirty or forty years ago?

Les: I'd say there are more good musicians around now than ever, and it's such a shame that they can't get a decent job. Woody had a pipeline to the best. I never heard kids like that play so well. And I say kids, because I don't believe there's anybody in the band except Frank Tiberi, the leader, and the road manager who is over thirty. Everybody else is anywhere from nineteen up, and they are wonderful. They are virtuosos.

Q: Who, in your opinion, had the greatest single influence on the development of big band jazz?

Les: Well, I'd say Fletcher Henderson, with his arrangements. As soon as I heard Benny Goodman play those Fletcher Henderson arrangements, my whole idea about big band swing changed. And, of course, all the great arrangements of Count Basie.

Q: What do you think's going to happen in the future for the big bands?

Les: Well, once the leader passes away, it's not the same. You can't tell me the Duke Ellington band is like it used to be. You can't tell me the Count Basie band is like it used to be. And let's face it. It's a financial thing. The lawyers that own the Glenn Miller band were thinking of putting out a second unit of the Glenn

Les Brown Band of Renown at the Carnation Plaza, Disneyland. (Courtesy of R. Gaynor).

Miller band. I don't think it happened, and I don't think it will. The Glenn Miller name is so legendary and so famous. You know he's been dead forty-four years. He had a very popular band, and he made a lot of good records.

Q: What leisure time activity do you enjoy?

Les: Well, I used to enjoy golf. I'm down to about once a week on golf now, because I'm playing so poorly. I'm embarrassed to get out there, but I still like the walk in the park. I do play bridge at least four or five times a week. That takes care of my leisure time, except reading. When we finish the evening news and have our dinner, we go to bed and read until 10:00 or 10:30, and then turn out the light.

The Bands Played On

The big band era began to draw to a close just after World War II. A number of factors contributed to the eventual demise. The war had ended, the service personnel now discharged, returned to civilian life. The government, apparently seeing the possibility of heavy unemployment while the nation retooled for a peacetime economy, gave the veterans the GI Bill which enabled them to further or complete their education. Thousands of ex-GI's entered the nation's college and universities, leaving the mainstream of public life. The effect on the music industry was disastrous in that a large segment of the population was now without funds for entertainment. Veterans (this writer included) received; free tuition, books, supplies, and 65 dollars per month. This left little money or time to attend dances or for other entertainment.

Another factor was the musicians themselves who through the years had become egotistical and disregarded the fact that the public was paying their salaries. They played music for themselves, often far above the comprehension of the audience. They wanted to play for/impress each other. Stan Kenton, accused by fellow musicians of playing not for dancers but for listeners, accepted the accusations as real. His was a classic example of the type of music that did not attract people to the ballrooms and dance halls. You could not dance to his 'progressive' style of music with its breakneck tempos and thunderous dynamics.

More than four decades after the end of the big band era, Americans find themselves dancing and listening to the music of the big bands. In most cases, the original leaders have died. The descendants/families have authorized the continuance of the bands. They act as the business managers and receive their share of the profits, if any, from the performances. In some cases a band might have a full calendar of performances, while another might just undertake occasional tours. Some of the bands restrict their travel, while others travel from coast to coast, depending on schedules.

These bands were inappropriately called "Ghost Bands," with the implication that the leader is traveling with the band in spirit. The term meets with disdain by the men leading these bands and by the players themselves. Some of the deceased leaders, in their wills, decreed that their band will not continue after their passing. "Buddy" Rich, Benny Goodman and Stan Kenton are three bands that have completely disbanded. Those that are continuing include: "Duke" Ellington, "Count" Basie, Harry James, Tommy and Jimmy Dorsey, Woody Herman, and Artie Shaw. While the latter leader is still alive, he no longer leads the band. Of all the big bands that are still in existence, The Glenn Miller band has survived the longest. It has continued for over forty years after Miller's death with several leaders including drummer Ray McKinely and clarinetist "Buddy" DeFranco. The band has been so successful that the Miller family is considering putting a second Glenn Miller band together in order to meet all the performance requests.

Finally, economics became a major factor. Salaries, travel, housing, etc. all were rising and the consumer would not accept higher prices for admission to hear the bands. The consumer stayed away! Musicians also found that they could (and still do) make more money in Europe than the United States. All these factors caused many of the bands to disband or go broke. The 20 percent entertainment tax (also called cabaret tax) resulted in less income for proprietors who in turn cut down the amount of live entertainment offered. Clubs had 'live' music on weekends only. A band could hardly afford to work such a schedule and still maintain steady, competent personnel. A final, fatal blow was television. It brought about a whole new form of entertainment.

Assisted by a few key agencies/management people like Tom Cassidy of Tom Cassidy Artists' Management (Woodstock, Illinois); Wayne Hutchinson (New York); Bob Bonis of the Phoenix Talent Agency (Great Neck, New York); VIN Attractions (New York); Dave McKay of Glenn Miller Productions (New York); Bill Curtis (Boston, Massachusetts); "Pee Wee" Monte (Los Angeles) and the "Count" Basie Enterprises, Inc. (New York), road bands are able to keep nearly full schedules. "Sonny" Anderson, who is connected with Walt Disney World, Epcot Center and Disneyland, is instrumental in bringing big bands to these areas for several summer evening concerts. As a result, thousands of big-band enthusiasts are able to listen to the music of these great bands.

Discussion Topics

1. What effect did the band era have upon the recording industry?
2. While the big bands were an extension of the bands of Dixieland, what made them so popular, and why then was the big band era so short lived?

Dizzy Gillespie (Ed Dwight, Sculptor).

CHAPTER **11**

Bop/Cool

The eras of 'bop' and 'cool', while closely related, should be treated as two periods although one followed and even transcended the other. Separately, they can be classified as the shortest periods in jazz history. Each had a life span of approximately five years as peak periods of popularity and productivity. Collectively they encompassed a decade, 1945–1955. Bop came first followed by Cool.

Bop

The name was derived from the scat singing of nonsense syllables which had their origin in the work song. It was associated with the riff, an outgrowth of the jazz in Kansas City during prohibition. 'Hey-ba-ba-rebop' were the syllables uttered to the riff and were repeated through an entire phrase (12 bar blues). The rhythmic figure was a series of long-short-short-short-short notes. The first note, a quarter note, followed by four eighth notes followed by a quarter rest. This pattern is repeated over and over throughout a twelve bar blues chorus. The term itself was shortened to 're-bop' and then to 'bop'. The musicians who played the music were called 'boppers' as opposed to the generalization that anyone playing jazz was, and still is, called a 'jazzer'.

Bop Riff

repeat 6 times

or

repeat 12 times

The music was conceived as a music of 'revolt' against racism. Originated by black musicians, it was a backlash against the indignities suffered by black musicians playing for the entertainment of the white society. It may even be viewed as a throwback to minstrelsy, where white audiences were entertained by whites in blackface doing an imitation of the lives of blacks. It was a revolt by the black musicians against the years of entertaining the whites but not being allowed to entertain the blacks, the years of being considered less of a musician because of skin color and not musical ability.

Bop was a revolt against the music of the dance bands. Dancers considered the music secondary in their social activity. It was a necessity for dancing but not music for its own value. The rebellious musicians wanted to be heard for their music and not as an adjunct to a form of social interaction and physical exercise. This could explain why the music of bop was based on European forms. Classical music was performed for the listener not the dancer. Duke Ellington's compositions (Black, Brown, Beige, etc.) were attempts to get the audience to listen to the music. Stan Kenton admitted that his band played music to be listened to, not danced to. He expanded the size of his organization to include orchestrally oriented instruments such as French horns and renamed his band a 'neophonic orchestra'. Critics labeled it 'progressive jazz'.

Finally, it was a revolt against the restrictions and constrictions placed upon the big band musician. Big band arrangements were restricted to three minutes (for recording purposes) giving the soloist little time to demonstrate artistry and talent. Likewise, playing in a section (saxophone, trumpet, etc.) became a monotonous, almost robot-like experience. Inhibited by these restrictions, and gifted with unused talent, the break was inevitable. The end of the big band era was welcomed by musicians who wanted to be 'front and center.'

The Pioneers

Someone had to be the originator of the change. In this case credit is given to two men—**Charles Parker** and **John Birks Gillespie.** They are by no means the only people involved with its development. The end of the big band era left large numbers of musicians unemployed. For them the search for other avenues had begun. Those that saw the 'handwriting on the wall' quickly began organizing small groups and working in small clubs. At the outset, the small bands were a condensed version of the big bands. Many of the establishments still catered to dancers but on a much smaller scale. For others the new style of music called bop created a new interest in jazz. It was a common practice of musicians playing in the big bands, to 'jam' with musicians from other bands, following an evening of playing formalized arrangements. It was an opportunity to be creative, competitive, and to continue to develop improvisational skill and technique. It allowed a musician the opportunity to extend improvisation over several choruses instead of only short passages, if at all. In a jam session, a player might be allowed to play several choruses giving adequate time to experiment with melodic lines, harmonic, and rhythmic innovations and to develop a 'style'. Jam sessions had been used by musicians since the early days in Storyville.

Charlie Parker (Courtesy: Institute of Jazz Studies, Rutgers University).

A large number of big band musicians became involved in bop, many of which contributed immensely to the development of the style. Following is a partial list of these men by instrument.

Trumpet

Clark Terry
Howard McGee
"Red" Rodney
"Fats" Navarro
Conte Condoli
Roy Eldridge

Saxophone

"Zoot" Sims
Phil Urso
Charlie Ventura
Dexter Gordon
"Flip" Phillips
Al Cohn
Lester Young
Coleman Hawkins
Stan Getz

Trombone

J. J. Johnson
Kai Winding
Frank Rosolino
Bill Harris

Piano

"Bud" Powell
"Dodo" Marmarosa
Oscar Peterson

Guitar

Johnny Smith
Tal Farlow
Charlie Christian

Bass

Jimmy Blanton
Ray Brown
Charles Mingus
"Slam" Stewart

Drums

Max Roach
Kenny Clarke
Roy Haynes
Jo Jones

Dizzy Gillespie. (Courtesy: Willard Alexander, Inc.).

Lester Young (Courtesy: Downbeat).

Clark Terry (Courtesy: Willard Alexander, Inc.).

The Author, left, Red Rodney, center, Louis Bellson, right.

The Combo

It is essential to acquaint the reader with the name given to the groups that performed the new music. 'Combo' was a name that immediately identified the group. The term 'combo' is an abbreviation of the word combination and referred to the varied combination of instruments. It was a new term for an instrumental jazz ensemble. Taking it one step further, the new groups were 'bop combos'.

The leaders of the bop combos did not use a name for the group. It was simply billed as the Charlie Parker Quintet or Quartet. The number of players in a combo determined its name and obviously described the group; trios, quartets, quintets, sextets, etc.

The Music

The music was based upon two components—the riff and improvisation. The format for a selection was optional introduction, first chorus—played in unison by the wind instruments (the riff), and followed by extended improvisational solos by the wind players or, to include one or all members of the rhythm section. The music of a selection was either based upon the 12 bar blues or the 32 bar song form (AABA). It was a practice of boppers to compose riffs based upon the chordal progression of standard songs (Parker and Gillespie were noted for this).

As mentioned in Chapter 9 (Tin Pan Alley) this usage of the chordal progressions was a form of plagiarism, though the melody was changed. Examples include "Donna Lee" based on "Indiana", "KoKo" from "Cherokee", and "Anthropology" came from the standard "I Got Rhythm".

The music became quite complex. Harmonies were extended to include additional notes in chords. The addition of ninths, 11ths, and 13ths were added to chords giving a polychordal sound similar to 'stacking' one chord on top of another.

Polychords

became F 11 Chord   became Dm 11 Chord

Another effect, not necessarily a harmonic development, was the use of the diminished seventh chord, which had as one of its notes, the flatted fifth. This became a musical trademark of bop.

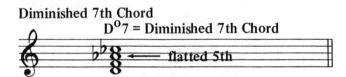

Also used, though not invented by the boppers, was the accenting of the notes that fell on the 'up-beat' in successive eighth note patterns. This was used in either riffs or solos.

Soloists, in their improvisations, began structuring lines based upon the upper notes of the chords, giving the feeling at times of playing in another key altogether. Rapid passages full of notes were interspersed with brief pauses (rests) which at times gave the audience a feeling of a disjunct series of notes with no correlation to the total solo. One had to be a very active listener to appreciate the improvisational artistry and skill of the musician.

The boppers added another new dimension to the music. Instead of beginning a phrase on the first beat of the measure which is traditional in most music styles, they began the phrase on the second beat, giving a delayed feeling to the phrase. They also broke tradition by playing phrases of odd duration. Most music is based upon duple (or multiples thereof) phrasing (four bar or eight bar phrases being the norm). It became a practice for phrases to be structured in odd numbers of measures; three and seven becoming standard among boppers.

The tempos of the up-tunes became quite fast with metronome markings of M. M. $\downarrow$ = 200–300 or faster. These fast tempos had two effects. Very few musicians could play consistently at these tempos, thereby limiting the number of players capable of playing bop. It also changed the playing style of the rhythm section. Playing 16th note phrases and passages at such a rapid tempo required utmost skill and technical agility. On the whole, the music of the big bands did not include music of these tempos as dancers could not dance to such fast tempos. As bop was not conceived for dancing, the combos could impress the listeners with their fast paced technical acrobatics.

Drummers had to change their style of playing. The steady beat in a selection with the use of the bass drum was no longer adequate. In the big bands the drummer was required to provide the beat via the bass drum on either all four beats of a measure or on the first and third beat while using the hi-hat cymbals to play the second and fourth beats. The hi-hat, when quickly depressed gives a sharp 'click' sound which is quite audible to the band. The alternating of beats in a measure by the bass drum and hi-hat became known as 'two beat' style of drumming.

In bop, the drummer no longer provided the continuous beat. It was physically difficult as a cramp would develop in the foot and calf after just a few measures. Now the string bass player, played a scalic or 'walking' figure, providing the initial pulse or beat plus indicating the chordal progression of the music. The drummer in turn used the bass drum for specific accents (known in bop terms as 'bombs') in conjunction with the musical phrases to give percussive impact to the music. The pianist, particularly on fast tempo numbers, adopted a punctuated style of playing, supplying the rest of the musicians with the necessary chordal changes. Count Basie had been using this 'light touch' punctuated style for years prior to bop.

In addition, drummers (Max Roach is credited with pioneering the development) began utilizing a large (19, 20, or 22 inch) cymbal to play 'time' and assist the bass player in keeping the beat moving forward. The cymbal became known as the 'ride' cymbal. It projects a 'ping' sound rather than a 'splash' or 'crash' and gives the listener a feeling of forward motion. A swing rhythm was used by the drummer

Bert Dahlander, drummer, left with the Author.

when playing this cymbal. The use of wire brushes on the snare drum, again played in a swing rhythm gave a new dimension to the drummers' sound.

Ride Cymbal – Swing Rhythm

Bop compositions were given names quite different from those of tin pan alley. "KoKo", "Parkers Mood", "Relaxin at Camarillo", "Shaw Nuff", "Dizzy Atmosphere", "Salt Peanuts", "Bussy", "Bird Gets the Worm", "Klactoveesedstene", and "Oop Bop Sh'Bam" all became bop standards.

The Times

Along with a dramatic change in the style of the music, there were also several social changes taking place among musicians and their audiences. The musicians no longer dressed in a uniform. They wore what seemed comfortable and what happened to be in their wardrobe. Some did however start fads among their followers. Dizzy Gillespie wore dark horn rimmed glasses, a beret, and sported a goatee. Soon young bop musicians along with their fans began doing likewise. The language of the bop musician became the language of double entendre, refined from that of the slaves, in that it related primarily to the language of the 'hip' musician. A 'hip' player played well, a 'square' did not. The instruments were 'axes' and a superb bopper was one who 'cuts' or 'carves' all others. A player, described as being 'cool', was a dignified professional. On the stage the musician showed very little emotion. Applause following a solo was acknowledged with a brief bow without any show of emotion such as a smile. It was to be music for the intellectual, the musically elite.

Alcohol was the nemesis of the professional musician during the major part of jazz history. The exception was the bop era. Before this musicians were known to have used drugs, primarily marijuana. Bandleader/drummer Gene Krupa's career was almost ruined as a result of having been arrested for possession. The bop era brought about the use of 'hard drugs'. It adversely affected the careers of many musicians. Charlie Parker's death was attributed to his drug addiction.

The Locales

The places in which the bop combos played were completely opposite those of the big bands. New York was the birthplace of bop and in that city were the ideal establishments, of the rights size and decor. Mintons, the Three Deuces, Birdland, the Royal Roose were clubs in New York where some of the first bop was played. In Chicago it was the Blue Note. The clubs were characterized by being small with intimate surroundings and 'postage stamp' size stages (stands) on which the combos were cramped for space. Many clubs had a policy of 'no cover charge' but required a 'two drink minimum'. Fifty-second Street in New York, housed a series of clubs where the top boppers appeared.

The Audiences

Bop audiences were almost a 'cult'. They came to listen and admire. Unfortunately, to the musicians, the audiences were not considered an important part of the total picture. The dance bands catered to their audiences. To bop groups, the audience was a necessary byproduct, not to be considered for their musical interest but rather for their economic value. Musicians expressed their disdain for the audience, at times turning their backs to them and playing to each other. Small wonder that it did not receive nationwide acclaim. Audiences always have been and will continue to be a viable part of all the performing arts. The bop musicians played for themselves much as the latter day big band musicians, with the same consequences.

Norman Granz, a promotor of jazz, and bop in particular, embarked on a venture which became known nationwide as Jazz at the Philharmonic (JATP). In 1944, at Philharmonic Hall in Los Angeles, he presented jazz at the first of a long series of concerts. He hired well known jazz soloists, presenting them in concert settings. He took the musicians on tour with great success. It gave audiences an opportunity to hear the very finest of jazz musicians without having to go to the small clubs in major cities. The concerts added a new dimension rarely done in the past, that of 'live', on the spot recordings, which he then produced and sold under the JATP auspices. It began a practice which is quite common today both in classical music and jazz.

Recording Developments

Following World War II, a recording machine was developed utilizing a spool of wire, a predecessor of the tape recorder. This allowed recordings to be made outside of the studio. In addition to the wire/tape recorder, the record disc was enlarged to 12 inches and the revolutions per minute of the turntable (RPM's) were reduced to 33-1/3. This created the long play (LP) record, capable of extending the playing time of a disc to 22 minutes, compared to the original ten inch disc with its three minute limit. The effect on the jazz musician was phenomenal. Solos could be extended over longer periods allowing time to 'develop' a solo line without the time restriction.

Cool

In 1949, when bop had been well established as the 'pure' jazz form, a number of musicians became disenchanted with the direction jazz was taking and formed what was to become known as the 'cool school' of jazz. Its principal location was on the West Coast (Los Angeles area), where many of the jazz musicians were located at the time. It took on the name 'West Coast Jazz' as opposed to the jazz of New York, 'East Coast Jazz'.

One of the leaders of the cool movement was trumpeter Miles Davis, who, for a period of time had played in a group led by Parker. An outstanding bop trumpeter, Davis moved to the West Coast and became influential in the development of West Coast jazz. Others who must receive credit for helping develop cool were Lennie Tristano, piano; Stan Getz, sax; Thelonios Monk, piano; Charlie Mingus, bass; Ted Macero, sax; Gerry Mulligan, sax; and Lee Knoitz, sax. These were but a few who were involved in the creation of what would in the future be called avant-garde jazz.

The cool movement, a much different style than that of bop, was much lighter in content. It was more closely associated with classical music. Where bop used a unison riff as its trademark, the cool style utilized more countermelodies and more complicated harmonies. It became known as 'chamber' jazz following the precepts of classical chamber music. Very controlled and well organized without the brash, raucous hard driving sound of bop, it was a fusion of jazz and classical music. The musicians began experimenting with odd tempos, getting away from the standard 4/4 meter used in bop. A classic example is the composition "Take Five" written in 5/4 meter. Composed by saxophonist Paul Desmond (Dave Brubeck Quartet) and recorded by Brubeck, "Take Five" became a top seller.

The music of cool included instruments heretofore unused as solo, improvisational instruments in jazz, but traditional in classical music. The French horn, bassoon, the tuba (having been absent from jazz through most of the big band and bop eras), the flute, and the cello became improvisational instruments. Gil Evans emerged as one of the top arrangers of this new form of music. Formerly with the Claude Thornhill band, Evans' arrangements for Miles Davis' "Birth of the Cool" album established the standard for the style of the era.

Hard Bop

As a counterattack to the cool movement, the bop musicians adopted an even harder style of playing. It became more frantic. Loud dynamics, faster tempos, and more punctuated accents became the vogue. During this period, "Dizzy" Gillespie hired an exciting drummer from Cuba, Chano Pozo. He was an extraordi-

Miles Davis (Photo Courtesy Institute of Jazz Studies Rutgers University)

Dave Brubeck (Photo Courtesy Institute of Jazz Studies Rutgers University)

nary conga player and Gillespie incorporated his talents into his group. It have birth to still another facet of bop called 'Afro-Cuban'. Unfortunately Pozo's contributions were short lived. He was murdered not long after his arrival in New York City.

Musicians/Composers

In addition to those mentioned in the section on Bop, the following are among the top names of the era in both East and West Coast jazz.

Composers/Arrangers	Drums	Saxophone
Thelonius Monk	Roy Haynes	"Sonny" Rollins
Charlie Parker	Art Blakey	John Coltrane
Gil Evans	Shelly Manne	Oliver Nelson
Errol Garner	Mel Lewis	Stanley Turrentine
Charlie Mingus	Chico Hamilton	Dave Pell
Dave Pell	Chano Pozo	Jimmy Giuffre

Composers/Arrangers	Trumpet	Piano
Dave Brubeck	Clifford Brown	Andre Previn
Bill Holman	Donald Byrd	Horace Silver
Gerry Mulligan	Thad Jones	George Shearing
Ralph Burns	Nat Adderly	Ramsey Lewis
"Shorty" Rogers	Art Farmer	
"Dizzy" Gillespie		

Bass	*Trombone*	*Vibraphone*
Percy Heath	Bob Brookmeyer	Milt Jackson
Oscar Pettiford	Milt Bernhart	Terry Gibbs
"Curly" Russell		"Red" Norvo
"Red" Callendar		
Eddie Safranski		

The Inventors

Charlie Parker, raised in the Kansas City area, played with the **Jay McShann** band for a period of time. He later joined the **Billy Eckstine** band, where he played with **"Dizzy" Gillespie.** While both were members of the Eckstine band, a liaison was formed which gave them the impetus to experiment with a new musical style, and eventually venture into the world of be-bop. Parker, a very talented individual, was considered the finest, most progressive instrumentalist in the country. His improvisational skills were the envy

Shelly Manne (Courtesy: Avedis Zildjian Co.).

of the music world. He was equally adept at composition. Musicians found him difficult to work with, primarily because of his personal traits and habits. Personal problems forced the eventual breakup between he and Gillespie. He drank often, and in large quantities, and became a victim of drugs which eventually contributed to his death at 35, in 1955. Nicknamed 'bird', the New York club, Birdland, was named after him.

Jazz producer **Dick Gibson** relates a tale which, describes Parker during one of the low points in his career.

> The "Count" Basie band was looking for a new alto player. "Buddy" Tate, a tenor player in the band, recommended Charlie Parker to Basie, who showed no interest. After five attempts Buddy became frustrated. "You've just got to hear this guy," Buddy pleaded, "He's turning every sax player in New York upside down." Finally, Basie said, "Alright, Buddy, I'll go with you tonight to hear him. But let me tell you, I've heard some strange things about this cat." They were sitting down in front, right up against the stage. Charlie walked out and threw up on the microphone. Buddy stared wide-eyed at Basie while Basie gazed serenely at the mess on the floor around the mike. After a moment, Basie turned to Buddy and said, "He'd sit by you in the band, you know." "Buddy" shook his head, "He don't play as good as he used to."

With all his inadequacies as a human being, his musical innovations set a style for others to follow. It is tragic that such talents were not developed to their fullest.

John Birks "Dizzy" Gillespie, born in 1917 in South Carolina began playing trumpet in Teddy Hill's band. There are two conflicting accounts as to the origin of his nickname. One is that he was named "Dizzy" by classmates while in school. The other, and perhaps more logical, was that his humorous antics while on stage got him nicknamed by the other musicians in the band. Rumor has it that he was fired from the Cab Calloway band as a result of his 'horsing around'. In any event, the name stuck and since has been shortened to "Diz". Credited with inventing a new style of trumpet playing, he was the pacesetter for trumpet improvisation for decades to come. During the latter part of the era he experimented with Latin rhythms, giving rise to the 'Afro-Cuban' style of jazz. For a period during the bop era he formed a big band and tried 'big band bop'. It was relatively short lived, in part because of the overall decline of big bands. He was a style setter, not only with his glasses, beret, and goatee but also with the upturned bell on his trumpet. An instrument manufacturer produced the "Dizzy Gillespie" model trumpet.

He influenced trumpeters such as Clark Terry, "Red" Rodney, Howard McGee, Thad Jones, and Miles Davis. Gillespie had modeled his playing after Roy Eldridge. Gillespie's technical facility coupled with his seemingly endless improvisational talent made him a giant among his contemporaries. As a composer, his musical creations have become standards of bop. "Shaw Nuff", "Grovin' High", "Salt Peanuts", and "A Night in Tunisia" still enjoy vast popularity after three decades.

The Singers

Bop was predominantly an instrumental era. The singers that performed with bop musicians adopted 'scat singing' as the general fare. Singers attempted to sound like one of the instruments rather than pronouncing the words of a song. Nonsense syllables such as 'a-biddle-le-be-bop' and 'ool-yo-koo' sung in unison with the wind instruments were typical. Two of the singers to perform will in this style were **Ella Fitzgerald** and **Sarah Vaughn,** both big band albums.

The End

The bop/cool period in jazz was popular with a small segment of the population compared with the big band era. Its sophisticated approach was difficult to digest for all but the most active listeners. The compositions were much longer than those of the big bands. With the format of first chorus unison riff, followed by extended solos, and then a closing chorus of the unison riff, the music became a quasi marathon. The attention span of music listeners is a few minutes at best, and, with the repetition of style by the soloists albeit on contrasting instruments, after a period of time, all tunes and all players sounded alike. It took on the flavor of a series of well organized jam sessions. Radio and recording companies did not 'push' it to the public. Compared to the song stylists even as far back as the race recordings of the blues singers, and into the era of rock with Presley, the Beatles, and the Rolling Stones, the records produced during bop/cool were insignificant in number. The era did bring about the formation of the independent record companies. While the major labels did produce recordings by bop and cool groups, small companies such as Dial, Clef, Savoy, Prestige, Verve, and Atlantic, made their presence know. It paved the way for a large influx of 'indies' during the subsequent periods of jazz.

While the bop and cool periods were not the most popular with the public, (Louis Armstrong termed it a 'modern malice') they exerted a tremendous influence on jazz instrumentalists of the future. The style of the music catered to a minority of the listening public. When the pioneers of Rock n' Roll made their debut in the 50s, the public smiled and listened, and bop/cool faded from an already dim limelight.

Discussion Topics

1. What was one of the major contributing factors to the invention and development of bop?
2. What is the difference between early bop and hard bop?
3. The cool period followed bop. Why did it emerge as a style called "chamber jazz"?

CHAPTER 12

Rock, the Beginning

Rock n' Roll began in the mid-fifties, at a time when the public was in need of a new type of musical entertainment. Bop and cool did not fit the needs of the youth. The song stylists, although popular with a large group of the middle-aged public, were not meeting the musical needs of the youth. The ballrooms and theaters were closed to live music which left radio and television as the prime entertainment source. Families on the whole became television oriented. Jazz recordings were low on the priority list of a family's budget.

The beginning of rock can be attributed to an amalgamation of country music and rhythm and blues. The pioneers of this music were Bill Haley and Elvis Presley. There were others influential in the development of the style, but these two men were the headliners. They brought the public new concepts in entertainment. Not only did they bring the voice into focus, but added the dimension of physical movement. The lyrics were simple to remember. The faces were pleasant to view and the physical antics were refreshing and exciting. The harmonies were simple in contrast to the complexities found in bop and cool. The instruments were basic rhythm instruments—guitars and drums. Dress was both conservative and flashy depending on the performer. The vocal techniques were crude and toneless. But the entertainment starved youth listened and bought it regardless of its musical quality.

Jazz musicians and followers felt it was a 'fad' and hoped it would fade into oblivion. They adopted the philosophy that if it was paid little or no attention, it would live a short life and die. Little did they know that it would last for four decades and take on numerous dimensions during that time.

The Voice

The voice was the leading component of rock. Singers emerged throughout the country and record sales soared. The leading singers during the mid 50s were Bill Haley and his group the "Comets"; Little Richard; Elvis Presley; Jerry Lee Lewis; and Chuck Berry.

In this vocal era, singers were the main attraction. The vocal style was a mix between singing and shouting. The voice often was thin and nasal in quality. Instruments, often played by the singers themselves, were used for accompaniment purposes. For the vocal soloist, the guitar was the most popular. The singers made no attempt to be accomplished guitarists in the class with jazz guitarists. They provided chordal accompaniment to their music and used the instrument as an assist in their physical antics. Early recordings of rock singers were accompanied by either solo guitar or small instrumental ensembles, of rhythm sections, piano, bass guitar, and drums. Occasionally the rhythm sections were augmented with a smattering of wind instruments.

The Lyrics

The words to the songs encompassed a variety of subjects from love to anti-establishment. The origin of the title of the era had strong sexual connotations similar to the word jazz itself. It was a double entendre used by black youth. While the youth of the country, black and white alike, understood the meanings, parents did not. The lyrics became very suggestive with sexual overtones. Socially, it created communication gaps between generations, creating the illusion that the music was causing moral ruination of the youth. The lyrics of a song, plus the suggestive body movements of the performer increased emotionalism in the listeners. The dances that followed did little to dispel the attitudes of parents and grandparents. It is credited by sociologists as one of the main contributors to disintegration of the family.

The Rhythm

During the previous eras of jazz, the uneven 'swing' rhythm was the foundation of the music. In rock the basic rhythmic structure was changed to an even eighth note pattern with the emphasis or accent on the second and fourth beats of the measure. This was a carryover of the two beat style found in earlier jazz. The music became duple as opposed to the jazz style of a triplet feeling. Drummers in playing 'fills' in rock used a duplet beat, while jazz/swing drummers used a triple beat.

The tambourine, used in Latin music to augment the rhythm section, became a percussion instrument in rock because of the quick splash sound produced by the 'jingles' on the instrument. This sound enhanced the accents of the second and fourth beats of a measure, and gave a more punctuated sound to the rhythmic accompaniment. In time, drummers expanded their drumsets to give them greater latitude of sound for a more emotionally explosive effect.

Dancing

The dances that evolved with rock were highly physical compared to the waltzes and fox trots of the swing era. The 'jitterbug' was quite tame by comparison. The dances associated with rock were very physical and required stamina in the dancers. While the swing era had three basic dances excluding those that were of the Latin style, the rock era produced and continues to produce innumerable variations of styles. Among the more popular over the years have been: the Twist, the Watusi, the Mashed Potato, the Frug, the Jerk, the Swim, the Popeye, and the list goes on. While the dancing was popular with the younger set, adults enjoyed the dances also. It gave them the feeling of youth. History notes that the 'Jet Set' discovered the dances of the rock era in a New York club called the Peppermint Lounge.

Recordings

The recording industry came alive. Records of rock stars sold millions of copies. A number of artists formed their own record companies. Elvis Presley's recordings alone sold more than ten million copies. Along with the recording industry, radio disc jockeys became the 'voice of radio' playing and replaying the top recordings of the day, providing the necessary exposure for the artists and the record companies. The 'top 40' replaced the 'hit parade'. Record companies such as Mercury, Dot, MGM, and Sun had sales comparable to such traditional leaders as Columbia, Victor, and Decca. Sheet music on the other hand decreased in sales. Many of the songs written and performed by the artists were never published as sheet music.

New Directions

Unlike the big band era which had but two major styles; hot and sweet, rock began to wear a variety of new hats. It diversified itself until it became confusing to the public, but still came under the label of 'rock'. Vocal and instrumental groups and combinations of both have dominated the scene through the decades. Groups from foreign countries including the Beatles and the Stones had impact on the style and trends. The amplification had a direct effect on the music and on the listener. The use of the synthesizer created new variables in sound which could not be produced by wind, string, and/or rhythm instruments, and exotic lighting effects gave the era a new aura. It became psychedelic. Influenced by socio-economic factors, the music has undergone changes and additions to its original concept.

As rock is vocal in nature, the singers and the types of songs are the dominant feature. The singers can be classified as one of the following:

Rhythm and Blues
Balladeers
Crooners
Shouters
Novelty
Monster

The styles of music can also be categorized. Each of the following has its own identifying style and sound.

Rock n' Roll   Country Pop
Soul   Punk Rock
Acid Rock   Funk
New Wave
Folk Rock

In each of the styles there are leaders. The listing of all is an impossible task. However, as with previous eras of jazz, there are individuals and groups who have contributed to the development and popularity of the era. A partial listing follows:

Individuals

Bill Haley	Janis Joplin	Carole King
Elvis Presley	Jimmy Hendrix	Joan Baez
Jerry Lee Lewis	Pat Boone	Bob Dylan
Fats Domino	Bo Diddley	Mick Jagger
Buddy Holly	Ray Charles	James Brown
Little Richard	Johnny Cash	Eric Clapton
B. B. King	Paul Anka	Stevie Wonder

Groups

The Beatles	Doobie Brothers
The Comets	Weather Report
The Platters	Chicago
The Beach Boys	Blood, Sweat and Tears
The Stones	Chuck Mangione
Led Zeppelin	Santana

The Effects

While some jazz purists denounce the era of rock as unmusical and akin to noise, it has made worthwhile contributions to jazz as an entity. As it is primarily vocal in nature, there is little opportunity for improvisation. Yet it has had a number of positive effects—it fostered a large listening audience, dancing, a prosperous record industry, musical composition, and continuous experimentation.

Discussion Topics

1. What activated such a phenomenal interest in the new music called rock?
2. Rock has undergone numerous changes in the four decades of its existence. What forces these changes, and when will it finally evolve into a style or format that will last?

CHAPTER **13**

Contemporary Jazz

Some call it third stream or avant garde, others call it free jazz, still others name it new age. Under the vast umbrella of contemporary jazz it many also be called fusion, a name which in itself implies elegance, and means a blending or melting together. Although quite different in structure, style and objective, they are all allied. Some of contemporary jazz is for dancing, but generally it is designed for listening. This is similar to the philosophy of bop and cool.

Maynard Ferguson, leader, Bop-Nouveau jazz ensemble.

Third Stream is a combination of classical music and jazz. In the mid-twenties, Paul Whiteman happened upon this by introducing what then was called orchestral jazz. In 1924, he commissioned George Gershwin to compose and perform the Rhapsody In Blue with his jazz orchestra in the first real jazz concert. Third stream became very popular in the 1950s and 60s. Bandleader Stan Kenton reorganized his band with the inclusion of orchestral instruments and named it the Neophonic Orchestra, designed for listening only. Composers found this a whole new areas in which to create. Of course, ragtime composer/pianist James P. Johnson was a pioneer of this form during the early days of jazz. But, perhaps because of his color, he was ignored by classical audiences. Today some of the leading composers, both classical and jazz oriented, are delving into the style and form. The leaders include, Gunther Shuller, Quincy Jones, Chick Corea, Lalo Shifrin, Johnny Richards, Allyn Ferguson, Dave Grusin, and John Lewis. Others who have made notable contributions but have since passed away are Charles Mingus, Gil Evans, Stan Kenton, Don Ellis, and "Duke" Ellington.

183

Free Jazz seems to be a continuum of bop and cool It gives the musician total freedom from constraints of traditional music. To be sure, the basics of music are still used. Melody, harmony and rhythm are still the main components. That will never change. What has changed and continues to evolve is freedom for the performer. The term "playing outside" refers to the structure of the improvised solos in which the performer is not restricted to key (tonal center), rhythmic, or chordal structure. Free jazz was and still is an experimental venture. The early audiences were the young intellectuals, again, a similar to the audiences of bop and cool. They were sophisticated listeners—not overly concerned with tempo, meter, or tonality, but rather with mood and expression, spontaneity, and a portrayal of innermost feelings. Nationally, the audience was limited. Internationally free jazz received wide acceptance. Early recordings had limited sales and record companies were reluctant to produce large volumes of releases regardless of the popularity of the performers—not unlike the bop and cool eras. The style was primarily instrumental. The inclusion of additional rhythm instruments instead of one drummer gave the ensemble a feeling of percussive arts expanding the rhythmic capabilities. Vocalists including **Bobby McFerrin** and **Abbey Lincoln** became classic innovators of the form.

Following is a listing of some of the headliners of this music, many of whom are quite active.

John Coltrane, Saxophone
Ornette Coleman, Saxophone
Anthony Braxton, Reeds
Roland Kirk, Saxophone
Eric Dolphy, Saxophone
Don Cherry, Trumpet
Hugh Ragin, Trumpet
Pat Metheny, Guitar
Cecil Taylor, Piano
Keith Jarrett, Piano
Sun Ra, Keyboards
Archie Shepp, Saxophone
Charlie Mingus, Bass, Composer
Tony Williams, Drums
Freddie Hubbard, Trumpet
Scott LaFaro, Bass
Roscoe Mitchell, Reeds
The Art Ensemble of Chicago

Fusion is a blend of several forms and styles of jazz. In its simplest form it is a combination/marriage of traditional jazz and rock. Some historians go further by describing it as a blend of the blues, rock, soul, pop, and new electronics with emphasis on the use of the synthesizer. It evolved and became popular during the 1970s and 80s. Supposedly the record companies, in search of a new marketing device called it fusion. It is instrumental in style and not considered music for dancing. Also appealing to the young intellectuals, it became a favorite form of entertainment. Musicians who had gained experience in jazz eras akin to fusion quickly assimilated the style and ran with it. The following individuals and groups represent a few who were important to the development and performance of the music.

Kenny G., Saxophone
Paul Winter, Saxophone
Grover Washington Jr., Saxophone
Wayne Shorter, Saxophone
David Sanborn, Saxophone
Miles Davis, Trumpet
Don Ellis, Trumpet

Tony Klatka, Trumpet
Art Farmer, Fluegelhorn
Chuck Mangione, Fluegelhorn
Herbie Mann, Flute
Pat Metheney, Guitar
Stanley Clarke, Bass
Chick Corea, Keyboards
Herbie Hancock, Keyboards
Joe Zawinal, Keyboards
Dave Grusin, Keyboards
Don Grusin, Keyboards
Gary Burton, Vibes
Billy Cobham, Drums
Tony Williams, Drums
Ed Uribe, Drums
Airto Moreira, Percussion
Dom Um Romao, Percussion

Groups:

Weather Report
Blood, Sweat & Tears
Spyro Gyra
Steely Dan

In many ways fusion had its real beginnings with men like Miles Davis during the cool period, when he incorporated electric piano, Fender bass, several drummers, and auxiliary percussion instruments with three wind instruments—trumpet, soprano sax, and bass clarinet. These all can be heard on the 1969 album "Bitches Brew." There is a similarity with free jazz in the use of multiple rhythm instruments and is apparent in both. Electronics are also a mainstay of sound production. Fusion relies to a great extent on the bass. The rhythmic structure portrayed by the bass is the foundation for much of the music. Quite often a Latin influence creeps into the rhythmic content of a selection. The term "funk" is also applicable to this style of music.

CHAPTER 14

High Technology, Movies & TV Music

One of the leading exponents of fusion is composer/pianist **Dave Grusin.** During his career he has continued to be active as both a writer and performer. In partnership with Larry Rosen they formed one of the foremost record companies. Today, GRP Records has amassed a group of outstanding performers in all phases of jazz including fusion. Grusin's album "Mountain Dance" is an excellent example, utilizing all the components of fusion. As a major part of composing, he has become involved in writing music for movies. Being nominated for Oscars for his music for "On Golden Pond" and "The Fabulous Baker Boys," he received an Oscar for his score for the film "The Milagro Beanfield War." In addition he has composed the music for the following films.

The Graduate
Heaven Can Wait
Ishtar
Tootsie
The Goonies
The Heart Is A Lonely Hunter
Falling In Love
The Champ
Three Days Of The Condor
The Little Drummer Girl
The Firm

What needs to be said in a film, and can't be said with words or pictures, is finally said with music. Oddly enough there is more possibility of misunderstanding the words and/or the images. Although the music is both more precise *and* more ambiguous, it is, surprisingly, always clearer. And when it works well it is so braided into the fabric of the film that it is inseparable from the final emotional result.

As a filmmaker you try to use all these tools of light and sounds and words and there is, sometimes, something not yet born in it. Like a slightly out-of-focus snapshot. So you put yourself in the hands of a magician-musician like Dave Grusin, who, by some alchemy, imagines these phrases and colors of music that pull it all together and bring it into focus.

The lucky ones, and there are many, who have worked with Dave will confess (under just a little pressure) that he often makes it into more than it deserves to be. More romantic, more frightening, more eerie, more nostalgic, more haunting, and indeed more resonant on every level.

Dave is a consummate orchestrator. Not all film composers are. Aside from having written some of the most memorable themes in modern movies, it is his voicings, the rich textures of his orchestrations that finally press the buttons that trigger the emotions.

Dave has scored six of my films, located in places as disparate as Kyoto, Japan, and St. George, Utah. His range is amazing. He can write the most symphonic, acoustic, classical score ever needed and next time up be as hip, electronic, and contemporary as any group out there. I don't think there is anything he can't do with film.

Sydney Pollack

Two of his recent albums; Grusin Plays Gershwin and Homage To Duke will become classics. To add to his credits are the numerous Grammies he has received.

An advocate of electronic music, he is aware of the impact of electronics on all forms of music from live performances, recording techniques, and music for movies and television. As a performer he played as a member of the Benny Goodman band in 1960 and with Quincy Jones from 1970–73. The following interview gives the reader a closer insight into the music industry of today. Throughout the interview it becomes readily apparent how the music of today has become "high tech."

Since the advent of the talking picture music has been an integral part of the action on the screen. Movie music replaced the pit orchestra or small ensemble which played music that was sent to the movie theaters along with the film. Occasionally, the house pianist was given the option to improvise appropriate music to coincide with the action on the screen. The music was to enhance the plot and dialogue when talking pictures became well-established. Love scenes required music that was tranquil and melodious but would not detract from the action or dialogue. The tempo was moderate to slow, giving viewers a relaxed and comfortable feeling. Scenes with fast-paced action including fights, automobile racing and crashes, and the ever-popular western complete with range war or Indian war, required music with faster tempos, played by the brass and percussion with explosive sound effects thrown in.

A very small but elite group of musicians became the composers and conductors for the movie industry. The music involves a complicated form of composition, much of it written by a mathematical formula that is required when the music has definite time constraints. Composer/arranger Sammy Nestico, in presenting a lecture-demonstration at a music conference, described the problems facing the composer. He indicated the necessity of coordination between film and music in a hypothetical situation. Scene: Car goes over cliff and will crash in rocks at seashore and explode. Music must be timed perfectly so when the car impacts on rocks, a heavy chord is played by the orchestra. If the chord is played prior to impact, scene is destroyed. If the chord is sounded after impact, scene is likewise destroyed. Everything must be synchronized so the impact appears and the music is heard at exactly the same moment. It is often the suggestions of the director and·producer that determine the type and style of music to be used for specific scenes, as well as for the whole production. Background music for "Keystone Kops" movies included much humor and a number of sound effects giving the whole scene a good deal of hilarity, whereas movies that indicate tragedy, war, religion, or serious, social-economic crisis will require music of a very serious heavy nature.

Composers such as Frank Skinner, Vladimer Bakalinikov, Max Steiner and John Cacavas were early masters at composing music for films. They were later joined by men such as Andre Previn and Henry Mancini, who put jazz effects into the movie scores. Today, Quincy Jones and Dave Grusin are the leaders in the field. Jazz-oriented, they have found a new freedom in writing for movies. No longer must they adhere to the restrictions that forced earlier composers to match the mood of the music with that of the scene. Actual recordings of some of the rock bands are permissible. Using excerpts of classical music with a contemporary instrumentation and rhythmic treatment is also quite acceptable. The opening scene of the movie "Bob and Carol, Ted and Alice" is accompanied by a rock band playing the "Hallelujah Chorus" from Handel's *Messiah*.

Movie and television composers have a tendency to favor composing for movies over television. Movies are produced in a time frame that includes an open end for completion. This give the composer flexibility in his work. Television, particularly a weekly series, has no open end. Everything has a definite deadline for completion. As composer Dave Grusin indicates in the following interview, with television composing, you have time for nothing else. The television show and the impending deadlines rule your entire life.

Perhaps the tight scheduling for composing was partly responsible for the use of synthesizers in movie and TV music. The composer, working with a synthesizer, could produce the sounds of a band or orchestra with the machine. This was faster than waiting until the film was complete, then hiring and rehearsing the orchestra, and working with the film in the studio. The major complaint of studio musicians in recent years has been that they are being replaced by the synthesizer. The musicians are convinced that the sounds produced by synthesizers do not compare with those of the actual instrument being performed. Studios, on the other hand, feel that movie and television audiences are not so perceptive that machine-produced music will distract them from enjoying the film.

188

A compliment to the movie composers is the inclusion of a category in the annual Academy Awards presentation for film music. It recognizes the importance that music has in a film.

Following is an interview with one of Hollywood's leading composers. Throughout the interview, readers will get an intimate look into the making of movie music. It should also give one an appreciation of music as an integral part of a movie.

David Grusin is a native of Denver, Colorado. He received his formal training at the University of Colorado, and maintains ties with the University's music program, serving on the music school's advisory board. A proponent of electronic music, he is aware of the impact of electronics on all forms of music, from live performances to music for movies and television. As a performer, he has played piano for the Benny Goodman band in 1960 and with Quincy Jones from 1971 to 1973. He is a consultant for the Yamaha instrument manufacturing company, and, along with a partner, has formed GRP, a recording company. They have produced a number of albums under that label. He received an Academy Award nomination for his musical score for the movie, "On Golden Pond." In addition, he is given credit for the theme music of the successful television series, "St. Elsewhere."

Dave Grusin Interview

April 14, 1988, Boulder, Colorado

Q: What percentage of your scoring for movie and television is done by high tech. as opposed to the traditional method of scoring for full orchestra?

Dave: I'm doing some scoring by synthesizer. The percentage, I guess would be a third electronically, two-thirds acoustically. The last film I did, "The Milagro Beanfield War," was done acoustically. I don't do that much television. The last thing that I did was "St. Elsewhere," which was about four or five years ago. That was all electronic. I think the nature of the project is going to determine how it's done. Certainly it has a lot to do with the size of orchestras and what kind of orchestra.

Q: Describe your "home" studio where you do your writing. What type equipment are you presently using in your writing/scoring?

Dave: My little home studio consists of a couple of synthesizers, Yamaha DX-7's, some effects, a small mixing board, a cassette player to record with, and a computer to actually make digital recordings of tracks. I have a computer called an Atari ST, and a software program for that called Hybrid Arts Midi-Track. This software is in the nature of a sixty-track recording studio, so that I can play a part on it and then play a part on another track, and then continue to over-dub. If I had enormous numbers of instruments, I guess theoretically I could put on up to sixty tracks, and they'd all be of different instruments. But, it does help to make demos of film scores, particularly. They're not the final product, but as I'm writing, it helps if I can record something in terms of the theme with a patch on the synthesizer that sounds vaguely like the ultimate acoustic instrumentation that it's going to be—in the case of the Milagro picture for Redford, there was a theme played on guitar with strings. I had both of those sounds available to me on the synthesizer, so I make a demo for myself to see if the theme would work with the picture, as well as to play for the director. And to play it that way for him, on a cassette, so that he can hear not the final product, but some kind of demonstration of what the final sound is going to be, it's pretty valuable for both of us. That's my little home outfit. When a project is finished, I just turn in a score, and in that case (Milagro), we then hired an orchestra. The demo was purely for our own "work in progress" use, so we could hear it as we went along.

Q: When you contract with a studio for a film or television program, how large a staff of assistants are you allowed and what are their roles?

Dave: I don't use orchestrators, normally, but if I did, I suppose they would be part of the assistants. I do use copyists, and the studio pays for them. They also pay for a music editor. The only time this wouldn't be true is if I took a package, I think. If I said, "You give me X amount of dollars, and I'll deliver the score to you, and I'll be responsible for writing it, recording it, having it copied, and having it edited to work with your film." I've never done that.

Q: Do you have any say in who the conductor will be?

Dave: I'm usually the conductor. I'm usually hired to do that, as well as to be responsible for the band. There's another person involved called a contractor, who is necessary to call an orchestra. Sometimes he is from the studio but not necessarily. Sometimes I use an outside contractor. He goes on the payroll as a sideman, right on the contract, as far as the union is concerned. The music editor first takes the film and times the musical sequence, so you know exactly how long the cues are, where they start, where they stop, and what the internal things are that happen. Then, after the recording and mixing, the editor will actually take the music that has been mixed, and cut that so that it is in sync with the picture. That's the function of the music editor. The editor usually has an assistant, because that's a lot of work.

Q: Describe the changes in film composing and scoring that have taken place during this past decade.

Dave: The primary change is the development of technology, since music is now made not only acoustically, but digitally as well. There's been a use of that technology in some areas to try to save money—to save salaries. Rather than their twenty-four strings, you put it on a couple of tracks with a synthesizer. Generally, that doesn't work so well. The best use of synthetic music is to do things that you can't do acoustically. That's the exciting use of that stuff, not to try to fool anybody or to replace existing sounds. That would be the biggest single factor. Another factor is that films have changed a lot in the last ten years. The majority of films coming out of Hollywood are clinically and scientifically directed at an audience, and I don't know what the age is, but I'd guess it would be between fifteen and twenty-four or so. There's a whole science now about who's going to see this picture, how many people can we expect to see it, and that will determine how much we're going to spend on making it. If you make a film for a certain demographic age group in that area, a logical choice of music for that picture would be music which that age group listens to. So that's why we see a lot of songs in pictures now, by hit name groups, Phil Collins and U2 and David Byrne and Talking Heads, and so forth. The film maker is using the ancillary contemporary media of music, to use in his contemporary film.

190

Q: What are the procedures for adapting music to film?

Dave: It's basically mathematics. Three feet of thirty-five millimeter film go by every two seconds. So if I have a scene in a picture that's sixty feet long that needs music, I have to know that the cue is going to be forty seconds long, so there's a three to two ratio. Now, what that means is, if the cue starts at zero and runs for forty seconds, we'll be at the sixty foot increment of film. The way it specifically works, I don't think about footage at all. I think about time—seconds. So my tempo might be four seconds per bar. That means I've got ten bars in forty seconds. So, you see, if does finally come down to be mathematical formulas. Now, the way I determine that my tempo is four seconds per bar is another matter. It's best that I determine the tempo first, and then measure it, and then I can find out where I'm going to be. The tempo can correlate directly with the action on the screen. You have the option of doing that. In the old way of scoring films, they tried to do that, absolutely. They tried to match action with tempo. A newer way to do it is to try not to do that; to try to do some kind of counterpart to the tempo of the film and speed of the action, and not hit every cue. You know, when the guy closes the door, try not to have the big chord hit on the door anymore. That used to be almost the gospel. Click tracks are a device to keep everybody on tempo. If I've got something going four seconds to a bar and I hear a clock on each beat, I'll hear it on each second, and therefore I'll know I'll be absolutely right on the tempo at the end of that forty second cue.

Q: What musical processes change when composing music for live public performances versus composing for the screen?

Dave: The nature of live music is that the music is the medium. The nature of film is that film is the medium, and it's absolutely the boss, so that you can't ever forget that you're serving this film. That's not to say you can't be musical in the process, but live music certainly is an entity of its own. That is the end, and in the other case, it's the means.

Q: What specific skills do you feel you possess that allowed you to enter the professional arena of Hollywood composers/arrangers?

Dave: When I first started to do this, I had an agent who had ninety-five composers on his roster, and he had them listed in terms of who was on top, and then the next guys down. I used to get jobs, I think, when the first guys were not available. Then they'd come to my name and he'd sell me. Then I'd have to find out who they'd called for, that they really wanted, so I'd know who I was supposed to be when I got there. And I'm talking about people like Mancini, and Burt Bacharach and Elmer Bernstein, and so forth. I tried to be somewhat eclectic. I tried to incorporate any style I could to do the film. My whole sense of my beginnings in this was a workshop nature. In retrospect, the whole thing was a workshop. Every film demanded different things. One of the things I could do was be somewhat of a chameleon and adapt to whatever a film needed.

Q: You still have opportunities to play live performances and produce recordings. What type of group and what specific instrumentation do you use?

Dave: We make recordings, but I don't have any specific size group that I am locked into in terms of recordings. My brother, Don, and I just finished recording, just the two of us, all electronic. He's a keyboard player, as well, and we did the whole thing with the computer that I mentioned before. We programmed it and played to it and played live with it, and so forth, and make the record so that nobody else was on the record except the two of us. That's one way to do it. On the one before that, I used the London Symphony Orchestra, for the Cinemagic album last year. So there's no set rule in terms of what I'm doing. I don't do much live performing. I sometimes play with a guy who does, one of the artists on our label, named Lee Ritenour. I'll got out and do concerts with him. In fact, we just got back from one in Europe with Lee and Tom Scott and a rhythm section. We did some one-nighters, but that's not my life as a rule.

Q: Looking to the future, what academic/musical preparation do you feel will be required for professional composers/arrangers in the twenty-first century?

Dave: I like that question, but I don't know how to answer it. I just talked to a kid who said, "Don't you think computers are going to ruin music? It's not going to be as sensitive as it once was, and shouldn't somebody be practicing their instrument instead of playing with their computer?" And I said, "Well, if you are a viola player, you better practice the viola and leave the computer alone. If you're going to be in electronic music, the computer is your instrument, so you'd better practice that." I think that the preparation in that area has to be addressed academically. I'm quite interested in this college (University of Colorado). I'm on the faculty board, and one of the things that I'm interested in seeing is intensifying whatever the electronic opportunities are. I'm not saying everybody should do it, but if a keyboard major wants to have a career later on, either as a composer/arranger or as a player in the studios, he should somehow get himself a good, solid electronic keyboard education. It's not easy to do that all at the same time. I'm still learning my computer. My children all grew up in the computer era, but it's really hard for me. I have to do it a step at a time. By the time I get one instrument figured out, it's obsolete. The state of the art changes every six months. With this stuff it's a constant learning process, and I think it would be great to formalize that a little bit academically. It is sometimes looked down on as the "stepchild" of music education, but for somebody who's going to be a player and actually make a living playing music in the future, he's going to have to know something about that, unless he's an acoustic virtuoso and only going to deal with symphony orchestras.

Q: What composers/arrangers do you enjoy listening to for your personal enjoyment?

Dave: I don't listen to much music, but when I do, I listen to classical music. I listen to Stravinsky. Stravinsky is maybe my all-time guy, if I had to pick one favorite composer, certainly of the twentieth century composers. Bach is always fascinating to me—the French composers like Poulanc, Milhaud, Debussy and Ravel. Brahms is something I get into. I don't listen to much jazz. I don't listen to much current stuff, except as it relates to our record company and my work.

Q: When you first entered the field of composition, who were the people that became your inspiration?

Dave: Nobody in particular. I thought when I was here at the university, in the early fifties, that maybe film music was some kind of frontier that I could look at in some kind of pragmatic way. Not too many American composers are making a living composing. So I thought about that. One man in particular stood out at the time, and that was Andre Previn, who was the head of the music department at MGM. He was this "wunder kind" from Berlin. I think he came to this country when he was eight years old. He was a marvelous pianist—a serious pianist and also a very good jazz pianist. I thought he was a great film composer. He didn't do that many films. He opted to bail out on that and do what he's doing now, which is dealing only with classical music, conducting. I have a lot of idols in that field, but I remember him specifically from those years, as being influential to me. He was one of the first modernists, changing the nature of scoring from the old Max Steiner school, and putting in these new elements, these modern, jazzy elements. (At that time I thought anything having to do with jazz was going to save the music world.) I picked up on that. Mancini was a master at it. The more one does it, the more one sees how hard it is to do, and the less pleased one is with the results. It's not easy. Quincy Jones is another one who did that same sort of jazz-oriented type of scoring, even more than I did. I've kind of drifted away from the straight jazz element, and I'll do a picture that has none of that in it now. I guess I've become more interested in serious writing and less interested in film writing, over a period of time, although it's been a wonderful profession, and the need for it continues.

Q: You are in the profession of music, but in that field you are divided between two major facets, that of a performer and that of a composer. How are you able to handle both areas so well?

Dave: I really don't spend much time on the performance part of my career. I do spend time with the record company, in production, and administration. Luckily, I have a partner who's a crazy workaholic that runs the company. It's grown so much now that there are thirty people working at GRP Records in New York. I

192

moved from there a little over a year ago. I just couldn't live in New York anymore, so I've moved to New Mexico, and it means that I do a lot of commuting, but it's still better than living in the middle of that city.

Q: One of your best known movie scores is for the film "On Golden Pond." How long did it take you to complete the score, and how were you involved in the actual recording of the music?

Dave: This was nominated for an Academy Award, but besides the nomination, the thing I remember most about "Golden Pond" is the fact that the film was a special film for music, because it had a lot of space in it, and a lot of need for a certain kind of ambience in the music. This is very rare. I have never worked on another film that had that kind of opportunity. The score has a lot of space in it as well, and usually there's not time in each segment of music to take that kind of time. It was a pleasure to work on. I don't know that that's my favorite picture, but in terms of my working experience, it's probably my best one, the one that I had the most fun with and that was the most satisfying. I must have spent six weeks on the picture. Prior to that I had gone to location and had a couple of talks with the director. I think we recorded it over a period of three days. The first day, I just did the piano part. I went in with the picture and had the picture streamered and marked and organized, and played only the piano part to the picture. Then the second two days we brought the orchestra in, and we played on other tracks to those same cues. It was great. One of the best parts of the experience was that the director loved everything from the beginning, and continued to love it until the film was released, which is rare. I met the Fondas on location. Jane actually had control over the music, because her company was the producer of the film, but she didn't surface in that phase of the film at all.

Q: On the television series, "St. Elsewhere," you are credited with the musical theme for the show. Are you also responsible for any of the music for the continuing weekly segments?

Dave: I only did the first show, and the theme. A fellow named J. A. C. Redford, to my knowledge, did all of the segments of the show, a really talented kid who's now blossoming and doing a lot of nice projects. I loved what he did, because he took the kind of generic quality of the titles of the theme and we extracted the first cues. He used that for over four years. We talk occasionally, and it's a very nice experience for me to have somebody dealing with my material in that way, in a way that I would have loved to do it myself.

Q: What is the difference in writing for a movie and writing for a television series? Do either have specific restrictions for a composer?

Dave: Mostly, it's in terms of time. Television is a voracious medium that leaves no time for anything. With film, at least you have a little breathing room. Most of the time you have six weeks. You're supposed to have ten weeks, but I don't think I ever have had that much time. But in television, if you're doing a series, and it's a show that's on every week, that's what your life is, because you only have the film long enough to barely get it done and get it copied and performed.

Q: How did you become involved with composing/scoring for movies and television?

Dave: I became involved with film television and movie through live television. I was working for a singer named Andy Williams. I had a band and was music director for a show he did in the early sixties at NBC. It was a television variety show. The producer of that show branched out and had a couple of other film shows going at Screen Gems. He asked me if I'd be interested in doing them. It was an opportunity to get into the film medium. I also did some bad sit-coms for a couple of years, but as I said before, my whole life has been a workshop, so I don't think anything is ever lost. There's never anything wasted there.

Q: Are you on any particular schedule of composing and if so, how many projects are you involved in during the same time period?

Dave: In composing, I try to do one thing at a time. otherwise I find it hard for my own sense of concentration. If I'm desperately trying to come up with a theme for one project, the idea of trying to come up with a theme for something else is horrendous. I try not to do that. A couple of times I've had to double up, but never on purpose. Sometimes I'll be on a picture that will go overtime. They'll make changes and I'll need to do some additional work, and I will have already started a new project, so I'll have to go back and do a little bit of double duty. I don't mind doing that, but the idea of trying to create two things at once is tough.

Q: On your personal goals, do you plan to continue both facets (composing/performing) indefinitely, and if not, which will you give up to continue the other?

Dave: I'm sure I would give up performing. I don't know that I would ever give up composing. If you write music, that's what you do and almost who you are.

Q: How do you spend your leisure time? Do you have any favorite hobbies or activities? Are you involved in anything outside of music?

Dave: I'm involved with alot of things. I love sports, specifically skiing and tennis. And, having grown up in Colorado, just getting back in the mountains is great. Probably my favorite sport is fly fishing. If I could ever figure out a way to make a living fly fishing, I would be doing that. I just think it's the best thing.

CHAPTER 15

Women in Jazz

Women in jazz have made valuable contributions to its development through the eras, even as far back as its African roots. Today, in large part due to music programs both in high schools and colleges throughout the country, women are playing a very active role. Women are singers and instrumentalists with jazz bands. The area of jazz in which there seems to be rather limited female activity is that of composition and arranging. Exceptions in this area include bandleader, pianist, composer/arranger Toshiko Akiyoshi, from Japan, who, along with her saxophonist husband, Lew Tabackin, have been favorites among audiences in this country and Japan for several years. Her published band arrangements have become standard literature with school jazz bands.

Lew Tabackin (left) and Toshiko Akiyoshi, bandleaders (Courtesy: Thomas Cassidy, Artist Management).

"The problem with women jazz musicians is that they simply cannot make the music swing." So stated a leading authority on jazz a number of years ago. That concept has not changed appreciably in recent years. Although strides have been made to disprove that statement, women are still a minority in the professional world of jazz. "They have been used out of necessity, to add a bit of charm and glamour to an otherwise unattractive body of persons in the beings of the jazz musician with wrinkled and unkempt attire and general slovenly appearance, and little or no personal pride in grooming." That, too, is an ill-conceived generalization. Society has often stereotyped the jazz musicians as anything but a stalwart citizen. The lifestyle was seen as one with alcohol, drugs, and tobacco. The musician had few roots and no direction in life other than playing jazz in some hovel called a nightclub. Both these views are erroneous.

The purpose of this chapter is to recognize the accomplishments of some of these women. Exploration into the lives of individual personalities can serve as inspiration and provide lessons for greater equality of opportunity for all in jazz.

Historically, women in the African tribes played an active role in tribal music. While men played the percussion instruments, the women adeptly performed on the kalimba, also known as the thumb piano. This instrument was constructed in a box-like fashion similar to the guitar, with a tone hole over which was placed a series of springs which were plucked with the fingers. Small in size ($6'' \times 10''$ to $8'' \times 10''$) it projected the sound quite well over the playing of the drums. The flutes and lutes were also played by women. Women were largely responsible for singing the songs of the tribe. The voice ranges of the women gave them much better projection than the men. In a time without sound reinforcement, effective projection was a necessity.

During the era of slavery and the work song, the woman's voice again was essential to make the songs heard above the instrumental accompaniments. It may be the quality of the female voice and the projection ability that made it a popular addition to the evolution of jazz. In early jazz, following the abolition of slavery, women were involved in minstrel shows as singers with emphasis on songs of the blues. Bessie Smith was a member of a minstrel troupe prior to becoming a solo singer and recording artist. Gertrude "Ma" Rainey was the first woman bandleader of any renown. Married to "Pa" Rainey, she was a singer in his band prior to forming her own Georgia Jazz Band, although in this capacity, she was a singer/leader and not an instrumentalist.

Of the women instrumentalists, Lillian Hardin (later to become Mrs. Louis Armstrong) was a pianist in a New York City music store. Her assignment was to play sheet music for customers who wanted to hear the piano arrangement prior to deciding whether or not to purchase it. (George Gershwin had a similar job many years later in a music store in the same city.) It was while she held this job that Louis Armstrong, then a member of the "King" Oliver band, was in New York and visited the music store where he met Ms. Hardin. Their friendship culminated in marriage. She so impressed Oliver with her musical ability that he hired her as the pianist with his band. She later became the pianist with several other Dixieland bands, including Armstrong's Hot Five and Hot Seven. Of her many compositions, the best known is "Struttin' With Some Barbecue." Louis claimed authorship of it and had his name placed on the music as the composer. Following their divorce many years later, she successfully sued Louis for title as the songwriter, and was paid a large amount of back royalties. Today, her name justly appears as the song's composer. It has become one of the classic standards of Dixieland music.

While Lil Hardin was very popular performing with an all-male band, a number of women were involved as members and featured soloists with all-female bands. Their territory was primarily as featured attractions on the Keith and Orpheum circuits during vaudeville. These bands appeared in shows as accompaniment for singers and dancers as well as having their own special places on the program. Women jazz instrumentalists, as well as singers, were to be found in the casts of Florenz Ziegfield's annual Follies and George White's Scandals. Both men changed stage shows each year during the twenties, featuring new acts and individuals. Drummer/entertainer Ann Pennington was an excellent musician and appeared in the Ziegfield Follies of 1924, during which she was rated as one of the highest paid stars in all of entertainment.

Anna Mae Winburn and the Sweethearts of Rhythm

In a boarding school for underprivileged black girls in Mississippi, 20 miles from the nearest community, an excellent music program developed. The school was Piney Woods and was funded by wealthy Iowans. Out of this program came an all girls' jazz band patterned after the Ina Rae Hutton all girl band. A young lady, Anna Mae Winburn from Omaha, Nebraska, was hired to front the band. She was attractive, with a fine singing voice as well as an outstanding stage personality. These characteristics contributed to the popularity of the band itself and the young women began their careers by playing for black audiences in nearby cities. As their fame spread, the Frederich Brothers Booking Agency picked them up and booked them on USO (United Service Organization) tours in Germany playing for black troops in World War II. The band also made appearances at the Savoy Ballroom in New York, The Apollo Theater in Washington, DC, The Regal Theater in Chicago, and the Royal Theater in Baltimore. They shared billing with such musical greats as Ella Fitzgerald, Fletcher Henderson, and Erskine Hawkins. Eddie Durham, noted arranger for the "Count" Basie band, wrote arrangements for his group. As the band began losing some of the original members, young women of various nationalities became members. The band became Anna Mae Winburn and the International Sweethearts.

Other female instrumentalists who were popular during the Twenties deserve mention. Bess Vance, drummer, played with Harry Waiman's Debutantes on the Orpheum Circuit. Gene Peterson, saxophonist/xylophonist also nicknamed the "musical doll," appeared with her group at the Bamboo Inn in Indianapolis. Ms. Percy Nolan, a dance band drummer with the Burch orchestra, played the territory in and around Seattle. Elsie Perry was the drummer/leader/manager of the Ladies' Nonpareil Orchestra in Circleville, New York. She was also the secretary of local 819 of the Musicians' Union, a position normally held by a man. Peggy Steele played the vaudeville circuits with Grace Simpson's Melody Girls and then became the leader of her own band, called the Mayflower band, which headquartered in New Haven, Connecticut. Mary Zoller, a vibraphonist, was one of the first instrumentalists to popularize the instrument with which Lionel Hampton became famous. She appeared in vaudeville shows as a soloist, and then moved to live radio, thereby gaining fame for both herself and her instrument, which was rapidly replacing the xylophone in jazz. Mitzi Bush was possibly the most famous of the female instrumentalists appearing in vaudeville. Rated on a par with the finest male drummers, she was the featured soloist with the Parisiene Redheads, the first female band to secure a recording contract on the Brunswick label. She then toured the Keith circuit as the featured member of the Bobbie Brice all-female band, called the "Brick-Tops." Sade Ruthe Rams, a drummer with Count Bernie Vici's Symphonic Girls, was a featured attraction on both the Orpheum and Keith vaudeville circuits. Drum manufacturer William F. Ludwig recounts a meeting with Ms. Rams when she visited his factory: Mr. Ludwig subsequently gave this advice to all drummers. "Drummers, if you are not well-versed in the rudiments, talk about the weather." He stated that she was one of the best lady drummers he had ever heard.

While there were a large number of all-female bands appearing throughout the vaudeville circuits, when that era came to an end, it also marked the sudden decline of women instrumentalists. There were several all-female bands that were quite prominent during the big band era, but the number was small compared to the vast number of male bands playing throughout the country. Ina Rae Hutton led a very fine all-female band for a number of years during the era. She later changed her format and made it an all-male band. Phil Spitalny toured extensively with an excellent all-female band that also appeared in movies. The band was rated as good as most all-male bands. The Hormel Meat Packing Company formed an all-female band during the late forties and put it on the road performing at business meetings, corporation activities, and promotional events. The band, however, was short-lived even though it had outstanding musicians.

Daily life was not easy. Why would women want to endure the torturous regimen of life on the road? In many cases, it meant doing a series of one-nighters across the country traveling in aging busses under horrible conditions. Being harassed both sexually and professionally by men in both the bands and the audience certainly could not have been conducive to first-rate performances. Some of the women singers that traveled with the big bands eliminated the harassment by marrying a member of the band. This posed problems when one or the other of the partners wanted to take up employment with another band. This situation would often lead to a breakup in a marriage or the retirement of one of the parties involved.

Today, Ada Cavallo is without doubt the foremost female leader of a name band. Appointed to the leadership in 1988 of the Xavier Cugat orchestra by Cugat himself, she along with pianist/husband Bob Kasha, has maintained the quality of the group with continued success. Its music is what Cugat termed "Musica Latina" which can simply be described as presenting the music of South America to the American public.

A native of the Dominican Republic, her full name is Adelfa Cristiana Genara Schavarria Cavallo. Her father was a music teacher at the Conservatory of Music in Santo Domingo where Ada studied voice and piano. Upon arrival in the United States she continued her studies at the Peabody Institute, hoping for a career in opera. While living in Washington DC, she broke into the world of popular music as a singer, working in small clubs with quartets, and began developing "an act." MCA gave her a five year contract and sent her to Las Vegas to appear in the lounge at the Tropicana. Further work with small groups in the New York area included gigs at the major hotels (Statler-Hilton chain, Copacabana, Waldorf-Astoria) during which time she met, worked with, and married pianist Bob Kasha (who was to become the vice president of the Willard Alexander Booking Agency). Her one woman show was included in performances with Bob Hope, Henny Youngman, and Jackie Mason.

Ada Cavallo, Leader, The New Xavier Cugat Orchestra. (Photo courtesy: ACK Enterprises).

Upon taking over the leadership of the Cugat orchestra, she devoted all her energies and efforts into that vein. The orchestra continues to have a full schedule of bookings throughout the country and has recently produced its first CD titled "Ada Cavallo And The New Xavier Cugat Orchestra - Get Hot Hot Hot."

In many cases, women appear as solo performers or with a small combo in an intimate nightclub setting. Two of the finest in the professional music world are pianists Marian McPartland and Ellen Rucker. McPartland, a native of England, is the former wife of Austin High Gang trumpeter Jimmy McPartland. The two met when he was stationed in England with an army band during World War II. Following the war, she moved to the United States and has gained an enviable reputation as one of the finest jazz pianists in the country.

One of the more exciting big bands in the nation is an all-female band in the Los Angeles area called Maiden Voyage, led by saxophonist Ann Patterson. While it is considered a rehearsal/kicks type band, it has made appearances as a feature on "The Tonight Show," and presents concerts in the Los Angeles area. Comprised of excellent musicians, the band generates true musical excitement when it performs. As jazz critics would state, "it swings."

However, through the eras of jazz and through the years of its development and eventual change, the prime role of women in jazz has been as vocalists. Song stylists such as Judy Garland, Lena Horne, Ethel Merman, Mary Martin, Barbra Streisand, Whitney Houston, Aretha Franklin, Diane Schur, Liza Minelli, Dionne Warwick, and Tina Turner did not have to endure the tortures of road travel with male bands. Credit must be given to those women who paid their dues as the big band vocalists, many of whom are still very active performers. Others have either retired completely from music or redirected their careers into other professions. All have made a definite contribution to the development of jazz. The blues singers performing on the old T. O. B. A. circuit including: Bessie Smith, Mamie Smith, Ma Rainey, Ida Cox and Sippie Wallace had all retired or died prior to the big band era. The late Alberta Hunter, the last of these singers, retired and in the late seventies made a brief but rather successful comeback.

Marian McPartland, pianist (Courtesy: ASCAP).

Ralph Levy, saxophonist with the Gene Krupa band when Anita O'Day was the band's vocalist, was asked what made her such a fine singer. He stated, "Anita had and still has the qualities necessary to make a tune swing. She had a great ear, a superb sense of time, and the creative mind with which to improvise. This, plus a style that was unique, captivated the listener. Her vocals made the band swing even harder. She was an asset to both the band and the era."

Professional musicians rate Ella Fitzgerald as the finest jazz singer in history. She was the vocalist with the Chick Webb orchestra and for a time, following his death, was its leader. Her improvisational skills set the standard for singers in the be-bop era. Her voice became an instrument, phrasing the riffs with the winds. She is still very active in jazz circles. Sarah Vaughn, Pearl Bailey, Keeley Smith, and Peggy Lee, although not affiliated with a specific band, made notable contributions to the development of vocal jazz.

Others who were renowned vocalists with bands were: Doris Day, Helen Forrest, Dinah Washington, Ivie Anderson, Dinah Shore, June Christy, Chris Connor, Pat Suzuki, Jackie Cain, Margaret Whiting, Paula Kelly, Kitty Kallen, Edythe Wright, Connie Haynes, Martha Tilton, Helen O'Connell, Helen Humes, Jo Stafford, Rosemary Clooney, and Billie Holiday.

Billie Holiday, also nicknamed "Lady Day" by saxophonist Lester Young, was one of the finest singers in all of jazz. A play entitled "Lady Day" and the movie "Lady Sings the Blues" recognizes her talent and tribulations. Her career ended much too soon due to an addiction to drugs. She was, for a brief time, the female vocalist with the Count Basie band. Unfortunately, lack of personal discipline and drug addiction was not tolerated by Basie. She was fired from the band and began a series of solo engagements throughout the country, including a number of record dates, the results of which have become classics in the eyes of record collectors.

Maiden Voyage, Ann Patterson, director (Courtesy: David Shaner Collection).

Singer Anita O'Day (Courtesy: David Shaner Collection).

Billie Holiday (Courtesy of the Institute of Jazz Studies, Rutgers University).

The women in jazz are here to stay. They have made valuable contributions in all forms of jazz. The last area of participation for women has been in instrumental music. Perhaps the most significant reason for this acceptance is due to the participation of women in the school jazz programs. Men and women playing in bands alongside each other are developing equality.

Today, both men and women are studying and playing jazz in schools throughout the country. This assures that women will be an integral part of the total jazz picture, both as vocalists and instrumentalists. The women listed here set the stage for others of their gender to be accepted, recognized, and praised for their contributions. Well-schooled, diligent individuals, they have made very positive marks in the field of jazz.

Coda

A coda is a form of tag ending, giving the music listener a feeling of finality. Many writers make the statement that 'jazz is alive and well'. This may be true but with certain reservations. Rudi Blesh, in his book, *They All Played Ragtime,* alludes to the fact that ragtime is here to stay. To you the reader, let me ask, "How often do you hear pure ragtime played on the radio?" Several years ago, a music equipment manufacturer (music stands, brass instrument mutes, portable stages) distributed bumper stickers which read, "Big Bands are Back". This is wishful thinking. The only place big bands are to be found in abundance are in schools—high schools and colleges, where the music education program includes jazz/stage bands. Even at that, many schools do not use the word jazz because of the connotation of the word, but rather call their bands, stage bands or swing bands. Dixieland has had the most notable success of enduring. Radio stations have been subjected to 'go with the flow' and at this writing, rock in one form or another, and country music are dominant. While there are some 'pure jazz' stations on the air, they are the exception. Also in the minority are jazz producers such as Dick Gibson of Denver who produces jazz concerts, featuring the finest jazz artists to come out of the eras of big bands and bop. His annual 'jazz party' held over the Labor Day weekend is a sellout. It provides attendees from the entire country, Europe, and the Far East an opportunity to hear the very best instrumentalists and vocalists. Other recognized jazz efforts that keep the music alive and shape its destiny and that of performers include the annual Newport (Rhode Island) Jazz Festival coordinated by George Wein, and Kool Cigarettes' sponsorship of jazz festivals/concerts in a number of locations across the country. Whether the development of jazz ended in the mid-50s is debatable. You the reader must judge for yourself.

Where will jazz go in the decades to come? I ask this question of the students in my classes at the end of each semester. The answers are a veritable mixture of personal likes and attitudes. Some feel it will return to a pure jazz form with no frills. Others feel it will continue on an experimental course with emphasis on electronics. The majority want to see something new and exciting take place. They feel that what happened in the past and what is taking place at present are a foundation for things to come in the future. All agree that society will dictate the musical needs and preferences of the future.

Yet, society has its moments of nostalgia. We tend to lean toward the music we were exposed to during our formative years. Our musical heroes are those to whom we listened and idolized. Whether we listened to jazz in a theater, an intimate club, or at a rock concert attended by tens of thousands, the choice is ours, and we need not defend our choice to anyone.

Bibliography

The individual seeking further reading on a selected period of jazz or a jazz personality is urged to pursue that interest by beginning with the books on this list.

Baxter, Derrick-Steward. *Ma Rainey and the Classic Blues Singers.* New York, New York: Stein and Day, 1970.

Belz, Carl. *The Story of Rock.* New York, New York: Oxford University Press, 1972.

Blassingame, John W. *Black New Orleans,* 1860–1880. Chicago, Illinois: University of Chicago Press, 1973.

Blesh, Rudi. *Shining Trumpets, A History of Jazz.* New York, New York: Alfred Knopf, 1958.

Blesh, Rudi and Janis, Harriet. *They All Played Ragtime.* New York, New York: Oak Publications, 1966.

Brown, Charles T. *The Art of Rock and Roll.* Englewood Cliffs, New Jersey: Prentice-Hall, 1983.

Buerkle, Jack V. and Barker, Danny. *Bourbon Street Black.* New York, New York: Oxford University Press, 1973.

Case, Brian and Britt, Stann. *The Illustrated Encyclopedia of Jazz.* New York, New York: Crown Publishers, Inc., 1978.

Coker, Jerry. *Listening to Jazz.* Englewood Cliffs, New Jersey: Prentice-Hall, 1978.

Collier, James L. *The Making of Jazz, A Comprehensive History.* New York, New York: Dell Publishing, 1978.

Dexter, Dave, Jr. *The Jazz Story From The '90s to The '60s.* Englewood Cliffs, New Jersey: Prentice-Hall, 1964.

Ellington, Edward K. "Duke". *Music Is My Mistress.* Garden City, New York: Doubleday, 1973.

Feather, Leonard. *The Pleasures of Jazz.* New York, New York: Dell Publishing, 1976.

Gleason, Ralph J. *Celebrating the Duke and Louis, Bessie, Billie, Bird, Carmen, Miles, Dizzy, and Other Heroes.* New York, New York: Dell Publishing, 1975.

Gridley, Mark C. *Jazz Styles.* Englewood Cliffs, New Jersey: Prentice-Hall, 1978.

Hamm, Charles. *Yesterdays, Popular Song in America.* New York, New York: W. W. Norton & Co., 1975.

Handy, William C. *Father of the Blues.* New York, New York: Macmillan Co., 1941.

Heilbut, Tony. *The Gospel Sound: Good News and Bad Times.* Garden City, New York: Anchor Books, Doubleday, 1975.

Jaffe, Andrew. *Jazz Theory.* Dubuque, Iowa: Wm. C. Brown Publishers, 1983.

Kaufman, Frederick and Gukin, John P. *African Roots of Jazz.* New York, New York: Alfred Publishing, 1979.

Kingman, Daniel. *American Music: A Panorama.* New York, New York: Schirmer Books, 1979.

Kmen, Henry A. *Music in New Orleans: The Formative Years,* 1791–1841. Baton Rouge, Louisiana: Louisiana State University Press, 1966.

Lombardo, Guy and Altshul, Jack. *Auld Aquaintance.* Garden City, New York: Doubleday, 1975.

Merriam, Alan P. *A Bibliography of Jazz.* New York, New York: Da Capo Press, 1970.

Meyer, Hazel. *The Gold in Tin Pan Alley.* New York, New York: Greenwood Press, 1977.

Morgenstern, Don. *Jazz People.* New York, New York: Harry N. Abrams, Inc., 1976.

Nanry, Charles. *American Music: From Storyville to Woodstock.* New Brunswick, New Jersey: Transaction Books, Rutgers University, 1972.

Nanry, Charles. *The Jazz Text.* New York, New York: D. Van Nostrand Co., 1979.

Ostransky, Leroy. *Jazz City.* Englewood Cliffs, New Jersey: Prentice-Hall, 1978.

Ostransky, Leroy. *Understanding Jazz.* Englewood Cliffs, New Jersey, Prentice-Hall, 1977.

Robinette, Richard. *Historical Perspectives in Popular Music.* Dubuque, Iowa: Kendall/Hunt Publishing Company, 1980.

Russell, Ross. *Bird Lives: The High Life and Hard Times of Charlie Parker.* New York, New York: Charterhouse, 1973.

Shaw, Ghita M. *The Rockin' 50's.* New York, New York: Hawthorn Books, 1978.

Shuller, Gunther. *Early Jazz: Its Roots and Musical Development.* New York, New York: Oxford University Press, 1968.

Simon, George T. *The Big Bands.* New York, New York: Macmillan Co., 1967.

Southern, Eileen. *The Music of Black Americans.* New York, New York: W. W. Norton & Co., 1971.

Stearns, Marshall W. *The Story of Jazz.* New York, New York: Oxford University Press, 1973.

Tanner, Paul O. W. and Gerow, Maurice. *A Study of Jazz.* Dubuque, Iowa: Wm. C. Brown Publishers, 1981.

Tirro, Frank. *Jazz, A History.* New York, New York: W. W. Norton & Co., 1977.

Tobler, John and Frame, Peter. *Rock N' Roll, The First 25 Years.* New York, New York: Exeter Books, 1980.

Walker, Leo. *The Wonderful Era of the Great Dance Bands.* Berkeley, California: Howell-North Books, 1964.

Williams, Martin. *The Jazz Tradition.* New York, New York: Oxford University Press, 1970.

Discography: Part A

Suggested recordings for additional listening:

Akiyoshi, Toshiko-Tabackin, Lew, Big Band—Insights, RCA–AFL–1–2678.
Armstrong, Louis Louis Armstrong and His Hot Five, Columbia CL 852.
Armstrong, Louis West End Blues, Columbia G 30416.
Armstrong, Louis The Armstrong Saga, Harmony Records—KH 31326.
Armstrong, Louis Hello Dolly, MCA–538.
Basie, Count Basie Plays Hefti, Emus ES 12003.
Basie, Count Basie's Best. Olympic 7121.
Basie, Count Hollywood . . . Basie's Way, Command RS–912–SD.
Basie, Count On the Road, Pablo D–2313112.
Basie, Count The Best of Count Basie, MCA Records MCA2–4050.
Basie, Count Super Chief, Columbia Records, #G31224.
Basie, Count Paradise Squat, 2-volume set. Verve, #VE22542.
Bechet, Sidney Blue Horizon, Blue Note BSP 81201.
Bechet, Sidney Superb Sidney, CBS 62636.
Brubeck, Dave Newport 1958, Columbia CL 1249.
Brubeck, Dave Time Out, Columbia CS 8192.
Brubeck, Dave Quartet at Carnegie Hall, Columbia Records, #C2S826, 2-volume set.
Brubeck, Dave Adventures in Time, 2-volume set, Columbia Records, #G30625.
Burton, Gary Dreams So Real, ECM–1–1072.
Byrd, Charlie Sugar Loaf Suite, Concord Jazz, #CJP114.
Cole, Richie with Phil Woods: Side by Side, Muse Records, #MR5237.
Cole, Richie with Eddie Jefferson: Hollywood Madness, Muse Records, #MR5207.
Coleman, Ornette The Best of Ornette Coleman, Atlantic 3D 1317.
Coltrane, John The Gentle Side of John Coltrane, ABC Records ASH–9306–2.
Corea, Chick Light as a Feather, Polydor PD 5525.
Complete Birth of the Cool, Capitol Records, M 2310–742.
Condon, Eddie The Liederkranz Sessions, Commodore Records, #XFL15355.
Davis, Miles Birth of the Cool, Capitol M–11026.
Davis, Miles Miles to Go, Columbia GS 8163.
Davis, Miles King of Blue, Columbia CL–1355.
Davis, Miles Bitches' Brew, Columbia, 2-volume set, #GP26.
Davis, Miles Nefertiti, Columbia #CL2794.
Desmond, Paul Paul Desmond and the Modern Jazz Quartet, Finesse Records, #FW37487.
Dorsey, Tommy The Best of Tommy Dorsey, RCA Records ANL1–1087– e.
Dorsey, Tommy A Man and His Trombone, Coplix Records SCP– 498.
Dorsey, Tommy Sinatra, Frank, Joker Productions SM 3878
Ellington, Duke Festival Session, Columbia P 13500.
Ellington, Duke Pure Gold, RCA ANL–1–2811.

Ellington, Duke The Immortal Duke Ellington, Hall of Fame Jazz Greats, JG 625.

Ellington, Duke This is Ellington, RCA LPM–1715.

Ellington, Duke Up in Duke's Workshop: Duke Ellington and his Orchestra, Pablo 2310815.

Ellington, Duke Duke Ellington's 70th Birthday Concert, Solid State Records, a 2-record set, #SS19000.

Ellington, Duke & Johnny Hodges Blues Summit, a 2-volume set, Verve, #2V6S8822.

Ellis, Herb, Pass, Joe, Brown, Ray, and Hanna, Jake: Reserved Seating, Concord Jazz, #CJS1.

Ellis, Don Connection, #KC31766.

Fitzgerald, Ella Ella at Duke's Place, Verve UMJ–3286.

Fitzgerald, Ella Jazz at the Philharmonic, Verve 815 147 1.

Fitzgerald, Ella Carnegie Hall, 1973, Newport Jazz Festival, Columbia Records, #KG32557.

Fitzgerald, Ella Fitzgerald Sings the Cole Porter Songbook, 2-volume set, Verve Records, #VE2–2511.

Fitzgerald, Ella Ella and Louis: Ella Fitzgerald and Louis Armstrong, Verve Records, 2-volume set, 2–V6S8811.

Fountain, Pete A Taste of Honey, Coral Records, #CRL757486.

Franklin Mint Record Society Big Band Era, Greatest Recordings, 50 Volumes.

Gershwin, George George Gershwin Plays Rhapsody in Blue. Everest Records X–914.

Gillespie, Dizzy Dizzy Gillespie: The Small Groups: 1945–1946 Phoenix LP–2.

Gillespie, Dizzy, Parker, C. "Takin' Off", Jazz Greats JG–620.

Gillespie, Dizzy Dizzie Gillespie Plays and Raps in his Greatest Concert 2-volume set. Pablo, #D2620116.

Goodman, Benny Big Band 1936–1939, Joker Productions SM–3870.

Goodman, Benny Benny in Brussels, Vol. 1, Columbia P 13502.

Goodman, Benny Hits of Benny Goodman, Capitol T–1514.

Grusin, Dave Mountain Dance, Arista/GRP 5010.

Haley, Bill Rock Around the Clock, Decca DL–8225.

Hampton, Lionel The Complete Lionel Hampton, French RCA 731.048.

Hampton, Lionel Vilver Vibes, Columbia CL–1486.

Hampton, Lionel The Blues Ain't News to Me, 2-volume set, Verve Records, #VE2–2543.

Henderson, Fletcher The Complete Fletcher Henderson, Bluebird AXM2–5507.

Henderson, Fletcher Fletcher Henderson and His Orchestra, Columbia C4L 19.

Herman, Woody Light My Fire, Cadet 819.

Herman, Woody Woody Herman, Everest Records FS–281.

Herman, Woody Woody Herman at Carnegie Hall, Lion L–70059.

Herman, Woody Woody's Gold Star, Concord Records, CJ–330.

Herman, Woody Feelin' So Blue, Fantasy Records, #F9609.

Herman, Woody Live at Monterey, Atlantic Records, #790044–1.

Hines, Earl "Fatha" Earl Fatha Hines & His All Stars, Cresdeno GNPS–9042.

Holiday, Billie Strange Fruit, Atlantic #SD16140598.

Jackson, Mahalia I Believe, Pickwick SPC–3510.

Jackson, Milt Plenty of Soul, Atlantic Records, #SD8811.

James, Harry Mr. Trumpet and His Band, Pickwick PC 3006.

James, Harry The Shadow of Your Smile, Pickwick SPC–3K26.

Jefferson, Lemon Early Blues, Olympic 7134.

Johnson, James P. All Original, Columbia CL 1780.

Joplin, Scott The World of Scott Joplin, Biograph BLP 10060.

Kenton, Stan Adventures in Jazz, Capitol T–1796.

Kenton, Stan Artistry in Rhythm, Capitol T–167.

Kenton, Stan Hits in Concert, Creative World ST–1074.

Kenton, Stan Kenton '76, Creative World ST–1076.

Kenton, Stan The Romantic Approach, Creative World ST–1017.

Krupa, Gene Gene Krupa and His Orchestra, Columbia C2L 29.

Leadbetter, Huddie The Legendary Leadbelly, Olympic 7103.

Lewis, Ramsey The Best of Ramsey Lewis, Cadet LPS 839.

Lombardo, Guy A Legendary Performer, RCA CPL1–2047.

McPartland, J. and Barbarin, P. Dixieland Now and Then, Hall of Fame JG 621.

McPartland, Marion At The Hickory House, Capitol T–574.

McShann, Jay The Big Apple Bash, Atlantic Recording Corp., #90047–1.

Miller, Glenn Parade of Hits, Camden ACL–7009.

Mingus, Charles Stormy Weather, Impulse AS–9234–2.

Monk, Thelonious Live at the Jazz Workshop, Blue Note 1510.

Monk, Thelonious Piano Solos, Everest Records, FS336.

Monk, Thelonious Something in Blue, Black Lion Records, BL 152.

Modern Jazz Quartette At Music Inn, Atlantic 1299.

Modern Jazz Quartette More From The Last Concert, Atlantic Records, #SD8806.

Modern Jazz Quartette Modern Jazz Quartette at Music Inn with Jimmy Giuffre, Atlantic Records, #90049–1.

Morton, Jelly Roll Jelly Roll Morton 1938–1940, Almac Records QSR–2424.

Morton, Jelly Roll Stomps and Joys "Red Hot Peppers", RCA LPM 1649.

Norvo, Red & Ross Tompkins Red and Ross, Concord Jazz, #CJ90.

O'Day, Anita SS' Wonderful, Emily Records, AR 92685.

Oliver, King The King Oliver Jazz Band 1923, Olympic 7133.

Ory, K., and Noone, J. New Orleans Jazz, Olympic 7109.

Parker, Charlie Bird Encores, Vol. 2, Savoy MGV 12009.

Parker, Charlie Charlie Parker, Vol. 2, Everest Records FS–232.

Parker, Charlie Charlie "Bird" Parker Performs Historical Masterpieces, Charlie Parker Record Corp. #PLP701.

Parker, Charlies The Verve Years, 1950–51, 2-record set, #VE22512.

Peterson, Oscar Oscar Peterson and Harry Edison, Pablo Records #2310.741.

Presley, Elvis Elis, RCA Victor LPM–1382.

Rich, Buddy Big Swing Face Pacific Jazz Records LN–10090.

Rich, Buddy Swingin' New Big Band Pacific Jazz-Liberty Records, PJ–10113.

Rodney, Red Red Rodney Returns, Argo LP–643.

Schuller, Gunther Footlifters, Columbia M 33513.

Shaw, Artie Black Magic, MCA Coral CB–20035.

Smith, Bessie The Bessie Smith Story, Vol. 4, Columbia CL 858.

Smith, Bessie The World's Greatest Blues Singer, Columbia GP 33.

Smith, Willie Willie "The Lion" Smith: The Original 14 plus 2, Commodore Records, #XFL15775.

Smithsonian Collection of Classic Jazz, Smithsonian Institution.

Sutton, Ralph Piano Solos, Sackville 2012.

Sutton, Ralph, Stacy, Jess Stacy 'N' Sutton, Affinity Records AFS 1020.

Sutton, Ralph The Last of the Whorehouse Piano Players: Ralph Sutton and Jay McShann, Vol. 1 & 2, Chaz Jazz Records, Inc. #CJ103, #CJ104.

Sutton, Ralph and Eddie Miller We've Got Rhythm, Live at Hanrattie's, Chaz Jazz Records, Inc. #CJ110.

Sutton, Ralph Ralph Sutton and the Jazz Band, Chaz Jazz Records, Inc. #CJ113.

Sutton, Ralph and Peanuts Hucko The Big Noise from Winnetka, Chaz Jazz Records, Inc. CJ#112.

Striesand, Barbra The Broadway Album, Columbia OC 40092.

Tatum, Art Art Tatum Masterpieces, Pablo Records, #2310775.

Taylor, Billy Life at Storeyville, West 54, #WLW8008.

Teagarden, Jack Trombone 'T' from Texas, Afinity Records AFS 1015.

Terry, Clark Ain't Misbehavin', Pablo Records, #2312–105.

Various Artists America's Musical Roots, Festival FR 1008.

Various Artists . . . and Then We Wrote . . . American Composers and Lyricists Sing, Play, and Conduct Their Own Songs, New World Records NW 272.

Various Artists Brother, Can You Spare A Dime: American Song During the Depression, New World Records NW 270.

Various Artists Come Josephine in My Flying Machine: Inventions and Topics in Popular Song 1910–1929, New World Records NW 233.

Various Artists Jazz Volume 9, Folkways FJ 2809.

Various Artists Maple Leaf Rag: Ragtime in Rural America, New World Records NW 235.

Various Artists Praise the Lord and Pass the Ammunition: Songs of World Wars I and II, New World Records NW 222.

Various Artists Ragtime Piano of the 20's, Folkways RBF 42.

Various Artists Sathchmo Remembered: The Music of Louis Armstrong at Carnegie Hall, Atlantic SD–1671.

Various Artists The History of Jazz, Vol. 1, Capitol T–793.

Various Artists The History of Jazz, Vol. 3, Capitol T–795.

Various Artists The Music Goes Round and Round: The Golden Years of Tin Pan Alley, 1930–1939, New World Records NW 248.

Various Artists The Red Back Book: Early Band Ragtime, Folkways RBF 38.

Various Artists The Roots of Dixieland Jazz, Everest FS–274.

Various Artists The Vintage Irving Berlin, New World Records NW 238.

Various Bands Greatest Recordings of the Big Band Era, Franklin Mint Record Society.

Various Bands Kings of Swing, Pickwick SPC–3281.

Vaughn, Sarah No Count Sarah, Mercury SR–60116.

Vaughn, Sarah The Magic of Sarah Vaughn, Mercury MG–20438.

Waller, "Fats" A Legend in His Lifetime, Trip Records TLX–5042.

Waller, "Fats" The Complete Fats Waller, Bluebird AXM2–5511.

Waller, "Fats" Piano Solos, 2-volume set, Bluebird Records, #AXM25518.

Weather Report Heavy Weather, Columbia PC 34418.

Wilson, Teddy Teddy Wilson, Everest Records FS–263.

Woods, Phil Phil Woods Quartet, Vol. 1, Clean Cuts Jazz, #702.

Discography: Part B

Through the eras of jazz beginning with ragtime and the first recordings of this new music, musicians have been identified with their best known works. In numerous cases, it would be difficult to ascertain just which particular selection either vocal or instrumental is the singular most popular for an individual, particularly since the recording artist might cover a vast span of time during which many recordings were produced, all of which could be considered hits.

Each year, magazines such as Downbeat, Metronome, Playboy, Modern Drummer, would undertake a poll to determine which artist is tops in the field for a particular year. So too, the record industry awards Grammies to the outstanding performing/composing artists.

With this as a format, it was felt that while artists listed in either a category or decade were all prominent performers, it would be of interest to determine which of their recordings or compositions, they are best known.

Using professional musicians, music teachers, and students as a population for a poll, the following recordings (not albums) were found to be those for which the artist is most remembered.

Ragtime:

Eubie Blake	Memories of You, Charleston Rag
Scott Joplin	Maple Leaf Rag
Huddie "Leadbelly" Ledbetter	Eagle Rock Rag
"Jelly Roll" Morton	King Porter Stomp
"Fats" Waller	Ain't Misbehavin'

Dixieland:

Louis Armstrong	Hello Dolly
Bix Beiderbecke	Swinging the Blues
"Wingy" Manone	Tailgate Ramble
"King" Oliver	West End Blues
"Kid" Ory	Muskrat Ramble

Big Bands:

Charlie Barnett	Skyliner
Count Basie	April In Paris
"Bunny" Berigan	I Can't Get Started
Les Brown	Sentimental Journey
Cab Calloway	Minnie the Moocher
Bob Crosby	Big Noise from Winnetka
Jimmy Dorsey	So Rare
Tommy Dorsey	Marie
Duke Ellington	Take the "A" Train

Maynard Ferguson   Gonna Fly Now

Maynard Ferguson	Gonna Fly Now
Benny Goodman	Stompin' at the Savoy
Glen Gray	Sunrise Serenade
Lionel Hampton	Flyin' Home
Fletcher Henderson	Nagasaki
"Woody" Herman	Woodchoppers Ball
Harry James	Ciribiribin
Stan Kenton	Artistry in Rhythm
Gene Krupa	Sing, Sing, Sing
Guy Lombardo	Auld Lang Syne
Glenn Miller	In The Mood
"Buddy" Rich	West Side Story
Artie Shaw	Begin the Beguine
Charlie Spivak	Stardreams
Paul Whiteman	Rhapsody in Blue

Be-Bop/Cool:

Art Blakey	Moanin'
Dave Brubeck	Take Five
John Coltrane	Naima
Miles Davis	'Round Midnight
Erroll Garner	Misty
Stan Getz	Early Autumn
"Dizzy" Gillespie	Night in Tunsia
Howard McGhee	Thermodynamics
Thelonious Monk	'Round Midnight
Wes Montgomery	Bumpin'
Charlie Parker	Ornithology
Oscar Peterson	Just Friends
Django Reinhardt	Crazy Rhythm
George Shearing	September in the Rain
Joe Venuti	After You've Gone

Singers:

Tony Bennett	I Left My Heart In San Francisco
Nat Cole	Unforgettable
"Bing" Crosby	White Christmas
Billy Eckstine	Caravan
Ella Fitzgerald	A Tiskit A Tasket
Judy Garland	Over the Rainbow
Billie Holiday	God Bless the Child
Lena Horne	Stormy Weather
Mahalia Jackson	Amazing Grace
Peggy Lee	Fever
Lizzie Miles	Bill Bailey
Liza Minnelli	New York, New York
Anita O'Day	Let Me Off Uptown
Frank Sinatra	My Way
Bessie Smith	Empty Bed Blues
Mamie Smith	That Thing Called Love

Barbra Streisand	The Way We Were
Jimmy Rushing	Harvard Blues
Mel Torme	The Christmas Song
Sarah Vaughn	Misty
Dinah Washington	What A Difference A Day Makes
Joe Williams	Everyday I Have the Blues

Rock:

50's

Chuck Berry	Johnny B. Goode
"Chubby" Checker	The Twist
Elvis Presley	Hound Dog, Love Me Tender
"Fats" Domino	Blueberry Hill
Bill Haley & the Comets	Rock Around the Clock
"Buddy" Holly	Peggy Sue
Jerry Lee Lewis	Great Balls of Fire
Little Richard	Tutti Fruitti, Good Golly Miss Molly

60's

Beach Boys	Surfin' U. S. A.
Beatles	Hey Jude, Yesterday
Four Tops	I'll Be There
Aretha Franklin	Respect
Grateful Dead	Truckin'
Janis Joplin	Me & Bobby McGee
"Smokey" Robinson	Tears of A Clown
Rolling Stones	Satisfaction
Supremes	Stop in the Name of Love
Temptations	My Girl
The Who	Talking 'bout my Generation

70's

Blood, Sweat & Tears	Spinning Wheel
David Bowie	Major Tom
Chicago	Saturday in the Park
The Doors	Light My Fire
Eagles	Hotel California
Genesis	ABACAB
Led Zeplin	Stairway to Heaven
Pink Floyd	Another Brick in the Wall
Bruce Springsteen	Born in the U. S. A.
Frank Zappa	Valley Girl

80's

Squeeze	Black Coffee in Bed
U-2	Sunday, Bloody Sunday

American Folk Music

Alabama	Mountain Music
Chet Atkins	Certified Guitar Player
Joan Baez	Diamonds and Rust
Glen Campbell	Rhinestone Cowboy
Johnny Cash	I Walk The Line
Patsy Cline	Crazy
Judy Collins	Send in the Clowns
Crystal Gayle	Don't It Make My Brown Eyes Blue
Arlo Guthrie	Alice's Restaurant
Waylon Jennings	Luckenback, Texas
Loretta Lynn	Coal Miner's Daughter
Willie Nelson	On The Road Again
Nitty Gritty Dirt Band	Mr. Bojangles
Oakridge Boys	Elvira
Dolly Parton	Nine to Five
Peter, Paul & Mary	Puff the Magic Dragon
Charlie Pride	Behind Closed Doors
Kenny Rogers	Lady, The Gambler
George Strait	Amarillo by Morning
Hank Williams Sr.	Your Cheatin' Heart
Tammy Wynette	Stand By Your Man

Glossary

Accent: Emphasizing certain notes by playing them louder than others.

Accompaniment: Providing a musical background for a solo instrumentalist/singer.

Accoustical Recording: Early method using large horns/megaphones instead of microphones, into which the instrumentalist/vocalist played/sang to create a disc.

A. F. of M.: American Federation of Musicians, the musicians union.

Afro-Cuban: Style of music with African and Spanish (from Cuba) influences.

Arrangement: The rewritten work of another composer, scored for an instrumental or vocal group.

A. S. C. A. P.: American Society of Composers, Authors, and Publishers. Founded in 1914 to protect the copyrights and performance rights of its members.

Attack: Beginning of a sound by either voice or instrument.

Back Line: Rhythm section of a jazz ensemble, consisting of rhythm instruments—piano, bass, drums, guitar, banjo.

Ballad: Composition characterized by slow tempo, smooth style, and romantic nature.

Bar: A measure of music. Standard blues choruses have a total of 12 bars/measures.

Beat: Pulse of the music.

Be-Bop: Also Bop or Re-Bop. A style of music during the mid 1940's describing a new trend in jazz based upon complex harmonies, riffs, and improvisation. The pioneers were Dizzy Gillespie and Charlie Parker.

Big Band: Expansion of instrumentation to include sections/families of like instruments instead of one of a kind; reed section, brass section.

Big Band Era: Period from 1935 to 1945 during which the big bands and dancing to their music prevailed. Also called; Swing era, and Dance Band era.

Blue Notes: Lowering of the third, fifth, and seventh notes of a diatonic scale.

Blues: Style of folk music originated by the slaves. It has two forms—city blues and rural blues. General themes dealt with sadness and tragedy. Originally eight or 16 bars in length, it was standardized to a 12 measure chorus. The chordal structure evolves around the first, fourth, and fifth chords.

B. M. I.: Broadcast Music, Incorporated. A licensing organization controlling fees for radio-television stations in use of music for broadcasting.

Bomb: Strong accents by the bass drum.

Boogie-Woogie: Steady repetitious figure played by the left hand on the piano, while the right hand plays melodic figures.

Book: The music library of a band.

Break: Point in music where all instruments cease playing for a period of time while the soloist continues.

Bridge: B section of an AABA composition. Usually eight measures in length consisting of a new theme, either in the same key or a related key. Designed to give the composition new life. Also called a release or channel.

Cadenza: Long break in which time/tempo stops while the soloist(s) plays/sings, freely without restriction, specific number of measures or a regulated tempo.

Cakewalk: Dance developed during slavery. A dance contest in which the winning dancers were given prizes. During slavery, the prize was a cake furnished by the slave owner, hence the term cakewalk.

Call and Response: Musical form employing two factions; solo vocalist/instrument sounding the call with a response by the chorus/band. Found in religious services in which the minister sounds the call and the congregation sounds the response.

Carving Contest: Improvisational duel among musicians.

Changes: Chords or chord progressions of a composition.

Charleston: Dance popularized during the Dixieland era.

Chart: Arrangements used by a musical group.

Chicago Style: During Dixieland, the two-beat style which was developed by musicians in Chicago.

Chord: Group of notes sounded at the same time.

Chorus: Complete performance of a tune with all its sections, AABA.

Chromatic: Semitones of a scale; C to C sharp, A to A flat, etc.

Classic Blues: Also city blues. A type of blues utilizing a central theme developed around sexual, racial, or social issues.

Cliches: Frequently played solo passages of short duration.

Coda: Closing section of a composition giving a feeling of total finality.

Combo: Small group (combination) of instruments, usually from three to seven.

Comp: To accompany, as in accompaniment.

Congo Square: Also Place Congo, a park in New Orleans where slaves gathered to sing, dance, and play instruments. Location of early jam sessions.

Cool: Also Cool School. Style of jazz developed in the mid 1950's. Also used as a complimentary term for a jazz musician.

Copyright: Right of a composer, author, or publisher to the exclusive use and control of original material.

Countermelody: Secondary melody accompanying a primary melody.

Counterpoint: Two or more lines of approximately equal importance sounding together.

Country Music: General form of popular music supported at one time by people in the rural South and West. Presently, popular nationwide.

Creole of Color: Originally the French word 'creole' referred to a person of French heritage born outside of France. The name 'Creole of Color' is applied to the offspring of a French father and an African mother.

Cutting Session: Also 'cutting contest', a competitive jam session in which one player attempts to outplay another.

Dixieland Jazz: The sound of bands through the 1920's which had their origin in New Orleans. Primary instruments included, trumpet, clarinet, trombone, banjo, guitar, piano, bass (tuba and string), and drums. The music was based upon the march but was changed through melodic and rhythmic improvisation.

Double Time: To double the original tempo. Double time feel is to have the rhythm section of a band double the tempo (beat) while the remainder of the players play in the original tempo. Sometimes called 'cut time'.

Double Entendre: Two different meanings and applications for the same word. 'Cat' as in a feline animal versus 'cat' as a colloquial term for a musician.

Duet: Two performers playing together, music of equal importance.

Dynamics: Changes in volume from either loud to soft or soft to loud. Also refers to the intensity level of the music.

Eight-to-the-Bar: Phrase used to describe boogie-woogie. The playing of a repetitive figure by the left hand on the piano sounding eight notes in a bar (measure).

Electrical Recording: Method of recording with the use of microphones.

Embouchure: Shaping and holding of the lips to a mouthpiece in order to produce a sound on a wind blown instrument.

Ensemble Out: Last full chorus of a composition/arrangement played by the entire ensemble.

Falsetto: Singing or speaking in a pitch higher than the normal voice range of an individual. The tone quality becomes thin. Similar to yodeling.

Fermata: Pause or holding of a note or chord.

Field Holler: Yell or shout by slaves as they worked in the fields. Sometimes used as a secret/coded means of communication. An early form of vocal music utilizing the bending or raising of notes. Forerunner of the blues.

Fill: Notes by the drummer in areas in the music during which no one else is scheduled to play. Assists in the forward flow of the music.

Flag-Waver: Fast paced, 'flashy' composition/arrangement used at the beginning or ending of a show/act.

Fluff: Mistake, a missed note.

Fours: Alternating or trading of four measure improvisations between solo instruments or sections.

Free Jazz: The playing/singing of jazz that is free of restrictions such as key, meter, predetermined chordal progressions, or precomposed melodic line.

Frontline: Wind instruments positioned forward of other instruments in an ensemble.

Funky: Also Funk. Music that is earthy, lowdown, sexy, and/or bluesy in nature.

Gig: Professional engagement or a job for musicians.

Glissando: Sliding effect between two notes. Can go either up or down.

Growl: Raspy, harsh effect played on wind instruments.

Half-Time: Playing at a tempo of one-half its original speed.

Hard Bop: Continuation of the bop style with faster tempos, harsh phrasing, louder dynamics. A form of rebellion against the 'cool school'.

Head Arrangements: Arrangements memorized by the entire group without the music being written on paper. A practice quite common with bands during the eras of Dixieland, big bands, bop, cool, and rock.

Hi-Hat Cymbals: Two cymbals struck together by a foot pedal mechanism. Traditionally played on the second and fourth beat of a 4/4 bar. Became very popular during the two-beat style.

Horn: Any wind blown instrument.

House Hop: Same as the 'rent party' occurring in large cities, in which tenants hosted a social event involving musicians, a fee was charged to raise money to pay the rent.

Improvisation: Playing extemporaneously.

Intervals: Distance between successive notes in a melody, or notes in a chord. Major, minor, diminished, or augmented, F to A being a major third.

Intonation: Relative precision of pitch.

Jam Session: Informal gathering of musicians for the purpose of developing or honing improvisational skills. Often found as an 'after hours' diversion following a formal gig.

Keynote: Tonic or first note of a key. F is the tonic or keynote in the key of F.

Laid Back: Playing/singing with a relaxed feeling, lazy or slow feeling. Sometimes used to describe performers who play/sing a little behind the beat.

Lay Out: To stop playing/singing while others continue.

Lead Man: Person playing the first part in a section, with the responsibility to see that the rest of the section performs together as a unit. The 'foreman' of a section. The first trumpet player in a trumpet section is called the lead man.

Legato: Playing of notes in a smooth style without interruption or pauses.

Lick: Short phrase or passage.

Master Drummer: Leader of an African drum choir/ensemble.

Measure: Space between vertical bar lines in music.

Minstrel Show: Entertainment developed in the 19th century by white and black performers in blackface depicting plantation life in a comical manner. Precursor to vaudeville.

Modulation: Moving from one key to another. Changing the tonal center.

Mute: Device placed into the bell of a brass instrument to change the quality of sound. May be a cup, harmon, straight, bucket, solotone.

New Orleans Style: Distinguishes between the Dixieland styles of Chicago and New Orleans. New Orleans was based upon the four-beat style as opposed to Chicago's two-beat style.

Octaves: Notes that are eight scale tones apart bearing the same identifying letter.

Out Chorus: Final chorus of a selection.

Patting Juba: Hand clapping, thigh slapping, and foot stomping to provide a rhythmic accompaniment in place of percussion instruments.

Pianola: Music machine using the pneumatic principle to activate a piano, a forerunner of the juke box.

Pizzicato: Method of playing a stringed instrument by plucking with the fingers instead of playing with a bow.

Playing Inside: Improvisation in which all notes played are contained within the given chord or scale.

Playing Outside: Improvisation in which few, if any, of the notes played are contained in a given chord or scale.

Plunger: Rubber toilet plunger, without the handle, used as a muting device by trumpet and trombone players.

Polyrhythm: Playing of two or more contrasting rhythms simultaneously.

Pot Tunes: Popular songs or tunes.

Progression: Complete sequence of chords contained in one full chorus of a song/tune. Also called chord progressions or chord changes.

Progressive Jazz: Mid 1940's development in which instrumentation of bands were expanded, harmonies became complex, frequent tempo changes were made which implied concert rather than dance music.

Quadrille: Dance popular in France and New Orleans designed for four couples. Popular during the 19th century. Used a 6/8 or 2/4 meter.

Race Recordings: During the 1920's, recordings made specifically for the Negro market. Paramount, Pace-Black Swan were popular recording companies for race records.

Ragtime: Style of piano playing at the turn of the century popular around St. Louis. It hit its peak of popularity during the early part of the 20th century. Based on the march form, it utilizes a great deal of syncopation.

Rent Party: Informal parties, sometimes advertised, given in the 1920's and 1930's among the Negro population, at which musicians were invited to play. Guests paid an admission fee which in turn was used to supply food, drink, and help pay the rent.

Repertoire: Complete list of compositions a person or group are prepared to perform.

Rhythm and Blues: Style of urban blues made popular in Chicago in the late 1940's. It contains elements of jazz blues and gospel. A predecessor of rock n' roll.

Rhythm Section: Instruments in a jazz ensemble consisting of; piano, guitar, bass, and drums. Primary function is to provide chordal progressions and keep the time (beat).

Ride Cymbal: Cymbal 19 to 22 inches in diameter, depending on the drummer's personal preference, suspended over the drum set, usually to the player's right. Used for playing timekeeping patterns.

Riff: Repeated short musical phrase, either used as a main theme for a selection, or as an accompanying figure for a solo.

Ring Shout: Song-dance in which dancers move in a circle while accompanists sit in an outer circle. A song involving call and response patterns.

Rock and Roll: Musical style popular in the mid 50's which has influenced popular music since that time. The rhythm is based upon even notes rather than the uneven 'shuffle' or 'swing' of rhythm and blues.

Rubato: Giving elasticity to the meter.

Scat Singing: The vocalist uses nonsense syllables instead of words in performing a song. Originated during the work song era and became popular during bop when the singer often sang in unison with the instruments.

Screech: Trumpet player who plays extremely high notes with consistent accuracy.

Secret Society: Fraternal organizations in New Orleans part of whose function was to assure their deceased members a proper funeral. Also financially sponsored bands within the society.

Shout: Style of singing in a forceful, shouting manner.

Sideman: Member of an ensemble other than the leader. A generalized term.

Spiritual: Religious song of Negro origin coming from black churches.

Standard Tune: Song which has endured the test of time and remained popular through the eras of jazz.

Stoptime: Process of playing a regular, but discontinuous rhythm in a short 'clipped' staccato fashion on the first beat of every measure. Often used as an accompaniment for tap dancers.

Storyville: Area in New Orleans, west of Canal Street, encompassing a section of approximately 34 square blocks in which were located the bordellos and 'sportin' houses.

Stride: Piano style characterized by using the left hand to provide a steady beat. Playing the first and third beats with a single note or octave, and the second and fourth beats with a chord.

Swing: Jazz style developed during the big band era, also called swing era. A complimentary term 'it swings', or 'he/she swings'.

Syncopation: Deliberate interruption of the meter, pulse, or rhythm. In simple terms, accenting the up-beat.

Tack Piano: Pressing of thumb tacks into the felt hammers of the piano in an effort to give the instrument more projection while sacrificing the tone quality. Used in early jazz when public address systems were unavailable.

Tag: Also 'tag ending'. A short (two-four measure) extension of a tune/arrangement, to give it an added feeling of finality.

Tailgate: Trombone playing in a countermelodic manner. Originated during funeral parades when the trombone player sat on the tailgate of the funeral wagon in order to have room to move the trombone slide freely. The ensemble rode on the funeral wagon upon its return from the graveside service.

Tempo: Speed of the beats (pulses) of the music.

Time Signature: Numerical symbols placed at the beginning of a selection to indicate the meter (number of beats per measure) (type of note to get a beat). The first number indicates the number of beats in a measure, the second indicates the type of note to receive each beat. 4/4 indicates four quarter notes per measure, 3/4 indicates three quarter notes per measure.

Tin Pan Alley: Area in New York City where the songwriters and music publishers were located.

T. O. B. A.:   Theater Owners Booking Association. A booking agency that booked Negro entertainers; singers, dancers, jazz bands, and comedians.

Unison: Simultaneous playing/singing of the same notes by two or more performers.

Vamp: Repetitive figure (used as an accompaniment). Usually used as an introduction. Of indefinite duration.

Vibrato: Slight fluctuation of the pitch (above and below it) of various speeds, designed to give the tone quality, warmth, and color.

Voicing: Manner of organizing the notes of a chord for various instruments/voices. The assignment of notes to the instruments.

Walking Bass: Style of bass playing in which the notes are played on or between the beats in succession. Usually in a scalic manner. The bass player is not relegated to playing only the notes found in the chord but can insert nonchordal notes (passing notes). Designed to give the rhythm a feeling of forward flow.

Index

Adderly, Nat, 175
Aeolian Records, 99
Akiyoshi, Toshiko, 195
Alexander, Willard, 140
American Federation of Labor, 100
American Federation of Musicians, 100
Ammons, Gene, 152
Anderson, Ivie, 139
Anderson, Marian, 92
Anderson, Tom, 85
Anderson, "Cat", 136, 147
Anka, Paul, 181
Arlen, Harold, 108, 116, 118, 119
Armstrong, Louis, 54, 80, 90, 91, 92, 93, 96, 97, 98, 100, 178, 196
Arnheim, Gus, 136
ASCAP, 73, 122
Associated Booking Corp., 140
Astaire, Fred, 91
Auld, Georgie, 136
Austin High Gang, 98

Bach, Johann S., 34, 112
Bacharach, Burt, 191
Back, Will, 140
Baez, Joan, 181
Bailey, Buster, 58
Bailey, Mildred, 139
Bailey, Pearl, 139
Baker, Dorothy, 97
bal de Cordon Bleu, 84
Band of Renown, 160
Bards, 30
Barnett, Charlie, 132
Barron, Blue, 128, 132
Barron, Lee, 127
Bartok, Bela, 116
Basie, Wm. "Count", 8, 86, 98, 132, 134, 145
Beach Boys, The, 182
Beatles, The, 182
Bechet, Sidney, 54, 58, 83, 90, 91, 96, 100
Beethoven, Ludwig V., 108, 112
Beiderbecke, "Bix", 91, 97, 100, 126
Bellson, Louis, 136, 147
Benny, Jack, 142
Berlin, Irving, 76, 93, 108, 109, 110, 114, 120

Bernhardt, Milt, 175
Bernie, Ben, 126
Bernstein, Elmer, 191
Berry, Chu, 136
Berry, Chuck, 59, 179
Bigard, Barney, 80, 100
Black Swan Records, 54, 58
Blake, Hubert "Eubie", 58, 62, 75
Blakey, Art, 175
Bland, James, 50
Blanton, Jimmy, 136, 147
Blesh, Rudi, 70, 203
Blood, Sweat & Tears, 182
Blue Bird Records, 54
BMI, 122
Bolden, Charles "Buddy", 75, 97
Boone, Pat, 181
Brahms, Johannes, 112
Brice, Bobby, 197
Brookmeyer, Bob, 175
Brown, Clifford, 175
Brown, James, 59, 181
Brown, Les, 8, 132, 156
Brown, Lawrence, 136
Brown, "Stumpy", 158
Brubeck, Dave, 8, 174, 175
Brunswick Records, 99
Burns, Ralph, 134
Busse, Henry, 132, 136
Byas, Don, 136
Byrd, Donald, 175
Byrne, David, 192

Cadillac, Antoine, 83
Callander, Charles "Red", 50, 176
Calloway, Cabwell, "Cab", 132, 134, 177
Camarata, Tutti, 134
Campbell, Jackie, 112, 113
Cannon, Hughie, 108
Capone, Al, 91
Carle, Frankie, 172
Carmichael, Hoagy, 108, 119
Carney, Harry, 147
Carr, Benjamin, 104
Carroll, Harry, 120
Carter, Benny, 132, 136

221

Student Profile I

Name _____

Major _____ Student Number _____

Year (circle)   Frosh   Soph   Junior   Senior   Grad   Other

Age (years) at last birthday (circle)

    < 16   17-18   19-20   21-22   23-24   25-29

    30-34   35-39   40-49   50-59 ≥ 60

Please indicate your heritage. Check those that apply (up to three) on the left. On the blanks following indicate specific country/area/tribe if you wish (up to three).

_____African

_____Asian

_____Caucasian

_____Hispanic

_____Middle East

_____Native American

_____Other (please list) _____

1. For the music types listed indicate the THREE you were most likely to listen to FIVE YEARS AGO (rank from 1—most to 3—least).

_____ Ragtime	_____ Bluegrass
_____ Dixieland	_____ American folk
_____ Big Bands	_____ Classical
_____ Be-bop/cool	_____ Opera
_____ Rock	_____ Popular/contemporary
_____ Fusion	_____ Religious/gospel
_____ Rhythm & Blues	_____ Other, list _____
_____ Country	_____ Other, list _____

2. Many people perform music—instrumental and/or vocal—as a job/career or for enjoyment, etc. Please check all the performances you have been involved in. **On the left,** check those you have participated in the past and **on the right** those you currently participate in.

Have been in   Are in now
_____ Instrumental   _____
     _____ concert band   _____
     _____ symphony   _____
     _____ jazz band   _____
     _____ other, list _____ _____
_____ Vocal
     _____ chorus
     _____ jazz/show choir   _____
     _____ church group   _____
     _____ other, list _____ _____

I performed/perform as a(n)
     _____ soloist   _____
     _____ ensemble member   _____

At my best I consider(ed) myself a(n) (check one)

_____ superior/outstanding performer
_____ excellent performer
_____ good performer
_____ average performer
_____ fair performer

3. My musical background and training includes lessons/classes (check all types that apply).

	High School	College	Other
Private individual lessons	____	____	____
School individual/small group	____	____	____
Class/group	____	____	____

4. My other music experiences include nonperformance courses (check the number you have had including in high school).

Course	0	1	2	3	≥ 4
Music theory	__	__	__	__	__
Music appreciation	__	__	__	__	__
Music history	__	__	__	__	__
Music literature	__	__	__	__	__
Ethnic/folk music	__	__	__	__	__
Psychology of music	__	__	__	__	__
Teaching music	__	__	__	__	__

5. My favorite musician/group is _____

Student Profile II — Music in Your Life

Name _____

Major _____ Student Number _____

Year (circle)　　　Frosh　　　Soph　　　Junior　　　Senior　　　Grad　　　Other

1.　For the music types listed indicate the THREE you are most likely to listen to (rank from 1—most to 3—least).

_____ Ragtime	_____ Bluegrass
_____ Dixieland	_____ American folk
_____ Big Bands	_____ Classical
_____ Be-bop/cool	_____ Opera
_____ Rock	_____ Popular/contemporary
_____ Fusion	_____ Religious/gospel
_____ Rhythm & blues	_____ Other, list _____
_____ Country	_____ Other, list _____

2.　For EACH type of music, indicate the approximate NUMBER of records, tapes, CDs, and/or music videos you have. If none, write 0 on the blank.

	Records	Tapes	CDs	Music Videos
Ragtime	___	___	___	___
Dixieland	___	___	___	___
Big bands	___	___	___	___
Be-bop/cool	___	___	___	___
Rock	___	___	___	___
Fusion	___	___	___	___
Rhythm & blues	___	___	___	___
Country	___	___	___	___
Blue grass	___	___	___	___
American folk	___	___	___	___
Classical	___	___	___	___
Opera	___	___	___	___
Popular/contemporary	___	___	___	___
Religious/gospel	___	___	___	___
Other, list _____	___	___	___	___
Other, list _____	___	___	___	___
TOTAL number of each recording	___	___	___	___

3.　Do you borrow/exchange recordings for listening?
_____ No
_____ Yes, from/with whom (check all that apply)

_____ friends/neighbors	_____ library
_____ family/relatives	_____ other, list _____

4. Do you belong to a tape/record/CD club (sends you a selection monthly).
   _____ No
   _____ Yes, check how frequently you order (receive and keep recordings)
              _____ usually make a purchase monthly (10 or more per year)
              _____ usually make a purchase every other month (4–10 per year)
              _____ make few selections (3 or less per year)

5. How many recordings do you usually purchase each month (all sources)?
   _____ None   _____ 5–8
   _____ 1–2   _____ 9 or more
   _____ 3–4

   How many of these are new releases? (write in number)

   Are these purchases
   _____ all new?
   _____ some new, some used?
   _____ mostly used?

6. When/where do you usually listen to music? Indicate the percentages of your listening time to total 100 percent.

   _____ at home   _____ at work
   _____ in your vehicle   _____ other
   _____ when biking, exercising, walking   _____ 100% Total

7. What audio equipment do you own? **Check all you have.**

   HOME   PORTABLES (indicate number of each)
   _____ Shelf/rack system   _____ AM radio
        _____ Receiver with AM/FM tuner   _____ AM/FM Radio
        _____ CD player   _____ AM/FM radio with cassette
                                               player
        _____ cassette player   _____ CD player
        _____ turntable   _____ mini-disc player
        _____ headphones   _____ boom box with cassette
                                            _____ boom box with CD
   _____ Component system   _____ short wave/world band radio
        _____ receiver   _____ other, list _____
        _____ amplifiers
        _____ single-disc CD player   AUTO/VEHICLE
        _____ multi-disc CD player   _____ in-dash cassette player
        _____ cassette deck   _____ in-dash CD
        _____ turntable   _____ CD changer
        _____ speakers, how many_____   _____ AM/FM radio
        _____ headphones   _____ car stereo amplifiers
                                            _____ headphones

8. For your radio listening what TYPE OF MUSIC do you usually tune it? List the two you most frequently listen to by type (jazz, country, etc.).

   _____   _____

9. Which live music performances do you attend? Check the TWO you most often attend.
   _____ musicals   _____ symphony
   _____ country western   _____ choral groups
   _____ jazz   _____ rock
   _____ opera   _____ other, list _____

Listening Guide

As assigned during the course, complete three listening guides.

Name _____ Student Number _____

Course _____ Date Completed _____

1. CIRCLE the style of music listened to

    Minstrelsy   Blues   Ragtime   Dixieland

    Tin Pan Alley   Rock   Fusion   Free Jazz

2. Complete the following about the recordings and selections.

    Format(circle)   CD   Record   Tape

    Artist(s) _____

    _____

    Selections (songs) _____ Minutes ___ : ___
    _____ Minutes ___ : ___
    _____ Minutes ___ : ___
    _____ Minutes ___ : ___
    _____ Minutes ___ : ___
    _____ Minutes ___ :

    Recording label (company) _____

    Date (year) recorded _____

3. Equipment used for listening to recording. (Example: CD player, Sony)

    SHELF/RACK SYSTEM: _____ What? _____ Brand?

    COMPONENT SYSTEM: _____ What? _____ Brand?

    _____ What? _____ Brand?

    _____ What? _____ Brand?

    AUTO/VEHICLE: _____ What? _____ Brand?

4.   Choose ONE of the selections and analyze it for each of the following.

Selection/song: _____

Rhythm:

Improvisation:

Syncopation:

Vocal solos:

Background to vocal:

Instrumental solos:

Use of auxiliary instruments:

Overall reaction to selection: